C000194861

A book from
ımaGine, Evesham

INSIDE THE BELLY OF THE BEAST

The REAL Bosasa Story

Angelo Agrizzi

As told to Phillipa Mitchell

Truth Be Told Publishing

Cover design and typography: W. Booysen
Editor: Melinda Ferguson
Proof reader: Kelly-May Macdonald
Set in EB Garamond

First published by Truth Be Told Publishing 2020
First edition, first impression

ISBN: 978-0-620-90284-7
ISBN: 978-0-620-90285-4 (epub)

To Sophia Ella, Avery Ruth, and every child born in South Africa post-2019. Always speak your truth, even if your voice is shaking. Guard against the mistakes made by my generation that took our beautiful country to the precipice of disaster.

"In a time of universal deceit, telling the truth is a revolutionary act."
– George Orwell

Contents

PUBLISHER'S NOTE

"There can be no faith in government if our highest offices are excused from scrutiny – they should be setting the example of transparency."
– Edward Snowden

At a time when corruption has become the most urgent scourge to address, *Inside the Belly of the Beast* plays a critical role in further exposing the corporate and political crimes that redirected billions meant for the citizens of this country. The public is owed this information since much of it directly relates to the criminal pillaging of state coffers.

The name "Angelo Agrizzi" first burst into public consciousness when, in late January 2019, an audio clip of him using the K-word a number of times was played at the Zondo Commission. Many South Africans were sickened to the core. But, if publishers only represented writers with whom they wholeheartedly agreed, the world would have a very barren lists of books.

Agrizzi owned up to his racist outburst at the Zondo Commission and subsequently paid a R200,000 fine to the Barney Mokgatle Foundation. There are many more racists in this country, hiding behind boardroom doors and uttering their bigotry in the privacy of their own homes, at braais and at cocktail parties. They just haven't been exposed yet. And besides, who are we, the public, to cast judgement on the man when we are also flawed?

Inside the Belly of the Beast is far bigger than the man himself. Agrizzi has written a hugely important and compelling memoir, tracking almost two decades of bribery, politicking and corruption that he witnessed and was part of as the COO of Bosasa under the leadership of Gavin Watson.

Truth be Told Publishing salutes the whistleblowers of this world – the Snowdens, the Assanges, the Mannings, the Agrizzis and the Magaqas – courageous men and women who have been exiled, besmirched, imprisoned and even murdered for telling the truth. At the time of going to print, Agrizzi had been deemed a flight risk by the state, denied bail and incarcerated. Was this to silence him? Were there greater forces at play?

South Africa needs to heal from the brutal legacies of apartheid as well as from our corrupted "democracy". More than ever before, we are at a time when the country's dispossessed should be receiving the long overdue blessings of freedom and prosperity. As a nation, we thirst for a new moral compass.

There is an extensive cast of "corruption characters" in this book. Most of the players implicated either have been or will be provided with an opportunity to testify at the Zondo Commission to dispute the allegations made by Agrizzi against them. Those who have not may approach the Zondo Commission to dispute what has been alleged in this book.

Truth be Told Publishing
October 2020

PREFACE

In this vivid account of the inner workings of corruption, whistleblower Angelo Agrizzi – due to his own failings – finds himself trapped in a dark and vicious den of bribery, corruption and state capture. When he finally manages to look into his own darkness to reconnect to his Life Source, he summons the courage to speak against a deeply corrupt system which, if left unattended, has the potential to destroy everything we stand for as a country.

The revelations in this book come at a time when our nation has become so used to corruption that many people have grown resigned to it. But it's also a time that is galvanising our people into collective action against the scourge. *Inside the Belly of the Beast* charts Agrizzi's personal story, his rise to occupying an influential role as the COO of Bosasa, and how bribery and corruption not only consumed a company but were turned into an art form.

The book also documents Agrizzi's assessment of South Africa's political economy, the culture of patronage and how public tenders can be systemically rigged for private accumulation and personal enrichment.

While real accountability is yet to come for the culprits, the cost of corruption continues to be exemplified by our country's increasing inequality, spiralling debt and poverty.

This magnificent work gives valuable insights into how our post-apartheid society is permeated with capitalist values like self-aggrandisement, greed and consumerist temptations. It also offers hope as we witness what happens when a heart transforms. Despite the breath of power on his neck, Angelo Agrizzi has chosen to stand up for what is right in a culture that rewards people for doing the opposite – keeping quiet about the extent of corruption in public tendering and not taking ownership for wrongful actions.

While corruption has reached epic proportions in our country, it is my hope that this book will give courage to whistleblowers to rise up and stand their ground when the lions of our culture roar against them. Courage can crush the crises we are facing as a nation.

Buang Jones – Provincial Head at the South African Human Rights Commission (Gauteng)

THE CAST

Angelo Agrizzi – Chief Operating Officer (Bosasa)
Gavin Watson – Chief Executive Officer (Bosasa)

SUPPORTING CAST

Carlos Bonifacio – Head of Accounts (Bosasa); Retracted as whistleblower

Danny Mansell – Co-founder, shareholder and Managing Director (Bosasa)

Dr Jurgen Smith (Doc Smith) – Founder Consilium Business Consultants; Meritum shareholder

Tony Perry – Group Company Secretary (Bosasa)

Andries van Tonder – Chief Financial Officer (Bosasa); Whistleblower

Frans Vorster – Logistics Manager (Bosasa); Whistleblower

Richard Le Roux – Regional Technical Coordinator, Sondolo IT (Bosasa); Whistleblower

Leon van Tonder – IT Manager (Bosasa); Whistleblower

Petrus (Peet) Venter – External Accountant and Auditor to Bosasa; Director of Consilium Business Consultants; Retracted as whistleblower

Linda Mti – Acting National Commissioner of Correctional Services (2001-2007); National Commissioner of Correctional Services (2007-2008)

Patrick Gillingham – Former senior prison official (since the early 1990s) who went on to become Chief Financial Officer (Department of Correctional Services) between 2004 and 2010

Nomgcobo Jiba – Appointed Deputy Director of Public Prosecutions in 2001. In 2006, she was appointed Senior Deputy Director of Public Prosecutions. In December 2010, she was appointed Deputy National Director of Public Prosecutions (National Prosecuting Authority), a position she held until September 2016

Vincent Smith – Head of both the Portfolio Committee on Finance for Standing Committee on Public Accounts (SCOPA) and the Department of Correctional Services between 2014 and 2018

Dudu Myeni – Executive Chairperson (Jacob Zuma Foundation) since 2008

Nomvula Mokonyane – Dyambu shareholder, MEC for Safety and Liaison (1999-2004); MEC for Housing (2004-2009); Gauteng Premier (2009-2014); Minister of Water Affairs and Sanitation (2014-2018)

Gwede Mantashe – Secretary-General of the African National Congress (2007-2017); Chairperson of the African National Congress (since December 2017)

Lawrence Mrwebi – Special Director of Public Prosecutions and Head of Specialised Commercial Crimes Unit (National Prosecuting Authority) (2011-2018)

Jackie Lepinka – Manager: Executive Support (National Prosecuting Authority)

Nosiviwe Mapisa-Nqakula – Minister of Home Affairs (2004-2009); Minister of Department of Correctional Services (2009-2012)

Joe Gumede – Executive Chair (Bosasa)

Papa Leshabane – Executive Director (Bosasa)

Ishmael Dikane (Mncwaba) – Director (Bosasa)

Carol Munirah Oliveria (Mkele) – Director and shareholder (Bosasa)

Nomazulu Thandi Makoko – Chairperson, Youth Development Centres (Bosasa)

Jackie Leyds – Executive Director (Bosasa)

Trevor Mathenjwa – Managing Director, Sondolo IT (Bosasa)

Lindie Gouws – Gavin Watson's lover (also Bosasa employee)

Brian Biebuyck – Attorney and Legal Consultant to Bosasa

Leigh-Ann Watson – Gavin Watson's wife

Roth Watson – Gavin Watson's son

Lindsay Watson – Gavin Watson's daughter

Daniel "Cheeky" Watson – Gavin Watson's brother

Valence Watson – Gavin Watson's brother

Ronnie Watson – Gavin Watson's brother

Jared Watson – Valence Watson's son

Valence Nkosinathi Watson – Valence Watson's son

Mark Taverner – Gavin Watson's brother-in-law; Procurement Officer (Bosasa)

Sharon Taverner – Gavin Watson's sister; Mark Taverner's wife

George Papadakis – Senior SARS Consultant

Sesinyi "Commander" Seopela – Consultant to Gavin Watson (under Consilium Business Consultants)

Riaan Hoeksma – Owner, Riekele Construction

FEATURED EXTRAS

Andries de Jager – Private Investigator hired by Gavin Watson

Allister Esau – Function Coordinator (Bosasa)

Barney Mokgatle – Founder, Barney Mokgatle Foundation

Claudio Agrizzi – Angelo Agrizzi's brother

Dr Denise Bjorkman – Manager, Bosasa Wellness Clinic

Glynnis Breytenbach – Former Prosecutor for the National Prosecuting Authority; Democratic Alliance Shadow Minister of Justice (since 2014)

Gerhard Wagenaar – Angelo Agrizzi's first attorney at the Zondo Commission

Hilda Ndude – Dyambu shareholder

Jacques van Zyl – Accountant (Bosasa)

Johan Helmand – Head of Technology (Control Rooms), Sondolo IT (Bosasa)

Jacob Zuma – President of South Africa from 2009 to 2018

Jarred Mansell – Danny Mansell's son

Mannie Witz – Angelo Agrizzi's Advocate at the Zondo Commission

Natasha Olivier – Company Secretary (Bosasa)

Retief van der Merwe – National Operations Coordinator, Sondolo IT (Bosasa)

Willie Hofmeyr – Head of Special Investigating Unit (SIU) and Asset Forfeiture Unit

EXTRAS

Anwa Dramat – Hawks Boss (2009-2014)

Archie Mkele – Carol Mkele's husband; Vulisango shareholder

Berning Ntlemeza – Hawks Boss (2015-2017)

Brian Blake – Owner of Blakes Travel

Daniel (Danny) Witz – Angelo Agrizzi's Attorney at the Zondo Commission

Grace Molatedi – Regional Commissioner, Groenpunt Management Area; Official at Department of Correctional Services

Hein Späth – Former owner of F&R Diesel

Hennie Viljoen – Head of Maintenance and Technical (Bosasa)

Jackson Mafika – Regional head (National Union of Mineworkers)

Jenny Schreiner – Acting Commissioner (Department of Correctional Services) (2009-2010)

Khotso De Wee – Chief Operations Officer in the Department of Justice and Constitutional Development (2005-2015); Zondo Commission Secretary (2018-2019)

Marijke De Kock – Senior Prosecutor (National Prosecuting Authority); Deputy Director of Public Prosecutions at the Serious Commercial Crimes Unit

Menzi Simelane – Director of National Prosecuting Authority (2009-2012)

Mike Bolhuis – Private Investigator hired by Angelo Agrizzi

Nontsikelelo Jolingana – Acting Head of Bid Adjudication Commission (Department of Correctional Services); Appointed as Acting National Commissioner of Correctional Services in 2013

Sam Sekgota – Lobbyist liaison between Department of Correctional Services and Bosasa during 2016

Sandy Thomas – Personal Assistant to Nomvula Mokonyane

Syvion Dlamini – Director of the Mogale Youth Development Centres

Thabang Makwetla – Deputy Minister of Justice and Correctional Services (2014-2019)

Tom Moyane – National Commissioner of Correctional Services (2010-2013)

The Cast of Characters listed here mentions most of the individuals referred to in the book. Their inclusion, however, does not suggest that all or even most of them are implicated in corruption or wrongdoings. Their relevance to the events described in the book will be apparent in the contents of the book, which readers are urged to read in full.

HOW TO ACCESS QR CODES

The integration of QR codes within *Inside the Belly of the Beast* creates a unique interactive experience for the reader, bringing to life key video evidence, articles, interviews, testimonials and documents from the Zondo State Capture Commission of Inquiry.

SCANNING A QR CODE

Download a QR Code Reader app on your smartphone – either from the iOS App Store or the Android Google Play Store. Mozilla Firefox has a built-in QR Code scanner that can be downloaded onto any device.

Once the QR Code Reader has been installed onto your smartphone or device, you are ready to start scanning the QR codes.

Follow the quick steps below to get started:

1. Open the QR Code Reader app on your device or smartphone.
2. Hold your device over the QR code so that it clearly displays within the scanning field on your device's screen.
3. Once the QR Code Reader has identified the code, it should scan the code automatically. If not, you can activate the scanner by pressing the capture button on your device.

Once the QR code is captured, your device or smartphone will automatically navigate to the web site where the content or desired media can be viewed.

 Access a wealth of information at
www.insidethebellyofthebeast.co.za
www.itbotb.com

PROLOGUE

"If you have a garden and a library, you have everything you need."
– Marcus Tullius Cicero (106 BC-43 BC)

On the 16th of January 2019, I took the witness stand at the Zondo Commission. Named after Judge Raymond Zondo, the Commission was established as a Judicial Commission of Inquiry into allegations of State Capture in South Africa. When I first met Gavin Watson face to face in the old mining town of Krugersdorp, never could I have imagined where our journey together would take us. Bosasa would become deeply embedded in the capture of various State departments, and I would become the company's chief whistleblower.

My revelations shook the country. There was enormous international media interest. Few testimonies in history have implicated so many people by name with such astonishing facts, insights and descriptions of what went down behind the scenes, deep down in the belly of the beast which thrived on greed and bribery.

While much of the production line of corruption was revealed at the Zondo Commission, I am now at liberty to tell the full story, the way I lived it.

I am often confronted with questions like, "Why did it take so long? Are you not just trying to cover your arse?" or "You gained from the corruption – shouldn't you be prosecuted?" or "Is this about a personal vendetta?"

My intentions and actions to bring the truth into the light were always noble, as were those of my fellow whistleblowers. I turned down a R50-million cash offer to halt my testimony. I waved away a substantial separation package for my nineteen years of service at Bosasa. After years of being in service to Gavin Watson, I wanted none of it. I had had enough. I wanted the truth to be known. I wanted to set a trend that would encourage other potential whistleblowers in South Africa to come forward – without fear – to bring about much-needed change.

It is important that one never confuses a cult with a corporate culture. In my experience, Bosasa was like a cult – no more and no less. And in a cult, there is always a Master – a kingpin. That kingpin, in the case of Bosasa, was none other than Gavin Watson – the Master who dictated to his followers how they may (or may not) think and behave.

Within the Bosasa cult, there existed a strong need for acceptance. Followers believed their lives (and livelihoods) were entirely dependent on their Master and that they were nothing without him. Many were prepared to leave no stone unturned in their efforts to please him – even if it meant walking over everyone else. For years, I watched people cultivate lies to make others look like failures. It is easy to become a colluder when all you want is for The Master to look upon you with favour. For many years I found myself in the same trap.

Every member of the Bosasa cult was, at some point in their tenure, privy to manipulation and intimidation. Disgracing one's followers in a public forum was The Master's favourite game. With the clever use of derogatory words – masked as healthy criticism – he was able to influence the thoughts and behaviour of his followers, break down what remained of their integrity, and destroy all possible opposition.

"Don't cry, Gina!"

"Stand up, Jacques!"

These belittling commands – some as derogatory as telling people they were fat or useless – were as staged as they were frequent. I cringed watching a video sent to me by one of the whistleblowers – which was later shown at the Zondo Commission – of an imbizo[1] held at the Silverstar Casino in 2017 with the middle management team. Gavin used the opportunity to endorse his authority and remind them of their inferiority and dependence on him. He might not have been educated at an Ivy League institution, but he was well-read on strategic and tactical matters and, I believe, a master of manipulation. Machiavelli served him well.

While it was standard procedure that anyone who came on board was

---

1   An isiZulu word meaning "meeting". Amongst the Zulu people, an imbizo is a gathering called either by the king or a traditional leader.

made to feel indispensable, it rarely lasted. After being inducted into the politics of the organisation, many Bosasa cult members would eventually reach the end of the honeymoon period or fall from grace with The Master, going from hero to zero. Gavin and his board of directors derived great pleasure from dismissing people with a wave of the hand and the words: "You're fired."

These broken people inevitably became my problem, and without any legitimate reasons for firing them, I had no choice but to work them back into the company and find a way to actualise a return on them. Since Gavin liked people to believe they had power, it was often tricky getting these people off their pedestals once Gavin had put them there. In many instances, I transferred people away from our headquarters so that Gavin wouldn't realise they were still working for the company.

Bosasa's "cult-ure" probably started out as well-intentioned. It was established to empower its members, to teach them that God had created them as originals and that each one had the innate ability to make a difference in people's lives and build on their God-given talents. Personnel were encouraged to innovate and improve their divisions.

But it all went horribly wrong when the glory was bestowed upon mortal beings, instead of being placed on the Lord God Almighty. People have egos. Stroke that ego too much, and eventually, the ego will consume the person. Chaos was deliberately introduced. Accusations of Satanism, witchcraft, and demonism were commonplace. Two-hour solemn prayer meetings often evolved into discussions about dreams of snakes and other premonitions. The company's boardrooms – and sometimes even my office – were often used to exorcise "evil" spirits from the campus.

The need for self-validation was fuelled by greed. Cult stratagems restored the pecking order, exercised control and destroyed identities. Cult acolytes would target and destroy anyone who overstepped the mark in their quest for personal glory. For many, the erratic withdrawal of approval from the Master led to depression. Dedicated employees quickly became demotivated. People would lie awake at night wondering whether they would be the subject of public ridicule the following day. Their lives became a daily fight for psychological survival.

After listening to the same old Gavin Watson rhetoric, day in and day out, it wasn't long before I too was swept up in what I thought was not only the gospel truth but also the Gavin Watson way and the Bosasa life. My senses began to dull, common sense became blurred, and the act of making important decisions became a complicated process, riddled with self-doubt and mental strife.

This was the machinery of the cult at work. The wings of well-meaning, aspirant glory-seekers were adroitly clipped. The acclaimed freedom that Gavin raved about as part of the Bosasa culture became nothing more than a myth.

The way Gavin treated his people reminded me of the story of Stalin's Chicken. Whether it happened or not is immaterial – the lesson remains as relevant as ever.

It is 1935, and Stalin invites his senior advisors to a meeting where he intends to drive a point home, using the most evocative of methods.

When everyone has settled down in anticipation of what is to be discussed, Stalin calls for a live chicken. Clenching it in one hand, he sits down and proceeds to vigorously pluck out the chicken's feathers in clumps. Despite its agonised shrieks and squawks – and oblivious to the disgust on the faces of the people (too afraid to express their unease) – Stalin continues to denude the poor bird until there is not a feather in sight.

Eventually, he places the bloodied bird down on the ground, close to a small pile of maize sweepings. Standing up to complete the final scene in his act, he watches his audience observe the chicken moving towards the maize. While the chicken pecks away hungrily, Stalin places his hand into his jacket pocket and pulls out a fistful of seeds and places them down in front of the wounded bird. To the audience's utter surprise, the chicken turns and drags its broken body weakly back to the dictator, eagerly pecking the fresh grain out of his hand – the same hand that only moments ago had inflicted untold trauma and pain upon it.

"This is how easy it is to govern stupid people," Stalin said. "They will follow you no matter how much pain you cause them, as long as you throw them a little worthless treat once in a while."

Many of the people who ran Bosasa appeared to thrive in this hostile environment, consciously and deliberately encouraged conflict, creating their own "thief-doms" so that they could catapult themselves into greatness and earn themselves their sought-after acknowledgement from The Master.

Added to the mix was the inherent nature of politicians and political processes. When a company plays a political card, psychological and financial value is introduced. The politicisation process that took place at Bosasa created a welcome bilateral dependency between the company and those in government, who offered themselves up – wittingly and unwittingly – to be stakeholders in a corrupt game. With their political status their only value, it became their calling card, used by unscrupulous people to further self-motivated ends. Sometimes this was implied, while other times it was discussed openly for trade-offs. For years, I witnessed this first-hand at Bosasa.

Being awarded shares in a listed company might create personal wealth and access into the world of business, but it does not necessarily suggest an understanding of the sector or its processes. There are few politicians who understand business or who are appropriately productive in a specific sector.

Take politicking out of the equation and deconstruct its greasy effectiveness in the workplace – by removing those who manufacture and sustain this reliance on "smoothness" and guile – and productivity will increase dramatically for the right reasons. Work teams are able to focus on their key performance areas and tasks, instead of constantly being on high alert for a potential rear attack by one of their teammates.

There are lessons to be learned from economic history that might describe what happened at Bosasa. For one, while we like to believe we live in a democratic society, I believe that it is more feudal in nature. For years we've been witnessing a widening of the gap between the rich and the poor, and the powerful and the weak – essentially, the employer versus the employee.

From its roots in the Industrial Revolution, the market ensured that the rich became richer through the control of debt and capital. Start-ups born of initiative and passion flourished. Die-hards emerged from uncertainty and turmoil. As private entrepreneurial ownership boomed, the millionaires next door – the private owners – gave way to the super-rich elite.

The market shifted again, where the control of capital by the individual was replaced by a more centralised form of ownership. For the ordinary man on the street, this dream of being the captain of his own ship quickly became nothing more than a fantasy. He was simply a cog in somebody else's machinery, paid by the hour for the sacrifices he made in terms of his time, based on his skill set and experience. The trade-off was for money and what it could buy. Hegemony reigned. Nobody dared question the capitalistic process to which they had become enslaved. Asking for more was taboo, and so we removed the phrase from our vocabulary.

Today not much has changed. We fulfil the roles allotted to us by society. To feed and nurture the family and pay our debts, we need to work. We become salary slaves. We dare not raise questions about unscrupulous dealings, lest we lose our jobs or – God forbid – find ourselves being publicly reprimanded or humiliated. We learn to curb our speech while the very fabric of our moral fibre is slowly stripped away.

Cult masters have studied the working class's emotional and financial needs, whims and aspirations in great detail. Much like Stalin and his chicken, masters understand how captive we are to the little clumps of sustenance occasionally fed to us. They are cognisant of the fact that we are reliant on a system that entraps us into believing that the tormentor is the indispensable provider. Some call it Stockholm Syndrome.

While providing for our families, our emotional core and our inner callings are tossed into the back seat. We think we are in control, yet we control nothing. Control is a fantasy. We control neither the land nor the industry built upon it. Coincidently, we don't even control those who work there. Management of self is an illusion of time, labour, tasks and outcomes. As labour, we have utilitarian value only.

I saw people arrive at Bosasa with an inner passion and a purpose that inspired them to work hard – but it was soon destroyed. Providing for the table became the nebulous driver, not that which the company stood for in its mission statement.

Our culture is largely one in which our worth as an individual is determined by the persona and position of the organisation into which we have chosen to slot ourselves. My sense of achievement became entangled in the prestige of a company's name. The more prestigious the name, the more I believed I had achieved. And so it was with many others in Bosasa's employ. For many years, my need for the Master's approval and my fragile ego blinded me.

Was I any different from that poor plucked fowl? For years I put my tormenter at the helm, I sold my soul for a heap of maize, and I grinned and bore the pain. I found myself ensnared in fear of upsetting my tormentor and not being able to provide for myself and my family. I became the chicken. So many of us did.

To get out of this box, something radical needs to happen, beyond surviving having our feathers plucked. My radical personal shift happened when I emerged from a coma after emergency heart surgery, only to discover that my employer had laid claim to the R30-million Key Man death benefit and dread disease cover held in my name – and I wasn't even dead yet. Fuelled by this shocking discovery, I realised that neither I, nor my spirit, was moribund.

After this near-death experience, my eyes were opened and my journey to freedom began. It started with a singular and conscious decision – to let the truth be told about what really happened inside the belly of the beast.

PART 1

CHAPTER 1

In the Beginning

"Be yourself – everyone else is taken."
– Oscar Wilde

I was born one of twins on the 3rd of December 1967, the same momentous day that Dr Chris Barnard performed the world's first human-to-human heart transplant at Groote Schuur Hospital in Cape Town. While Dr Barnard was giving new life to one person, my twin brother, his tiny, deformed body hooked up to pipes and machines in the hospital's neonatal ICU, was fighting for his own. He lived only forty-eight hours before he took his final breath.

My parents never named my twin brother. The family, sworn to secrecy by my mother, promised never to speak of him again. It was only much later, when she was on her deathbed and in her final hours, that my mother broke the news to me. While there was no time for her to explain the rationale behind her silence, I remember reeling with shock that this secret had been kept from me for over two decades.

Claudio – my younger brother, born six years later, and, as far as I was concerned, my only sibling – and I were raised in a strict lower-middle-class family in the railway town of Germiston, east of the city of Johannesburg in Gauteng, South Africa. My father came to South Africa from Italy as a young man, hungry for opportunity. Having grown up during the Second World War, much of his young life was difficult and, being a tradesman, South Africa seemed like the perfect place to find prosperity, settle down, and raise a family. Although he spoke little English, he met and fell in love with my mother, a nurse who had grown up on a peanut farm in the Northern Transvaal (now Limpopo). While my father worked as an electrical engineer specialising in the manufacturing of transformers, my mother ran a crèche. She became quite a legend in the Germiston community, with thousands of children passing through the doors of Bambi Crèche before making their way into the formal schooling system.

As an Italian migrant worker during that time, my father was treated with almost the same prejudice as the non-white people of apartheid South Africa. Second-class citizens, migrant workers were never guaranteed work, unlike the English and the Afrikaners who, at the time, hardly ever sat without jobs. Although as children, we were showered with love and well taken care of, there were no luxuries. We attended government schools, and a university education was little more than a pipe dream. At the end of the day, if we wanted something, we had to go out there and work for it.

And then there were times when we had to chance it.

I remember running away from home when I was thirteen. I had just driven my father's silver Datsun ZX through the garage door. They were those metal doors that were popular at the time, the ones with the weights hanging from either side. That car was my father's pride and joy, his "afternoon car" as he used to call it. It was 5 p.m. My parents had gone out for the evening, my brother was having a bath, and I was bored. I got inside the car and started it, giving it a few long revs. I put the car in reverse and, before I knew it, it was hurtling backwards into the garage door. I had no idea where the brakes were, but in my panic, I found first gear, dropped the clutch and ended up driving the car through the garage wall.

"I'm out of here," were my first thoughts. Without saying a word to my brother, I stuffed some clothes and supplies into a rucksack, grabbed my bicycle, and high-tailed it out of there. I had no idea where I was going – Durban, perhaps even Cape Town – all I knew was that I was never going back. I'd find a job and start a new life. Anything was better than facing up to what I had just done.

As darkness fell, I found myself in the sleepy town of Heidelberg, about forty kilometres from the scene of the crime. I was frozen to the bone and terrified. It was then that common sense prevailed. I found a ticky box[2] and called Vic Hangar, my scoutmaster. Something told me that Vic, aged fifty-four, would be the perfect mediator between my parents and me when it came to diffusing their anger. His mother answered the phone and told me Vic was out looking for me. Unbeknown to me, my parents had phoned every police station, every ambulance service in the area, and everybody who knew me. I waited at the ticky box until Vic returned home and called me back. He told me to wait right there and that he was on his way to fetch me.

---

2   A payphone

34

"You're bloody daft," he said, struggling to stifle his laughter as we drove out of Heidelberg, my bicycle wedged into the trunk of his car. "The police are even out looking for you." When we arrived home, the entire neighbourhood was there. It must have been about 2 a.m. My mother wrapped me in a blanket and handed me a cup of hot chocolate. I remember thinking that I should get into trouble more often. My father never reprimanded or punished me for my misdemeanour, but I made sure that before he drove off in his prized Datsun ZX every day, that the bent garage door was already open. I did that religiously for the remainder of my days in that house.

It was 1981 and, although I loved my sport and my boy scouts, I had other aspirations – I loved nice things. I knew not to expect favours from anybody, least of all my parents, and so, at the tender age of fourteen, I decided to go knocking on doors to find myself a job. I had a bit of a crush on a Greek girl at school and, knowing that her father owned a bakery, he was my first port of call. I asked that she put in a good word for me, and then I knocked on his door. "What kind of work do you want to do?" he asked when I approached him. "I'll do anything," I said, thinking about the new pair of shoes and the new shirts that I would be able to buy. "Go and put this on," he said, handing me an overall. "You can start work now."

I was relegated to the kitchen where I found myself cleaning giant, greasy baking pans. For seventy-five cents an hour, it was gruelling manual labour for a tall, lanky teenager who was as thin as a rake, weighing in at only seventy-two kilograms. The black kitchen staff taught me everything I needed to know, and there was great camaraderie amongst us as we worked together in the kitchen. Entering the kitchen in the early mornings, we would be greeted with the stale smell of cooking oil that permeated the air, the gas from the griller and the salamander's pilot lights adding to the noxious odour. The pot of stock would be bubbling away as usual, never to be switched off. Within the short space of an hour, the once desolate and eerie kitchen would churn to life as each chef and baker would get his division going, with freshly baked puff pastry oozing with butter, the first batch of bread for the day coming out of the oven, and the fermented smell of the sourdough bread proofing in the double steamer. The almond-crusted croissants filled with almond paste mixed with crème pâtissière, which only Solly could master, were my favourite.

Solly Monaheng, born and bred in the sprawling township[3] of Katlehong, and having worked at the bakery since its inception, was not only fully conversant in Greek, he could read and write the language too. His hands, the size of dinner plates, were as soft and gentle as his nature. Solly had an aura of authority about him and, as the back-of-house success story, everybody respected him. Solly's wife, Trifinia, worked across the road at the roadhouse, and together they had three children – Moses, who was my age; followed by Calvin and their little sister, Adelaide.

Solly was the one who inadvertently started me smoking. I would always take my breaks with Solly because that was when his famous stories about his life and his bakery pranks came out. Sitting at the delivery bay, it was also the only time that he would take out his pack of 20's Gold Dollar Red and offer a round of cigarettes to the shift. Often, the others would reciprocate. Keen to become part of this clan, I too purchased my first packet of Gold Dollar Red and offered them around.

With my sporting and scouting commitments beginning to encroach on my new-found cash-earning abilities, breaking the news to Mr Rockley Montgomery, the head coach of Germiston High School's rugby team that I would no longer be attending practice after school was no mean feat – but it had to be done. I knew where my true passion lay – making cold, hard cash motivated me far more than any time spent on a sports field, or going all-out pushing our boundaries at the annual World Scout Jamboree.

Before I raced in through the school gates every day, my mornings began with a 4 a.m. walk to my pick-up point at the train junction on the corner of Baird Avenue and Grace Avenue in Parkhill Gardens, Germiston, where my bakery boss would meet me. It was a relatively short walk, and I never understood (or asked) why he did not collect me from my front door, but this was how it worked, and it went on like this for years. I was never quite sure how to address him as I got into his car. Some days it was Mr Pagonis, while other days it was Uncle Pagonis or Sir, but I knew never to call him by his first name, Nick – even Uncle Nick was forbidden.

As I walked through the streets of my childhood neighbourhood, the 04:05 train headed from Elsburg and Tedstoneville to Park Station in central Johannesburg would break through the silence of the early winter morning, sending out plumes of white ash-laden smoke as it started out on its day's journey. Passing the houses along Baird Avenue, I would reflect on my memories of the families who lived inside. First up were our neighbours, the Gulles, and, more especially, the unfortunate Mrs Gulle. She had a constant battle with our Ridgeback, who would jump the fence

3   An informal settlement

between our properties and either steal her freshly-purchased groceries (including bottles of Sta-soft fabric softener and Handy Andy) or the occasional chicken she had left out on her windowsill to defrost for that evening's roast. The wayward hound would proudly present his takings at my father's feet when he arrived home in the evenings, leaving either Claudio or myself to trek next door and return the stolen goods to their rightful owner.

Next up were Brett and Tamryn Leppington. They lived over the road and formed part of the Baird Avenue Gang, the name bestowed upon those who had resided in our little neighbourhood from what seemed like time immemorial. Then there was Mr Herschelman, our version of The Nutty Professor, who also happened to be my science and biology teacher. As a teenage boy, the need to study the scientific tables eluded me, but I do recall having learned from Mr Herschelman that, and I quote, "We were born to have sex and procreate – that's what it all boils down to."

Further down the street was our esteemed local town mayor, Mr Eckstein, who was elusive at best – but then again, there weren't any blue light brigades back in the early eighties. At number sixty-two was Billy Landman, who acted as the local security and KGB for the street. While ADHD had not yet made it into mainstream medical diagnoses, Billy would have most certainly been identified as a sufferer. I remember how he enthralled us with his conspiracy theories, going as far as building escape routes and lookout points on his garage roof. That man was ready for war.

As it was in any pleasant street, we had the aspirant upper class. The quaint little sign on the gate bearing the words "The Boyd's Nest" said it all. Mr Boyd was a Chartered Accountant and held a prominent position at the local Perm Building Society. Mrs Boyd was a reserved, distinguished lady who spent many afternoons tending to her manicured garden in preparation for the following week's elaborate afternoon tea parties. John, their eldest – who would, in later years, go on to become the lead drummer in the popular local band, The Parlotones – could be heard pounding out his craft – much to the dismay of the neighbours who longed for a few hours of respite.

Reaching the end of Baird Avenue, I would wait patiently for the silver Nissan Skyline to approach. When he turned the corner, Mr Pagonis would always flash his headlights twice. I never asked him why he insisted on doing that – it seemed rather pointless at that time of the morning – but it is, interestingly, something that I began doing when I started driving a few years later. For the remaining fifteen minutes en route to the iconic Roxana Bakery on the corner of Angus and President Street in the heart of

Germiston, I would endure the uncomfortable employer-employee silence that ensued.

I worked Mondays to Fridays before and after school, and full-time over weekends. We were paid by the hour, and I remember having to write my hours in Mr Pagonis's little book. It wasn't long before I graduated from washing pans to kneading dough, and then onto confectionary work, piping icing onto wedding cakes. Fridays at the bakery were always my favourite because it was kitka day – the Jewish community was prevalent in that area. I remember being mesmerised by how the bakers laced together and carefully plaited the sweet dough.

I must admit that greasing pans and kneading dough by hand was far from glamorous, but being paid seventy-five cents an hour most certainly made up for it. A bonus was the admiration of the young ladies who came into the bakery who, seeing me clad in my spotless white coat and baker's hat, presumed I was the creator of the magnificent, multi-tiered wedding cakes that were proudly on display in the bakery's front window and on the island in the middle of the store. I remember, on more than one occasion, proudly explaining to my admirers how painstakingly the cakes were prepared, only to have the romantic chick-magnet moment interrupted by Mrs Pagonis's booming voice thundering down from the small office upstairs: "Angelo, fill up the fridges with Coca-Cola for the after-church rush at eleven! Quickly, please!"

I remember once asking Nick why there was always a bottle of milk and a loaf of bread at the cash register. He told me to watch and learn. A customer would approach with their basket, and Nick would ring the milk and bread up as part of the transaction. When the unaware customer realised what was going on, it was always too late. "Oh," Nick would say, "I'm sorry, I thought they were yours." The customers would generally accept the "sincere" apology and forgive the indiscretion, paying for the bread and milk anyway.

After a year of working at Roxana Bakery, I was approached by a French gentleman, Jacques Cantillon, who often frequented the bakery and took a keen interest in what I was doing. He was the head chef of Jordan's, a restaurant specialising in French cuisine, owned by a Mr Jordan Papadopoulos. "Why don't you come and work for me?" he asked me on one of his visits. "I'll teach you how to be a chef." My mind was in a whirl. I was fifteen, and I was hungry for growth and opportunity. Without hesitation, I accepted Jacques' offer, and my career as a chef at Jordan's in Wadeville, the industrial hub of Germiston, began. My parents were mortified when I broke the news to them. Being a cook at the age of fifteen was certainly not a career path they wanted me to follow. But I saw things differently. I pictured myself not just as a chef, but a master chef – a brand that would one day transform the culinary world.

I cycled to the restaurant every day after school, and spent every weekend there, mastering my craft with Jacques as my mentor. I served up crêpes Suzette and flambés and other French specialities that most people had never seen or tasted before – delicacies like salmon and frogs' legs, and onion marmalades. By the age of sixteen, I had mastered most of the dishes in the restaurant. I made quite a name for myself in the area – I was even featured in the local newspaper.

Jordan's was one of the first restaurants to offer carveries and buffets. On Sundays, we would go the whole hog, quite literally. I remember an offended patron reporting the restaurant to the NSPCA for serving suckling pig, complete with an apple in its mouth.

Jordan's was also one of the first restaurants in the old Transvaal to serve live lobster. I negotiated that we had an aquarium out front where Freddy the lobster would be on display. I would take him out of the tank and walk around the restaurant holding him like a pet – it was quite the show. People would place their orders for Lobster Thermidor, thinking it was Freddy they were eating. What they were blissfully unaware of was that I had quietly slipped him back into his tank and replaced him with the abundant supply of frozen lobster that was always on standby in the kitchen freezers. Freddy must have been sold over forty times, with nobody any the wiser.

Having completed my schooling, I enrolled myself at the Wits Hotel School in Johannesburg without my parents' knowledge. They always presumed I was out working, and it never crossed their minds to ask me what else I was up to. We were like ships in the night – I would arrive home at midnight and be gone again by 4 a.m. With all that mattered being a certificate with a qualification on it, I funded my own tuition with my earnings from the restaurant, knowing that my parents did not have the means to cover the costs of my tertiary education. At the end of my first year, I was awarded Best Student, much to my surprise.

I'll never forget being called in by Mr Jorn Dionet, the head of the catering school, only to find my parents sitting in his office. It was my second year of studies, and I was struggling to juggle my academic and work commitments. I remember asking the girls in my class to cover for me during practicals. They would mark me as present on the register, and the lecturers never checked. In return, I would make sure that I was always available to help them with their projects.

I thought I was in Dionet's office to be reprimanded for non-attendance, and my parents thought it had something to do with me wanting to enrol at the school. Being a boisterous and arrogant young man at the time, I looked at my parents and then back at Dionet and said, "Doughnut (as I affectionately called him), what do you want?" The meeting began cordially with Dionet explaining why he had called us all in. With his attention focussed on my parents, he said, "I thought that since you are paying for Angelo to be here, you should know that your son's interest in his education has dwindled quite significantly this year. After being awarded Best Student in his first year, it has come to our attention that he is spending more time moonlighting at a restaurant as a chef than attending lectures."

"Oh Doughnut," I interjected, "you're just upset that I didn't come out to see you when you dined at Jordan's the other night." I remember seeing Dionet and another lecturer, Patterson, entering the restaurant that evening, but when they asked the maître d' to call me, I arrogantly refused, saying I was too busy. Although they may not have been able to fault me on the Chicken Sandeman and Beef Wellington I had prepared for them, I suspect they were utterly unimpressed that I had not acknowledged their presence. They left the restaurant later that evening, entirely unamused.

My mother sat in Dionet's office with her mouth open while my father was visibly emotional. "But..." my mother stammered, her eyes as large as saucers, "we're not paying for Angelo to be here. We thought you had called us in to discuss giving him a place at your institution. We had no idea that he was studying here." With that, the meeting was over. It was the first time my father had ever reached out and hugged me. It was also the first time I had seen him shed a tear.

I still get emotional when I think about that moment. It was all quite bizarre. I told Dionet, rather nonchalantly, that in all honesty, I preferred working. "There's not much you can teach me anymore, Doughnut," I said.

And that was that – the end of my studies, the beginning of my full-time career in the hospitality industry, meeting my wife, Debbie, starting a family, and moving from province to province, uprooting my young family every six months in search of the ultimate job. There were countless times that I would arrive home late at night and say to Debbie, "Girl, get packing, we're moving." She would protest, but her cries always fell on deaf ears. I was chasing a dream, and I wasn't about to let anything get in the way of it.

CHAPTER 2

Gencor – Transforming the Hostels

"Always ask yourself if what you're doing today is getting you closer to where you want to be tomorrow."
– Paulo Coelho

In the early 80's, Gencor's then-Human Resources Manager, Ronnie Lousteau, offered me an opportunity to work in the mining sector. Based in Evander, the Gencor Group was in its heyday – the gold price was soaring, and general managers on the mines were treated like gods and idols, while the conditions for migrant mineworkers in the industry were usually appalling.

I was tasked with converting the traditional hostels at the Winkelhaak mine into more comfortable living units by impacting on the quality and variety of meals served to the miners. The management skills I learned during my time at Gencor were invaluable, especially when it came to handling strikes and riots with composure, empathy and professionalism. I'll never forget the 31st of December 1992. Debbie (who was pregnant with Natasha at the time) and I were ringing in the New Year at home with my parents, enjoying an informal braai[4] around the swimming pool. At about 5 p.m., just as I was about to put the last of the steaks on the grill, my two-way radio suddenly went berserk, its familiar crackle echoing in my ear. There was trouble on the mine – the Indunas[5] needed me there, and it couldn't wait.

"But how can people be unhappy on New Year's Eve?" my elderly Italian father asked. I explained that there were twelve thousand men in that hostel and

---

4   Barbeque
5   A tribal councillor or headman

that situations frequently became volatile when not addressed immediately.

I gathered my belongings and rushed out to the car, my father following in my footsteps. "Angelo," he said, "what now?"

"Dad," I insisted, "stay with Mom, Debbie and Giancarlo – I'll be back as soon as I can."

He was having none of it. "I'm coming with you," he said stubbornly, getting into the passenger seat and fastening his seatbelt. Having never been on a mine, much less in a densely occupied hostel, he wanted to see what all the fuss was about.

Arriving at the hostel, we climbed the stairs to the mezzanine level, where the tribal officers were housed. The Indunas and tribal representatives explained that they had run out of meal tickets for the hostel dwellers. If the nightshift mineworkers were not handed meal tickets when they surfaced from underground the following morning, all hell was going to break loose.

A crowd began to form. Eventually, ninety percent of the hostel dwellers had gathered around us. With an intoxicated few rallying the snowballing crowd with chanting and toyi-toying[6] , the noise levels eventually became deafening.

My father stood rooted to the floor, the blood draining from his face, turning him a lighter shade of pale. After spending much of his adult life being brainwashed by anti-black government propaganda that created fear and fed the racial divide, all he saw was imminent danger. After two hours of negotiations, I resolved the matter with the tribal chiefs, Indunas and hostel monitors, and we left the building. Leaving the hostel grounds, the car was silent except for the sound of the old man muttering under his breath, "Never again, never again," over and over. By the time we arrived back at the house, my father had regained some composure. "Angelo," he said, "I am not happy that you work in that place. It's dangerous."

"What?" I laughed – and then casually added, "That was nothing, Dad."

I watched him fumbling in his jacket pocket. "Look," he said, producing a 1965 Beretta 6.35, a small handgun he had purchased for my mother many years earlier, "I was ready to use it – I would have emptied it to protect us. But thank God it wasn't necessary."

Thankful that he had not decided to pull it out during the chaos, I teased him. "Ah, Dad, I know why you kept it in your pocket – you saw that I had it all under control."

I watched my father's face and neck turn crimson. "You had bugger-all under control!" he erupted, throwing in a few choice Italian expletives for

---

6   A dance performed during protests

good measure. "I had already done the calculations," he continued, his hands shaking. "I knew I had to keep two bullets – one for me, and one for you. I didn't want to be left to the mercy of our attackers. But the bloody problem was, I couldn't remember if I had six or eight bullets loaded," he added sheepishly.

For weeks afterwards, I received daily telephone calls from my father, checking to see whether I had resigned. It was not long before I was offered a more senior position at Western Platinum Mines in Mooinooi in the North West Province. Unfortunately, this grouping was somewhat more militant, and I decided that this time, it was in my parents' interest that I did not disclose where I was working.

I travelled from town to town, opening one office after another. In the back of my mind, I knew I was building up the experience and the knowledge to run an empire. I was young and self-confident, with an insatiable desire to be successful. I had seen enough hardship in my life – particularly the stigma and sorrow that accompanied abject poverty. I dreamed of spearheading a business that would create jobs for thousands of families; where everybody had the means to a brighter future. Back then, it was never about the power I could wield, or living off the reputation I had gained.

CHAPTER 3

Growth at Grantham Foods

"Business opportunities are like buses – there's always another one coming."
– Richard Branson

In 1995, I moved on to Nissan in Rosslyn for about a year, managing their facilities and catering, and then joined Grantham Integrated Foods as their Regional Operational Manager. For the first time, I was running various operations
instead of a single kitchen. I travelled around the country, putting out fires at
problematic sites. During this time, a little company called Dyambu, run by
someone called Gavin Watson and Danny Mansell, kept popping up everywhere, knocking on our clients' doors and trying to take business from us.

Over the three years I spent with Grantham Foods, I was promoted
through the ranks, eventually being appointed as Inland Director. During
my tenure, I became friendly with Sam Molope, one of our black-empow-
ered suppliers who owned two bakeries in the Ga-Rankuwa and Brits areas. Our conversations often centred around cash flow, and his lack of it.
On one occasion, I suggested that he list the company to raise funds. "It's
an easy way to give your business a large cash injection," I told him. He
must have liked the idea because, not long afterwards, he visited me and
told me he was in final discussions with people at JCI Limited, the Fourie
Brothers, Anthony Block, Frank Davidson, and even Cyril Ramaphosa.
They were going to buy up a number of different companies, his included,
and list them on the Johannesburg Stock Exchange as The Molope Group.

"Angelo," he said, "I want you and Grantham to be part of this."

And so, in 1996, Grantham Integrated Foods became Molope Foods. I met
with Cyril Ramaphosa on three different occasions, and he worked with the
company to bring in new business. Molope grew and grew and grew. The
directors were all given special share options, and we all made a great deal of

money out of them. Debbie, who had been working with me, was appointed as P.A. to the Managing Director, and we became one big, happy family.

And then, the one thing that every child dreads, but knows is inevitable, came to pass. It was 1997, and Debbie and I were on our way overseas. I had won an incentive trip for running the best all-round operation at the Molope Group that year. My mother, although fighting liver cancer at the time, offered to take care of Giancarlo while we were away. Natasha would spend time with Debbie's parents. We met at the airport and shared a meal before saying goodbye to the children and boarding our flight.

While I knew my mother was ill, she tried hard not to show it, and I never fully realised just how much of a grip the cancer had on her. Back in South Africa, I arrived at my mother's home to find a shadow of the woman I had waved goodbye to ten days earlier. In a matter of a week, the cancer had taken charge. This once strapping woman was now bedridden and writhing in agony.

It was only the two of us in the room, and I sat down beside her. "Mom," I said, fighting back the tears, "this isn't right. It's just not fair. Have we not endured enough?"

My mother looked at me sternly. "Stop playing the victim, Angelo," she rasped.

My parents died within a month of each other. My mother succumbed to her cancer on the 10th of January 1998, and my father committed suicide exactly a month later. I was thirty-one at the time.

Whatever inheritance we might have received from my mother was cleaned out by a family member, who was appointed executor of my mother's estate. There was a small policy that my father had in place that paid out a little money every month, but it barely covered the costs of supporting my brother Claudio and putting him through college.

Stop playing the victim, Angelo – my mother's poignant words reverberated. Even today – whenever I find myself facing seemingly insurmountable challenges, I hear her voice. *Stop playing the victim, Angelo.*

I knew that the only way out was through. I would wake up at 3.30 a.m. every morning to start my day – something that is now firmly ingrained in my DNA – with my primary goals being financial independence, contributing towards my family and, most importantly, making a difference in the world.

Although I felt like a victim of circumstance, I refused to allow it to define me. Filled with the passion of youth and driven by a strong sense of purpose, nothing was going to stop me from going out there and grabbing hold of everything life had to offer – with both hands.

CHAPTER 4

Dyambu's War on Molope Foods

"Without labour, nothing prospers."
– Sophocles

Throughout my career at Molope Foods, I recall that Dyambu continued to show up at the hostels, wearing their yellow T-shirts, upsetting the unions and creating havoc for me. The unions would grant Dyambu permission to bus the hostel dwellers to their presentations, usually after free yellow caps and T-shirts were handed out to everyone. It became a regular thing on a Monday morning – I would receive a call. *There are problems at the hostel. You need to go out. The unions are striking. They want Dyambu in and Molope out.* This was more of an irritation than a potential threat. I would drive to the hostels, sit down with the union leaders and hear them out.

The union members would walk into the meeting, decked out in their newly acquired yellow attire. "You're serving us rotten food," they would say. It was always the same old song, but when we unpacked everything, the truth would always come out – Dyambu had paid them a visit.

"We'll give you anything you want," I'd say. "You want caviar on toast? I'll give you caviar on toast if that's what you want. But then I need you to help me by speaking to mine management and getting them to increase the budget."

Ninety percent of the time, the matter was resolved within a few hours, usually culminating in a late lunch at the local Spur steakhouse. "Come," I'd say, "let's go out and have something to eat." And off we would go. With the ball thrown back into the mine's court, I paid for lunch, and Molope retained their catering contract.

The last thing the mines wanted to do was hand their catering operations over to a company who entered their hostels over a weekend, bussed their staff off to a conference venue, showed them presentations featuring a mine hostel catering utopia, and got them so agitated that, come Monday morning, the unions were all on strike, refusing to return to work until Dyambu was serving breakfast, lunch and dinner.

Gavin Watson referred to these sessions as "RDP Conferences". The term RDP[7] was an ANC buzz phrase that Gavin used to his advantage, telling the mineworkers that they had the right to choose who they wanted to prepare their meals, and where the budget should be spent. Gold Fields was dead set against Dyambu, thanks to Gavin's weekend rallies. Of course, they loved Molope Foods. I dealt with two procurement officers, Lynette Blysteiner and Philip Hayward, both of whom spoke freely with me when I visited about how much they disliked Dyambu and everything they stood for. I also recall hearing that Gavin was bribing the union officials to get them to work with their members against mine management. (I suppose some people could consider the Spur lunches that I treated officials to, as the same kind of business tactics that Gavin used.)

I believed that the rift that Dyambu seemed to be creating between mine management and their workforce was a dangerous threat to probably the largest industry in the country.

On one occasion, I was in a meeting with Lynette at the Gold Fields head office when Philip burst into her office, having been out on various site visits with union leaders to Molope, Fedics and Dyambu. This was standard practice, with unions having a major impact on how mine operations were run at the time.

"The paint on the walls at Dyambu is so fresh that you can see the cockroaches moving under it," he said with disgust.

Lynette shook her head. "The day Dyambu is awarded a contract at Gold Fields," she said, "I will resign."

At that stage, I had never physically interacted with Gavin Watson. I knew who he was, and I found his persistence impressive, albeit annoying. The amount of money he spent on buses, caps, T-shirts and venue hire must have run into the tens of thousands, and something told me that he wasn't going to give up until he got what he wanted.

At the same time, things were not all sunshine and roses back on my home

7   The Reconstruction and Development Programme was a government programme focussed on attending to the needs of the previously disadvantaged sectors of the South African population. Although they had achieved political freedom, economic freedom remained in the hands of the white minority. The RDP served to address this problem.

ground at Molope Foods. The business was strong, but the way the board of directors treated Sam Molope was getting under my skin. What I remember most about that old man was how, in the early days, he would collect all the unsold bread from his two bakeries at the end of each working day and give it away to pensioners and the poor. When his business was amalgamated into Molope Foods, he was given a beautiful vintage car to drive around in. There were times when we would sit together and reminisce about the good old days, and he would tell me how he was being ill-treated by the other board members.

Eventually, he was forced to leave, and the company insisted he give back the car. This upset him immensely and saddened me deeply. By the end of 1998, I had reached my pinnacle at Molope Foods. There was nothing holding me there, and I needed a new challenge.

CHAPTER 5

Meritum – A Sinister Sale

"In the end, all business operations can be reduced to three words – people, products, and profits. Unless you've got a good team, you can't do much with the other two."
– Lee Iacocca, President and CEO of Chrysler

It was a little-known company called Meritum that sparked the founding of Dyambu, which later went on to become Bosasa. Dr Jurgen Smith, whom everybody called Doc Smith, founded Meritum with Fanie van Zijl, a Springbok athlete. During that time, high numbers of juvenile delinquents were incarcerated in the same prisons as adult offenders. These children faced grave danger to their safety and wellbeing, and so eventually, Meritum evolved into the Lindela Repatriation Centre, a detention centre for undocumented migrants in South Africa.

With the ANC coming into power in the mid-nineties, Doc Smith, concerned about the lack of black participation and empowerment in the business, decided it was time to sell. He had heard about the Watson family in the Eastern Cape and their political connections and decided to reach out to Gavin Watson's friend, Danny Mansell, to see if he could broker a deal. Doc Smith had previously worked with Danny Mansell at the Small Business Development Corporation, where Doc Smith held a board position, and Danny managed the Eastern Cape branch.

Danny Mansell introduced Ronnie Watson to Doc Smith and Fanie van Zijl. In true Watson style – as explained to journalist, Adriaan Basson in an interview with Hilda Ndude – Ronnie said that the business would be sold to members of the ANC Women's League (ANCWL), with Hilda Ndude – an activist who had been closely involved with Nelson Mandela's 1990 release from prison – at the helm. The other women included Nomatyala

Hangana, Baleka Mbete, Nozuko 'Girly' Pikoli, Makho Njobe, Lindiwe Maseko, Mavivi Myakayaka-Manzini, Adelaide Tambo, Nomvula Mokonyane, and Nosiviwe Mapisa-Nqakula.

To the women, Ronnie pitched the idea as a business opportunity, a company that had already secured numerous catering and cleaning services contracts on mines across the West Rand of Johannesburg. Being struggle stalwarts, the ladies had had little time to bring in money, so this was a golden opportunity for them to become entrepreneurs in their own right. They could raise money for themselves, and the business would also distribute cash to the men, women and children at the various mining hostels, and later to poorer women from Limpopo and the Eastern Cape. Concerned about their complete lack of experience in running a business, Ronnie assured them that he would be bringing his brother Gavin on board to manage the business for them.[8]

Ronnie Watson gave the green light, and the deal was signed. The ladies named the company Dyambu (a Xitsonga word meaning "sun") and were later introduced to Gavin Watson as the company's CEO. Doc Smith and Fanie were convinced that they had sold their business to the women with their ANCWL ties, and they thought that they owned the company outright. What the sellers and buyers failed to realise was that the company was now primarily in the hands of Gavin Watson and Danny Mansell, who each owned 45% of the business. Only 10% belonged to the women, and they were none the wiser. To add salt to the wound, although Fanie van Zijl was clear that he wanted to retain ownership of the Lindela property, Doc Smith neglected to include this clause in the deal, leading to the bitter end of that particular friendship.

In the background, a master plan to hijack the Dyambu women of their shares was taking shape. Perks – or what they thought were perks – were plentiful. But as the expenses were going up, so the value of their shareholdings was going down.

As the women began taking up positions in the ANC government, Gavin and Danny took full control of the company. Three years later, in 2000, Gavin Watson handed Hilda Ndude a legal document and told her to sign it. While all of this was playing out, I believe that something far more sinister was being birthed – the rise of a company that would successfully manage to systematically capture an entire country.

---

8   Basson, Adriaan, *Blessed by Bosasa*, Jonathan Ball Publishers, 2019

PART 2

CHAPTER 6

Meeting Gavin Watson

*"If you have carefully examined a hundred people you met in your life jour-
ney, it means that you have read a hundred different books! Every person
you know is a book; the world is full of walking books; some are boring, some
are marvellous, some are weak, some are powerful, but they are all useful
because they all carry different experiences of different paths!"*
– Mehmet Murat ildan

My first encounter with Gavin Watson was as unplanned as it was memorable. At Molope Foods, everybody flew economy class but, thanks to
the Voyager Miles we accumulated during our travels, we were at least
guaranteed free access to the local airport lounges. During the course of
April 1999, having concluded my business in Port Elizabeth for the week,
I was whiling away the time in the airport lounge, waiting for my flight to
Johannesburg to be called. The silence was suddenly broken by a rather
arrogant gentleman – I guessed that he must have been in his fifties at the
time – bursting in through the doors, speaking so loudly that the whole
room could hear his telephone conversation. He brushed past me and sat
down in the seat behind me.

While following his conversation – and it was difficult not to – I picked
up on an undertone of black politics. Everything was "*comrade* this" and
"*comrade* that". By now, other people in the room were staring at him,
and, as soon as Gavin noticed, he would speak even louder. He ended the
call and made another, this time speaking fluent Xhosa. Understanding
the language myself from my time on the mines, I heard him say, "Do these
whites know what they're dealing with?" I sat up straight in my chair. Although I had never seen this man before, I wondered whether this was not
perhaps the infamous Gavin Watson from Dyambu. If it wasn't Watson,

it was another whitey spinning one of those "the whites have stolen from the black people" stories to gain credibility. I knew that game well. The conversation continued. "Comrade Mngomezulu," he said. I held my breath. There was also a "Mngomezulu" who had been giving me problems at Scott Hostel in Klerksdorp. This *had* to be Gavin Watson. I liked his chutzpah and his arrogance. I remember thinking to myself that this kind of attitude might be *exactly* what South Africa needed in order to move forward and grow. Despite my misgivings about Dyambu, I decided to contact Gavin when I was back in town.

When the boarding call was announced, I waited for him to get up and join the queue. When he was out of sight, I approached the receptionist at the entrance to the airport lounge and asked whether Gavin had perhaps handed in his business card. Although she was in possession of it, she refused to give me his number.

The following day, I called up an ex-colleague, Trevor Ronaldson, who had previously worked with me at SAMCOR and was now employed at Dyambu. Trevor told me how progressive the company was, and that, yes, my getting involved would be a positive move, for both parties. I picked up the phone, dialled Dyambu's number, and asked to speak to Gavin Watson. The receptionist refused to transfer me, so I asked to speak to David Sadie, Dyambu's Human Resources Manager at the time. David agreed to meet with me the following day, and it was there that I was introduced to Danny Mansell, Dyambu's Managing Director. Following my meeting with Danny, I was ushered into the boardroom, where I found myself face to face with the infamous Gavin Watson.

"Angelo," Gavin probed, offering me a seat, "give me your honest opinion. Tell me where we're going wrong?"

And so I told him. "Firstly," I said, "you are doing your costings incorrectly." I knew this because Molope had won numerous bids against Dyambu. Gavin motioned for me to continue. "You are budgeting for one hundred percent participation in meals, but not everybody eats every day. You should be budgeting at around ninety-one percent."

Gavin was visibly flustered. There I was, a young man in his early thirties, telling this business owner, twenty years my senior, how to run his shop.

"Tell me where else we're going wrong?" he asked.

"Gavin," I said, "your problem is management. You don't manage your business." His attention focussed solely on me, I continued. "If you think your politicking is going to pull you through, you're wrong. You are spending millions of rands on T-shirts, caps, drinks and buses, but you're getting nowhere. All I'm doing is taking the unions to the Spur for lunch, and we're winning the bids."

Right there and then, Gavin employed me. I resigned from Molope Foods with immediate effect, and they had no choice but to accept. Little did I know at the time that I was making a pact with the devil.

It quickly emerged that working for Gavin and being part of his circle meant demonstrating a profound display of loyalty – an irrevocable pledge of brotherhood, similar to that of a blood covenant.

On my first day at Dyambu, on the 12th of May 1999, Gavin paraded me around the office like his prize racehorse, introducing me as the new boy on the block, telling everybody that between the two of us, we were going to turn the company around. Within a matter of an hour, I was handed a laptop, business cards, and a large cash advance that I hadn't asked for. Oom (Uncle) Vossie Vorster, responsible for procuring Dyambu's fleet of company cars, was instructed to order a brand-new Audi for me. I was told to be at the Bundu Inn Conference Centre in Randfontein at 11 a.m. the following morning.

It was a Saturday, and everybody was in uniform – uniforms being compulsory. It being my second day on the job, I didn't yet have mine, so I stuck out like a sore thumb.

By the end of day two, I had a reasonably good idea of who Gavin was and what he was about. I remember thinking that the way he conducted himself with people he deemed weaker than himself was both demeaning and humiliating. He appeared to be extremely arrogant, abrupt and callous – it was his way or the highway. If you didn't take an interest in what he was talking about, he would blatantly call you out in front of everybody. I'll never forget him taking to the stage that day and preaching about love from the Book of Corinthians, and then switching into hate-mode and lambasting a gentleman by the name of Gert van der Walt, who ran Dyambu's butchery. Gert had asked Gavin if he could be excused from the company conference because his son was playing in an important rugby tournament, and he wanted to be there to support him. This did not go down well, and Gavin let the poor guy have it.

"You're a white male in the new South Africa," Gavin blasted from his podium. "You're never going to get anywhere if you lose your job here, so you'd better toe the line."

Gert van der Walt's only sin that day was being a good father.

It was the first time I had heard Gavin make a threat like this, but it certainly wasn't the last. If you were a pale male in your thirties or forties, Gavin relished the opportunity to use the white male threat on you.

Eventually, Gert *did* lose his job. Having decided that enough was enough, he opened his own butchery on the side, supplying meat to the Randfontein Mining Operations. When Gavin found out, he had Gert arrested. Some of the directors had contacts in the police force, so Gavin told them to arrange that a charge of theft be brought against Gert. Gavin was convinced that Gert had stolen from Dyambu to fund his new business, which was not the case. I remember Gert telling me at his disciplinary hearing that it was Gavin who had inspired the entrepreneur in him, and that after Gavin's threats he realised that as a white male in the new South Africa, he had better do his own damn thing – and quickly.

Something else that Gavin loved calling people out on was their weight, especially if it was the kind that tipped the scales. This shaming didn't only happen in a person's private office but in front of the whole company. There are video recordings of Gavin singling people out at conferences, saying, "All the fat people, get up!" Once they were standing, he would remind them that they were so overweight that they would never find work elsewhere. There were countless times where I had to intervene and calm the waters as people sobbed their hearts out in my office after he had belittled them and made them feel utterly useless. There wasn't much that I could do, other than to apologise on his behalf. Although I warned him that one day somebody was going to take him to the CCMA[9], he remained undeterred. He would pretend that he was listening to me and then make a joke about it afterwards. I never knew whether or not to take him seriously. The few times he tried that stunt on me, I fobbed him off or ignored him.

If Gavin liked a person, he'd take them out on a walk – or "on the prowl" as I preferred to call it – around the office park. Depending on the time of day, the walk would be followed by either a lunch or a dinner. Anyone taken on one of his walks knew they had been accepted into the pack. Of course, if Gavin decided he no longer liked a person, they'd be chased from the family.

Although I had no idea what I was walking into when I joined Dyambu, it didn't take me long to find out. Resources were limited, and finances were tight. Operationally, the company was a mess. Most of the basic elements essential to running a successful business were missing. There appeared to be no systems, no processes, and no procedures. It was no wonder that Dyambu was losing business. Gavin, in those early days, only came into

---

9   Commission for Conciliation, Mediation and Arbitration (CCMA) is a dispute resolution body established in terms of the South African Labour Relations Act.

the office on a Wednesday. When he wasn't at Dyambu's offices, he was consulting to Sun International's casino division. He stayed at the Indaba Hotel in Fourways, Johannesburg, and was living out of the boot of a borrowed car.

Something I've always been good at is building up businesses. To me, business is much like life – it works best when approached from a structured perspective. Decide on your outcomes, establish a strategy, put the right people in the right places, create synergies between these people so that they perform well together and enjoy the work they do, and then implement systems and procedures to manage the machine. When everybody understands what the playing field is, and you can help them not only to discover the benefits they can bring to the table but motivate them to become the best versions of themselves in the process, you have superstars in the making.

I've never been a marketer – I'm an operations person. I can solve problems and make things work, but don't ask me to sell stuff to people; I'm not good at that at all. Still, Gavin insisted that I would best serve the business in a marketing capacity. His modus operandi seemed to be along the lines of, "Fake it 'til we make it." Wherever you looked, there was smoke and mirrors. Even if Dyambu did not provide a particular service, we would have to tell our client, "Yes, we can." It wasn't long before I also took over human resources, procurement, and eventually tenders and bid submissions. The company mushroomed tenfold from its original staff complement of four hundred people, with about one hundred and eighty staff reporting directly to me.

Back in May 1999 when I first came on board, and before Broad-Based Black Economic Empowerment was written into law, it became clear to me that one of the many reasons Dyambu had not experienced any growth in years was because of something I termed "kitchen politicking". According to Gavin, everything that went wrong was politically motivated.

"The only reason we weren't awarded that contract is because of the old white South African mentality that black people should not be empowered," Gavin would say, moping around the office in defeat. In the meantime, the company, on paper, was far from black empowered – it was 91% *white* empowered. Although Gavin claimed that Dyambu was wholly owned by the ANC Women's League, I was suspicious – I rarely saw a female ANC politician on Dyambu's premises. Every time Dyambu lost a contract, it was because the "white capitalists" were against the Watsons. Gavin would stomp around with news clippings of Cyril Ramaphosa and Molope Foods, cursing them for stealing his idea to form a facilities management company – something that couldn't have been further from the truth.

Gavin had created the perception that Dyambu was not only owned by the ANC Women's League but that it *was* the ANC Women's League. This, according to the women involved in Dyambu, was never the case. Gavin believed that mine management was reluctant to bend to a company that was aligned to the ruling party. At the time, the South African mining industry was controlled by members of the old apartheid system – in other words, mostly old Afrikaner men – who, according to Danny in particular, felt that doing business with a company like Dyambu, owned by the very people they had fought to keep out of power for decades, was out of the question. This was hardly smoothed over by Gavin, who approached mine management with the antagonising premise of, "The only reason you're not giving us your business is because you're kicking back against change."

The mine managers loved their rugby, a sport the Watson brothers – Valence, Daniel, Ronnie and Gavin – had taken to the black townships in the Eastern Cape as teenagers. Daniel "Cheeky" Watson was renowned for being one of the first white South African Rugby Union players to participate in a mixed-race game of rugby – something that was forbidden at the time. I believe that many of the Afrikaner mine managers at the time, already annoyed with Gavin's antics with the unions and the strikes that ensued, saw the Watsons as misfits and sell-outs who, now that the tables had been turned were flexing their muscles, using their alliance with the ANC to strong-arm the mines into awarding contracts to Dyambu.

In those early days, Gavin continued to wreak havoc wherever he went. I remember attending a meeting with Colin Peens, the Human Resources Manager for AngloGold, a potential new client. Lindie Gouws, Dyambu's Client Liaison Manager, was there to facilitate the introductions. Exasperated with union interference in mine management decisions, Colin told me, "Angelo, you can't have the union telling the mines what to do – you can't have the tail wagging the dog." Lindie immediately relayed the message to Gavin, who, at his next meeting with the union leaders, showed them a picture of a dog with the word "Union" above it. Above the tail were the words "Union Leaders".

"Look," he said, pointing at the picture, "mine management is calling you dogs."

In June of 1999, I received a call from the *Beeld* newspaper. "I believe Dyambu is the reason for the current strike on the mines," the journalist probed. "Do you have any comment?" I told the journalist I knew nothing about the strike. In truth, I was terrified.

While Gavin was out riling up the mineworkers, my first port of call was to bring in some much-needed business. My focus was the tangible low-hanging fruit – in other words, ex-clients. While at Molope Foods, I identified the Gold Fields Mining Group as a potential client. Years and years of work and negotiations with Patrick Mayne, the Human Resources Manager at Leeudoorn Mine, bore fruit, with Gold Fields deciding to work with the Molope group to run their hostel catering division at the mine. Once the contract was signed, Molope would have been primed to take over Kloof, Libanon, and all the other mines in that region. Unfortunately, this coincided with me leaving the company, and so the deal was left to conclude in the hands of my successor – someone I had come to know as unreliable. Had I not handed in my resignation that Friday, I would have been due to sign the contract between Molope Foods and Leeudoorn the following Monday at 2 p.m.

I remember sitting with Gavin on that Monday, my first official day in the office, saying: "There's no way that they're going to be able to deliver on my promise – not with that guy in my place."

Gavin, who had also had his eye firmly on the Gold Fields Mining Group, posed a challenge. "Angelo," he said, "if you want to show me loyalty, get me into the Gold Fields Mining Group. Make sure that Molope doesn't sign that contract. You go in there and sign it for us."

This was a challenge I had not seen coming. "Gavin," I said, "do you realise what buttons you're pressing by asking me to do this?"

Gavin showed me the door. "Take Doc Smith with you," he added.

Driving out to Leeudoorn Mine that Monday morning, Doc hinted that his accompanying me to this meeting was a planned encounter. I sensed that Gavin wanted him to keep an eye on me and make sure that I did as instructed.

It was 9.30 a.m. and there Doc and I were, sitting opposite Patrick Mayne in his office. Charles Freeland, the regional National Union of Mineworkers coordinator, was seated next to Patrick.

I cleared my throat. "Patrick, I know you're supposed to sign a contract with Molope later today, but I'm going to ask you not to." Patrick looked at me strangely, but before he could open his mouth to ask me why, I explained that I had moved over to Dyambu. He was visibly shocked. "Give me one month," I said. "Let me prove to you that Dyambu can do a better job. And if we can't, then you sign with Molope."

"Angelo," said Patrick, looking at me, and then at Doc Smith, and then back at me, "we've been working together on the Leeudoorn contract for some time now. If you're not comfortable with Molope signing the deal, then I'm not comfortable. I'm going to suspend the signing of the contract." Doc Smith could hardly believe his ears. Although Patrick's compromise wasn't first prize, Dyambu was finally in with a chance. If we won this contract over Molope Foods, Dyambu would have first dibs on the other two Gold Fields hostels that were within a five-kilometre radius of Leeudoorn.

"I'm not going to simply hand the other two mines over to you, Angelo," Patrick added. "If you want the Kloof and Libanon contracts, you'll have to go and negotiate directly with them."

We all shook hands, after which Doc and I headed out to meet with the union leaders. It was no big deal. I didn't have to treat them any differently. There was no bribery or putting them on a pedestal, and they were happy with the potential switch.

"It's done," I said, arriving back at the offices later that morning. Gavin's eyeballs nearly fell out of their sockets. "But now," I added, "we have to start working." Convincing them *not* to sign with Molope was child's play in comparison to the amount of catch-up that lay ahead. Not only did we need to implement proper systems and develop sound strategies, but we also needed to apply stringent criteria to assure the mines that, in terms of their contract with us, they were permitted to impose penalties if we failed to perform. Most of all, we had to find a way to convince them that their negative perceptions around Dyambu were irrelevant when compared to the value we could add to their operations.

CHAPTER 7

The Hostel Takeover

"I found Rome a city of bricks and left it a city of marble."
– Emperor Augustus

As a twenty-five-year-old, I worked with a gentleman by the name of Ronnie Lousteau out at Winkelhaak Mine in Evander, Mpumalanga. He was the Human Resources Manager and came close to firing me on several occasions when he discovered I had pulled yet another one of my youthful pranks. While the gold mines were booming, it was also an uncertain time, and Ronnie did not always take kindly to my shenanigans.

It was the early 1990s, and the mine had just switched over to a computerised operating system. One of the systems brought in was a purchase order system called MATMAN. Whatever it was that you needed, you could order it. Once entered, the data moved up a level to your boss for approval, proceeding through the ranks until it reached the stores who issued the purchase order and sent it off to the supplier. Occasionally, there would be a special order for a non-standard item. These would be printed out for the mine's General Manager – who, in those years, was as terrifying and as revered as the Pope – to approve before going to the stores.

Willem van der Merwe (one of the hostel managers) and I had an acrimonious relationship. I didn't enjoy his dry sense of humour, and we were always finding fault with one another. I always said he had the IQ of a bread roll and the EQ of a railway sleeper. Two days before I left the mine to join a new company, I sat with Sean Elson, the only friend I had on the mine (who also happened to be a computer fundi), to place a special order. Most people had never changed their login details from the standard passwords provided, so I logged into the system as Willem van der Merwe and ordered him a second-hand brain. The order, elaborate in its specification, was a dig at his rather dry and militant personality.

Of course, this ended up on the General Manager's desk. Willem was called in and immediately suspended. Although he was dragged over the coals, Ronnie Lousteau knew I was the guilty party. If he could, he probably would have fired me, but by then, I was long gone.

And then, lo and behold, fifteen years later, Ronnie turns up as the Human Resources Manager of Kloof Mine – the next target on my client acquisition trail.

I called Ronnie up, and he agreed to meet with me for lunch. I told him about my move from Molope Foods to Dyambu, and he explained how he had been happily farming cucumbers in the Natal Midlands when Gold Fields had called him up and asked him to help them sort out their problems with the union – starting with their issues over the company's current catering contract. Although he had accepted their offer, and despite his previous experience working with the unions, he was struggling.

"You either want a corporate running the show," I said, "or you want a guy who has had experience in training and developing the unions." I explained how Gavin would deal with one of the union heads, Jackson Mafika, and resolve their issues, and I would work directly with Ronnie and his management team. Ronnie was impressed, and we entered into negotiations.

Although it was not within his power to simply hand the contract over to Dyambu, Ronnie promised me that he would support our application if we delivered on our promise and provided a solution that met the mine's requirements. I assured Ronnie that we would.

In the meantime, Gavin was out causing a strike at Kloof Mine.

Ronnie called me. "Angelo," he said, the sweat dripping from his brow on the other end of the line, "the unions are striking because of Dyambu." I promptly went in and sorted it out. Within a week, Ronnie remained true to his word, and Dyambu was brought on board. With our costings correctly (and profitably) calculated at R6.10 per person per day, we were able to offer every employee at Kloof Mine three square meals a day. We were in business. At the time, Lynette Blysteiner had been with Gold Fields for eighteen years, but she kept to her word and, as soon as that contract was signed, she resigned. Philip Hayward stayed on.

One thing I'm certain of is that business is about relationships. It's about trust. It's about delivering on your promises. Ronnie Lousteau knew me, trusted me, and, from what he had heard from colleagues at Molope Foods and Winkelhaak Mine, he knew my work ethic was vouched for. It was this that ultimately sealed the deal.

My second port of call was to clean up the way Dyambu did their tenders. While some of Gavin and Danny's excuses had a certain measure of validity attached to them, I called their bluff. Many tenders were being awarded to competitors purely because Dyambu was making critical errors. Not only were tenders being costed incorrectly, but they were making stupid mistakes in their proposals and presentations.

Sitting in our first meeting together, Danny showed me the figures for Bafokeng Mine in Rustenburg, one of the tenders that Molope Foods had been awarded. "There's no way that Molope should have won that tender," he insisted. "They costed out at R7.85 per person per day, while we costed ours at R13.75. They must have cheated on their pricing."

"Show me how you calculated your pricing," I asked. He handed me the calculations and, after examining them, I laughed out loud. "Danny," I said, "you've got marbles rattling around in that head of yours. We all know that not everybody sits down at every meal. You can't cost a piece of boerewors out at R5.50 if only 80% of the mineworkers and ancillary staff are sitting down for that meal – you've got to look at participation values. You could easily have costed that boerewors out at R4.85 per person."

Danny looked at me, the lightbulb in his head flickering wildly. Eventually, the penny dropped.

Although many of the mines were initially reluctant to outsource their catering operations, with Dyambu on board they began realising that it was in their best interests to focus their energies on what they were good at and allow us to run what we excelled in. Many were concerned that, once on board, our pricing would fluctuate dramatically. I personally assured the concerned parties that there would be no increases beyond the Consumer Price Index and, in fact, signed this into the contracts.

With Dyambu experiencing unprecedented growth, it dawned on Gavin and Danny that we were going to need to secure funding from the banks if we were to continue with sufficient operating capital to cover our monthly overheads. They knew the banks would laugh at us, but neither of them had a plan B. Well versed in thinking out of the box, I proposed that we allow the company to grow organically without the need for external funding. We would invoice clients on the 15th and the 30th of every month and request that they pay us within two days of presenting our invoice. That way, we could stretch our suppliers to forty-five days, thereby leveraging our creditors off our debtors. The plan was simple but effective.

Next up on my client acquisition trail was Libanon Mine. Wimpie Greeff had been my client at Oryx Mine at Molope Foods and had since moved over to Libanon as their Human Resources Manager. He had the utmost trust and respect for me, and a soft spot for Debbie and me as a couple. He signed an agreement with Dyambu, and the company was soon firmly entrenched in Kloof and Libanon mines, catering for about fourteen thousand people on a daily basis. One thing was certain – Dyambu had become a force to be reckoned with in the South African catering industry.

That same year, I decided to take the Human Resources teams from Kloof and Libanon Mines out to lunch. There were about fifteen of us, and we all met up at the renowned restaurant The Butcher Shop & Grill in Sandton Square. I took extra cash along just in case I maxed out my credit card and asked Debbie for her credit cards as well. I probably had about R45 000 to spend in total. I have never, and I mean never, in all my life, entertained a group of people who could drink as much as they did that day. Magnum bottle after magnum bottle of wine was ordered. They were quaffing it back as if it were water. One of the guys liked the bottles so much that he refused to allow the waiter to remove them from the table when they were empty. He was stashing them under his chair so that he could take them home and make lamp stands out of them. It wasn't long before the cigars came out.

I maxed out all my personal credit cards, all the cash, and each of Debbie's cards that afternoon. By then, I had learned two important things about the mining guys – one, they had expensive taste in well-aged wine, and two, they were exceptionally loyal to their employers and their suppliers. Nobody can break that.

I left my guests later that evening debating whether they were going to take the party to Montecasino or continue at Sandton Square. Driving home that night, I felt my chest swell with pride – I had single-handedly secured the largest contract ever outsourced to a facilities management company.

It wasn't long before we saw an influx of contracts. The mine managers were talking to each other, and we experienced a significant shift in attitude on their part – better service at a more competitive rate made logical business sense. At the time, there was disharmony at Randfontein Estates Gold Mine, which was owned by Randgold and managed by the

Kebbles. Harmony Gold, the mining giant that had recently taken over all the failing mines in the Free State and turned them around, was looking to acquire the operation. In early January 2000, Brett Kebble and the JCI conducted a hostile takeover of Randfontein Estates. We were the polony in the middle – Bernard Swanepoel, the CEO of Harmony Gold at the time, hated us, but the Kebbles loved us. Thanks to Roger Kebble's relationship with Ronnie Watson, I suspect Dyambu was invited to run the Randfontein Estates catering operation. We had barely gotten started when Bernard Swanepoel and Harmony Gold struck back and conducted a hostile takeover of their own.

With stringent rules and regulations to curtail reckless spending on independent contractors, Harmony Gold had a good reputation for low-cost mining. They did not like Dyambu one bit – so much so that I was once made to wait eight hours outside Leigh Bateman's office for a meeting.[10] I refused to move.

In the end, Harmony kept Dyambu on at Randfontein Estates and was soon so impressed with our service that they asked us to take over the catering operations at their Free State mines. Up next was Hartebeesfontein Mine in Klerksdorp.

It wasn't long before Dyambu was running most of the large mine catering operations in the region. This once floundering company, with its questionable past and only a handful of customers, was now beginning to make a significant impact on the mining industry.

Despite the significant growth spurt, profitability was low. Where we should have been attaining 30% to 32% profit margins, we were only obtaining in the region of 18% to 20%. I put it down to bad management, compounded by the additional costs associated with moving to our impressive new office park in Luipaardsvlei, Krugersdorp. With there being little time for me to get out to the different sites to check up on people, I employed a chap by the name of Leon Snyman – a streetwise past master in the catering industry and a maverick in his management style – and tasked him with running the Kloof and Libanon contracts so that I could focus on building the business. Leon had previously been my boss when I worked on the mines in the Rustenburg Marikana area.

As a compromise, I woke up at 3 a.m. every Saturday, collected the company's Volkswagen Combi and drove out to each of the different

---

10 Leigh Bateman was the Catering Manager for Harmony at the time.

operational units with Gavin Watson and a team of operational chaps. By 8 p.m., we were home, and up again at 3 a.m. the following morning. It was exhausting, but we were building an empire. I was always available, day and night. I worked for three years non-stop.

Although I had stopped attending site meetings, there was the odd occasion when I was present at some of them. It was during one of these meetings that I witnessed Gavin handing cash over to one of the union managers. When I questioned him about the incident, his response was, "Look, I'm helping them. There's been a death in the family. This is how I help my comrades."

Eventually, witnessing cash changing hands became the norm. "It's bringing us business, Angelo," Gavin would remind me every time I raised my eyebrows.

"Do you really need to pay these guys off?" I would ask.

"We're not the only ones paying the unions," he would insist. "These guys are used to receiving these payments."

Dyambu concluded transaction after transaction with relative ease. They were not influenced by the unions, or whether a bribe had been paid, or the company's Broad-Based Black Economic Empowerment rating. They were all above board. I knew that even if Gavin stopped handing money to the union members, business would continue as usual because management was already on our side. Yet Gavin was insistent that the payments continue.

After visiting Sasol and ironing out a few creases in Dyambu's costings, their management team agreed to give Dyambu another chance, and we were reappointed as their catering supplier. We would be servicing two of the mining hostels in the Secunda region – Brandspruit and Twistdraai.

While I thought it was my great work that had brought them back on board, I later discovered that Gavin had been bribing people behind the scenes. Sydney Manthatha from Bosasa was co-opted to manage and provide "favours" to the union bosses of Sasol. I would later submit evidence of these arrangements to the Zondo Commission. This underhanded way of conducting business was starting to get under my skin.

CHAPTER 8

Self-proclaimed Prophetess - Lindie Gouws

"Nevertheless, I have this against you – You tolerate that woman Jezebel, who calls herself a prophet. By her teaching she misleads my servants into sexual immorality and the eating of food sacrificed to idols. I have given her time to repent of her immorality, but she is unwilling. So I will cast her on a bed of suffering, and I will make those who commit adultery with her suffer intensely, unless they repent of her ways. I will strike her children dead. Then all the churches will know that I am He who searches hearts and minds, I will repay each of you according to your deeds."
– Revelation 20-23

Of course, no epic story is complete without a torrid love affair, and this one's star-crossed lovers came in the form of Gavin Watson and Lindie Gouws.

Although neither Gavin nor Lindie – who has said that Gavin was like a "father" to her – has ever admitted that they were involved in an affair, it was what one might have called "common knowledge" at Bosasa. I certainly believed that their relationship was about far more than business.

So you might be wondering why I am mentioning this story here.

If Gavin and Lindie's relationship had been a quiet and private matter, that would have been one thing. But it wasn't. It had a direct (and often devastating) effect on the employees at Bosasa and the way the company was run.

I believe this "love" story is central to understanding how a company, meant to be founded on strict Christian values, could become the poster child for corruption.

My first encounter with the melodramatic mess called Lindie Gouws took place in the middle of May 1998, a week after I joined Dyambu. She had recently returned from an exploratory tour to Israel with a certain pastor called Harold Weitsz from the Little Falls Christian Centre.

Gavin proudly introduced her as the company's marketing guru. She introduced herself as the person who dealt with all of Gavin's affairs. "If you need anything from Gavin or want to know anything about Gavin," she said, "come to me."

She reminded me of a typical busybody who wanted to stamp her authority on everything. I'd worked with people like her before at Nissan's Rosslyn plant with their gatekeeper mentalities, where the only way to get to the CEO or one of the directors or general managers was through their secretary. "Oh well," I thought, "this is par for the course. Lindie is just trying to stake her claim and show me who she's in charge of."

Although she held the position of Marketing Director, I soon realised that she didn't appear to know the first thing about marketing. The only people she had working under her were accountants. While Gavin insisted that I attend client meetings with her – which were usually cold calls – I quickly realised that her understanding of marketing seemed to extend no further than asking the clients how their wives were and other family-related small talk. While the mine managers loved her – perhaps because she was Afrikaans and from Randfontein – business was certainly never discussed and, after a while, I refused to attend these meetings with her. Whenever I asked Gavin about her background and qualifications, he skirted around the topic. From my early experience with her, all she seemed to be proficient in was making sure that Gavin had food in his house. She was openly convinced that she was supernaturally purposed by some form of divine intervention to be Gavin Watson's caretaker.

I remember a morning prayer meeting during which Lindie Gouws related "a divine message" that she had received at 3 a.m. about a virus that had evolved that was intent on attacking the directorate, the executive and, most importantly, Gavin Watson. She was insistent that we have the offices fumigated.

On one particular trip to Sasol in Evander to renegotiate a rejected bid for catering services at their coal mines, Lindie took the liberty of using the long, open road ahead as an opportunity to interrogate me about my background and ask for my personal opinion on matters close to her heart. "How do you feel about a man marrying the wrong woman?" she asked out of the blue.

Before I could open my mouth to give an answer – not that I had one – she continued. "I've had a fall-out with Gavin's brothers," she explained. "They say we're too close. They told me that, as a Christian man, he shouldn't be seen together with a woman who is not his wife."

We left Sasol later that day with the deal successfully renegotiated. One would have sworn that Lindie had secured the contract herself, based on her telephone conversation with Gavin that lasted the full duration of the drive back to the office.

Of course, I eventually put two and two together about the two of them but chose not to divulge my personal feelings on the matter. It seemed clear that something untoward was going on, and I wasn't going to be a part of it. I knew that Gavin spent three days a month in Port Elizabeth visiting his wife, Leigh-Ann, and their three children, but I also knew that he couldn't wait to return home. Andries van Tonder – the company's Chief Financial Officer – and I were frequently roped into his brothers' uncomfortable grilling sessions – sometimes right in front of Gavin – about why we tolerated Gavin having an affair with somebody at the office. On one occasion, Andries and I were summoned to Ronnie Watson's Houghton home, where he interrogated us for well over four hours, insisting that we take up a position with the other brothers to get rid of Lindie Gouws. A week later, I was called to the Michelangelo Hotel to attend a meeting with Gavin and his brother, Valence. While the meeting commenced with a discussion about a Chinese heavy-moving-equipment manufacturer, within fifteen minutes, the topic had changed. Valence launched an attack on Gavin's affair with Lindie, and the detrimental effect the community's "perception" of the relationship was having on the Watson family.[11]

When I took Gavin on about the family's attacks, he never showed any signs of embarrassment – it was easier for him to say that he didn't want to talk about it.

I suspected that Lindie believed she was destined to be Gavin's wife, despite the fact that he was already a married man. I believe Leigh-Ann knew about the affair, to the point that she apparently phoned Lindie and confronted her about it. Her message to Lindie was clear – "If you think I'm going to let him divorce me, you've got another thing coming."

Every year, on Leigh-Ann's birthday, I would make sure that one of the secretaries sent her a bunch of flowers or a gift voucher with a card from Gavin, just in case he forgot that it was his wife's birthday.

Besides the fact that Lindie believed her life was divinely anointed, as I will explain shortly, she also appeared to genuinely believe that she was

---

11 Valence Watson has publicly rubbished my Zondo Commission testimony, calling me a "pathological liar" and a "sociopath".

God's gift to Gavin and the company. This was premised off the fact that, in early 1999, there had been a burglary at the company's Stubb Street offices in Randfontein. Lindie was at the office when the so-called robbery took place. Her version of the story that I remember her frequently relating to staff was that the intruders were looking for Gavin because he had the keys to the safe – adding a spin to the story that involved an assassination attempt on his life – but he was not on the premises. The employees were forced to lie down on the floor while the robbers stripped them of everything. In an apparent desperate attempt to warn Gavin, Lindie managed to escape by jumping out of a bathroom window and running to the nearest roadside ticky box to call him. According to the other people who had been there that day, Lindie's dramatic escape had more to do with her fearing for her own life than Gavin's.

But I recall Lindie insisting that she was the hero that day. Later, when the company's name was changed from Dyambu to Bosasa, she told everyone that she had "given birth" to the new company. All she had done was register the new name.

And then there were the dreams and apparitions. She would arrive at work in a spin, saying she had woken in the middle of the night to hear her piano playing hymns to the Lord, all on its own. Or electrically-sparked charges had engulfed her bed. Or swarms of bugs, covered in colourful dots, had infested her home and the church at which she ministered. She saw God in every little detail, and the devil in any woman she perceived to be a threat to her relationship with Gavin. Sometimes, I recall, she would insist that a particular employee was demonically possessed – Danny Mansell was once accused of that – or that she had dreamt about an employee carrying a snake and that a witch-hunt had to be embarked upon immediately.

Her team would usually sit and listen to her while she carried on, hands flailing, nodding their heads in apparent agreement. When she was done with her rant, I'd pop my head into the team's office to check in on them. Sometimes they would relay their frustration and enquire about other vacancies in the company so they could escape "the sanatorium", as they called it. Most of the time, everyone would just shake their heads and share a good chuckle.

Another one of Lindie's stories involved dying and being resurrected, much like Jesus Christ. Apparently, she had flat-lined during a heart attack while on one of her trips to Israel and the paramedic had declared her dead on the scene, until she miraculously woke up.

When we moved to the Bosasa Business Park in Mogale City, Lindie arranged to have about four hundred brass plaques engraved with quotes from the Bible placed strategically around the premises. One of the more notable plaques was the one she placed at the entrance to the office park, which read:

YOU WILL BE BLESSED WHEN YOU COME IN AND BLESSED
WHEN YOU GO OUT
Deuteronomy 28:6

To say that Lindie was abusive in her behaviour towards Gavin (and other employees) would be an understatement. I remember many meetings in which Gavin would say something that upset her, and she would launch into him, hurling vitriol while grabbing him by the shirt. Her erratic behaviour, coupled with sporadic crying fits, eventually got the better of Gavin, and he would disappear into the sunset leaving me to deal with her – something that periodically brought me to a similar state of complete and utter despair.

Gavin was in a constant catch-22 situation with Lindie. She would often shout out while walking down one of the office passages, "Must I tell them, Gavin? Must I tell them?"

One day, unable to resist the temptation, I said to him, "Gavin, why doesn't she tell us?" Lindie backed off after I made that comment, but it was a long-standing joke in the company. Here he was, the mighty Gavin Watson, the only person in the entire organisation who didn't think that he was sleeping around with Lindie Gouws.

There were many times when I would arrive at his house and find traces that she had been there the previous evening. Gavin's elderly housekeeper, Joyce, often told me stories about his and Lindie's altercations. Joyce respected Gavin, but she couldn't stand Lindie. Once, Lindie tried to get rid of Joyce by telling Gavin that she had taken her to see a doctor and the doctor had diagnosed her with tuberculosis. Gavin then paid for Joyce to go home to be treated for the disease. Lindie may have thought she was victorious – that she had successfully managed to get Joyce out of the picture. When Joyce returned to Gavin's employ, Lindie was furious.

I received a call from Andries van Tonder one Saturday morning. Gavin had asked him to check whether there was a spare key for his car in the office safe. His story was that he and Lindie had been robbed outside her complex and that his keys and wallet had been taken. Miraculously, that same wallet, intact with all his bank cards and ID book, reappeared some two weeks later. Even the key that had cost him four thousand rands to replace.

When going on international business trips together, we would usually all meet up at Gavin's townhouse and head out to the airport in one car. On one particular occasion, we arrived to find Lindie there. She was not in a pleasant mood because she hated it when anybody went on a trip with Gavin and she was not invited. As we were about to leave, it became apparent that Gavin's car keys were missing. With time running out, everyone was frantically looking for the keys when Joe Gumede, one of the Bosasa directors, decided to go inside and inspect the house one more time. He walked up to where Lindie was sitting and moved one of the cushions aside, and voila! There were the keys. Joe emerged from the townhouse minutes later, dangling the keys in the air. "Look what I found," he said, grinning from ear to ear and trying not to look at Gavin.

Sometimes Gavin would miss the international trips completely. We were due to fly to the USA to visit a shrimp company in Florida when Gavin called an hour before Avis was scheduled to collect him and take him to the airport. He told me he'd left his passport in Port Elizabeth. I suspected him missing the trip had something to do with his love life. I told Debbie to pack her bags and get ready to fly first-class to Miami.

The Abu Dhabi trip I took with him in 2015 to watch the Grand Prix was peppered with drama. I had to stop by his room in the mornings to put a Voltaren patch on his back and give him an injection before going down for breakfast. He would always leave the door to his room ajar so that I could walk straight in.

It was the final day of the qualifying sessions – I was in a good mood and, not wanting to be late, arrived at his room twenty minutes early. The door was open, and Gavin was standing on his balcony, on the phone.

"I love you, Lindie, I really do," he lamented apologetically, "but I can't do that right now. It would be too dangerous." I could hear that he was on the brink of tears. Eventually, I made my presence known and signalled to him to end the call. He cut it immediately.

"Sorry, Angelo, that was Leigh-Ann," he said, trying to shrug off what had just happened. "You know how these bloody women are."

"I'd also be upset if I was your wife," I said sarcastically, urging him to hurry up. "You called her Lindie quite a few times."

Gavin immediately protested his innocence and accused me of trying to conjure up stories. His phone was on the table, and I could see the incoming call. "Lindie Gouws calling," it read. "Why don't you answer it?" I asked, imagining a hysterical Lindie on the other end. "Or should I answer it for you?"

He didn't take the call, so we headed down for breakfast. I took the opportunity to knock him down a little further. "Gavin," I said, "every day you ask God to bless your company and take away all the problems, but if you read 1 Peter 3:7, it tells you that if you don't honour your wife, your prayers will be hindered."

I'll never forget the glare he gave me.

Something else that Lindie was notorious for doing was smashing her car. Frans Vorster was responsible for the purchasing of company vehicles, and Lindie would find any reason to get behind the wheel of a new vehicle. At one stage, she drove a BMW Coupé with a personalised number plate that read "PHETIWE", meaning "It is done".

After being involved in a bumper bashing with the Beemer, she asked Frans to pull some strings and get the car in for immediate repairs. All the Bosasa vehicles were repaired by Rubicon Panelbeaters in Krugersdorp. When Lindie's car was ready for collection, Frans was tasked with taking her through to the workshop. As he drove in with Lindie in the passenger seat, young Nick, the owner's son, began frantically gearing his team up to present the car.

"Maak gou!" he shouted. "Dis die groot baas van Bosasa se cherrie."[12]

Lindie – unfortunately – overheard him. Up to that point, I didn't know that Frans could text in English. But there he was, frantically texting me to tell me that Lindie had instructed him to "get rid of Rubicon" and to find out who exactly had told them that she was "die groot baas van Bosasa se cherrie."

---

12 "Hurry up! It's the big boss of Bosasa's girlfriend."

CHAPTER 9

A Gentleman and his Toyota - Frans Vorster

"A man can stand up for himself, but it takes a stronger man to stand up for others. Such a man is a rare find."
– Angelo Agrizzi

If I had to do it all again, Frans Vorster would be the first person I'd call onto my team. Frans is your typical trustworthy, dedicated, committed Afrikaner chap from Randfontein. He is just like his salt of the earth father, Oom Vossie – who managed Dyambu and Bosasa's fleet back in the day. Before joining Bosasa, Frans was a Captain and Station Commander in the South African Police Force and, like every police officer, he has a deep-seated need to control everything. He is also the kind of guy who, as bright as he is, will run through a wall to fetch something on the other side if you ask him to, only to return and ask, "What was I supposed to fetch?"

When I first met Frans, he was based at Lindela Repatriation Centre. He'd sometimes go along on raids with the police to places like the (then) infamous Ponte City in Berea, arrest illegal immigrants, and take them back to Lindela to have them deported. If there was a raid at Lindela, he was always the man right out in front. I remember we had a riot once at one of the Youth Centres. The kids were running amok. Frans and I went out there to deal with the problem when, all of a sudden, it was like Road Runner – legs and dust everywhere – and there was Frans, taking the kids on, one by one.

The thing that impressed me most about Frans was how he excelled in every task he was given. Nothing was too great a challenge for him. I decided to invest my time in growing and developing him, and so I moved him into Procurement at the company's head office. He turned the department around, proving everybody who had doubted him wrong. Eventually, he stepped into his father's old shoes to manage the company's fleet. He followed Oom Vossie's rule to a tee – you could drive any vehicle, as long as it was a Toyota and it was white. If you were an executive, you could drive an Audi. Even after Vossie died, Frans still insisted that all new company vehicles remained either Toyotas or Audis.

In later years, when one of Bosasa's business units, Kgwerano Financial Services, was showing losses of between R2-million and R4-million a month, who better to put in there than Frans Vorster? With fourteen thousand vehicles to manage, it wasn't long before the company was turning profits of between R2.5-million and R3-million a month under his watchful eye.

Frans is much larger than me – despite the fact that he's a rugby coach – and has always been extremely conscious about his weight. I often joke with him that when we die one day, they're going to have to build bespoke coffins for the two of us. I remember Gavin once giving Frans an incentive – R10 000 to lose ten kilograms. Frans said it wasn't a large enough incentive, so Gavin upped his offer to R100 000. Frans decided that the quickest way to lose the weight would be to go for a gastric bypass. The only hitch was that he had to go through a consultative process with a team of medical professionals before the operation could go ahead.

One day I popped my head into his office to check in on him. "How are things going with the gastric bypass?" I asked.

"Angelo," he said, the blood rising up his neck, "I told that *donnerse*[13] psychiatrist where to get off, and quit the programme. I could handle everything, even the ten kilograms she asked me to lose, but then she told me that I had a psychological issue that I needed to work through before she would sign me off to the surgeon."

"A psychological issue?" I repeated.

"Yes," Frans said. "She wanted to know whether I was breastfed or not. I mean, what the hell does *that* have to do with anything?"

And that was typical Frans. His heart was as sensitive as a poet's. I'll never forget how he broke down in tears while on the phone to his daughter when we were on our way to the Hawks to be arrested many years later. He couldn't bear the thought of letting his family down.

---

13 Damned

PART 3

CHAPTER 10

Danny Must Go

"Weakness of attitude becomes weakness of character."
– Albert Einstein

In the early days of Dyambu, Gavin and Danny Mansell were inseparable. As fifty-fifty shareholders in the business, Danny basically ran the show, with Gavin popping in once a week to check up on everybody. But, when I joined the company, that camaraderie took a strange turn. Why he did it, God alone knows, but it seemed that Gavin began taking pleasure in pitting people against each other and creating divisions within the company, particularly when it came to Danny. There was an Afrikaner clique, an English clique and a Xhosa clique, and so it went on until I noticed two distinct camps forming in the organisation – the Gavin Watson camp, and the Danny Mansell camp.

Gavin started using any opportunity to mark his territory by openly bad-mouthing Danny in front of the team. While his antagonism towards Danny made me immensely uncomfortable, Gavin had me hooked to his line and was reeling me in. I noticed Danny becoming fearful and upset about my involvement in the business. Once Gavin had me firmly in his corner, he began painting a picture of Danny that had me believing that he had abused Gavin's goodwill and was a threat to the business. Gavin claimed that Danny had stolen money from him and that he was responsible for setting up the Afrikaner clique in the business. "I've done so much for that man," he said on repeat. "I've built him up, and look what he's done to me." After enough indoctrination, I took the approach of, "Well, Danny, you've done it to yourself."

One afternoon, Gavin told me to meet him at his house. Lindie Gouws was also present, but that was no surprise. "Angelo," he said, "from this day forward, I want you to have *no* relationship with Danny Mansell. Am I making myself clear?"

Later I would realise that this was all part of a grand plan. Gavin wanted Danny Mansell out – he had reached his sell-by date. Gavin planned to disempower Danny to such an extent that it would become untenable for him and anybody in his camp to stay on with the company. He wanted Hilda Ndude and the other Dyambu women out too. He wanted a whole new brand, without Danny and the Dyambu women. His masterplan was to have the company all for himself. Gavin would be its sole shareholder.

"Angelo," he added, as I turned to leave his house that day, "any new contracts you sign up from now on, sign them up as Bosasa. Just tell them that there has been a name change."

Back at the office, while Gavin point-blank ignored Danny, he didn't have the balls to confront him and ask him to leave. But I remember his stance being extremely passive-aggressive.

And then Danny made a fatal mistake.

Together with his son, Jarred, Danny decided to hire a helicopter and fly out to the different hostels and perform some routine checks. "Danny, are you bloody insane?" I exclaimed when he told me where he was off to for the day. "Do you realise the chaos you're going to cause by landing a helicopter at a hostel with eight thousand men inside? They're all going to want to see what it's about, and you're going to have endless crap getting out of there."

Danny went ahead anyway. News of the helicopter landings quickly reached Ronnie Watson and the Kebbles, leaving everybody fuming. Shortly after that incident, Gavin called a group of us to his house for a meeting – David Sadie, Doc Smith, Lindie Gouws, and me. Gavin claimed that he no longer trusted Danny and that he served no purpose in the company. Knowing that Danny and Doc Smith had a close relationship, Gavin instructed Doc to meet with Danny, negotiate with him, and make it clear that there was no room for two bulls in the company – which Doc duly did. With little resistance, Danny accepted Gavin's offer of R9-million for his shares in the business and headed off to the Eastern Cape to farm cattle.

CHAPTER 11

Bosasa's Dysfunctional Board of Directors

"It's funny how everyone considers honesty a virtue, yet no one wants to hear the truth."
– Anon

Bosasa is a Setswana word meaning "The future". Of course, the exact nature of that future was yet to be revealed, but, either way, the name had a nice ring to it.

Although the name change was primarily Gavin's way of stamping his signature and authority on the business, it also released the company from its apparent links with the ANC Women's League. By 1999, Mansell had exited, Hilda Ndude and her friends were a distant memory, and the company had made significant inroads into the mining sector.

The time had come to appoint a Bosasa board of directors. Instead of appointing high-level directors who could add significant value to the business; Gavin, who did not like being challenged, chose people he had worked with previously, people he thought would agree with him and support him, whether his decisions were sound or not. I referred to them as "The Stooges" because, in my experience, they did exactly as Gavin commanded and signed everything that he put before them.[14]

I lost count of the number of times he put it to the white management team that having a board of directors in place who challenged our decisions would be detrimental to the business. I suspect that Gavin believed that by surrounding himself with people who would not question him,

---

14 As referenced in (among others) – Basson, A., (2019). *Blessed by Bosasa*. Johannesburg: Jonathan Ball Publishers SA

he could easily manipulate them and make decisions on the spot without their input. It also made it easier for him to break fundamental company rules and ignore good corporate governance.

First up was Thandi Makoko, who was employed as a social worker at the Department of Social Development when she first met Gavin. He offered her a job as a Director and Chairperson of Bosasa's Youth Development Centres. She accepted. I called Thandi *Mother Teresa* because every-bloody-body who needed help at one of the Youth Centres would end up with soft-hearted Thandi. Sometimes it was a painter who needed paint for a job or a dressmaker who needed material to make a wedding gown, or it was a funeral that needed paying for. Whoever it was, she would make sure everybody had work, and she did everything she could to keep the whole world happy.

It was always a hard sell to me, but she refused to take no for an answer. I would invariably give her money to pass back down the line. Sometimes it was out of my own pocket, other times it was taken from petty cash for Corporate Social Investment, as we called it. When Thandi went to America, she wanted to save all the Americans. When she returned to South Africa, she wanted to save all the South Africans. As lovely as she was, she could never say no.

Next up on the board was Ishmael Dikane, a cook and cleaner from Buffelsfontein hostel. Ishmael was appointed as Director of Operations. Then came Papa Leshabane, a human resources officer who took care of staff issues at Libanon and Kloof mines. Gavin appointed him as Human Resources Director. Finally, there was Joe Gumede, a human resources officer from Leslie Mine. He was appointed as the Bosasa Group's Chairperson.

I had no interest in being appointed as a director, and neither did Andries van Tonder. Neither of us wanted the fiduciary duties that accompanied that role. With all the shenanigans going on, our personal risk and public liability would have sky-rocketed had we assumed the role of directors. So, Gavin gave us titles instead. I was named the Chief Operations Officer, and Andries the Chief Financial Officer.[15]

---

15 In hindsight, it was a smart move not to accept directorship. Nobody imagined that Gavin would die on the 26th of August 2019. Taxes in the region of R800-million still need to be recovered from Bosasa. It's the Joes and the Thandis and the Ishmaels of the world whose doors SARS is going to go knocking on now that Gavin is no longer around.

CHAPTER 12

Still Waters Run Deep – Andries van Tonder

"Men of few words are the best men. Andries is one such person. He is quiet and reserved and has the humility of Job. He has the heart of a lion and the stamina of a tiger. I often wonder what would have become of me if he wasn't around."
– Angelo Agrizzi

I spent the following months sitting around the boardroom table with Gavin Watson, David Sadie, Andries van Tonder, and a few of the directors, mapping out our focus areas going forward. Our plan was to infiltrate the mines, the education sector, the private sector, and hospitals with large-scale outsourced catering services. We identified specific regions that we would service and business units that we could develop to enhance the services we were already providing.

When I emphasised the need to bring influential, highly qualified administrative personnel on board, Gavin was overtly dismissive. He was convinced that if we didn't bring a younger generation on board, there would be no new thinking.

"Gavin," I pleaded, "when it comes to financial and operational matters, we don't want youngsters. We want old grey matter. Those are the people that the banks are going to listen to, not kids straight out of school."

Gavin found my suggestions preposterous, even using the opportunity to refer to his brothers. They had all studied abroad, yet they still relied on him to secure their business deals. He frequently pointed out that, despite his lack of formal studies, he had achieved far more than they had. "Look at Valence," he smirked, "he's got two degrees and three master's, and look where that's gotten him – he can't even run his own business. I've got nothing on paper, but guess who gets called in to run his business for him?"

Andries van Tonder and I didn't get off on a solid footing when we first met. As Bosasa's CFO, Andries was straight-up, prudent and hard-arsed, much like Doc Smith. While he referred to himself as an accountant, the thought of performing bank transfers and payments had him falling asleep at his desk. But when it came to being a financial strategist, to take a business from one level to the next, that had him working into the early hours of the morning. If a company was making a loss, he would make it profitable again. He took SeaArk, a prawn manufacturing plant that Gavin invested in, and turned it around. He was brilliant at problem-solving. Gavin couldn't read a balance sheet, so Andries drew graphs (up to eighteen at a time) to help him understand where the business was at.

While we had the financial systems in place to manage our accounting and payroll processes, when it came to business management standards and operational procedures, there was absolutely nothing in place. One of Andries's first responsibilities as CFO was to develop the computerised system that would manage and control the different cost centres that fell under the operational side of the business. He got hold of a company called Computer Initiatives and, R10-million later, the system was written. I went out and spent a fortune on new computers and waited in anticipation as the software was loaded onto each workstation.

Unfortunately, no sooner had we logged in than the entire system crashed. When we eventually got it working, we spent weeks going backwards and forwards, trying to get the program to spit out something that made sense.

One day, after a disastrous EXCO meeting, I walked into the Accounts department and threw my toys out of the cot. Andries was sitting on one side of the office, his brother, Leon (who managed the company's IT infrastructure) was on the other, and Gavin was sitting between them.

"Your program is bullshit," I said. "None of the figures gel."

"It's not the program," Andries said defensively, "it's the operating system. If you hadn't gone and bought open-source computers, we wouldn't be sitting with this problem."

There we were, swearing at each other and getting nowhere. "Andries," I shouted, "I'm not interested in your stories. Do what you want. I'll use my own program – a simple Excel spreadsheet!"

I turned around, stormed out of the room, and we didn't speak to each other for eighteen months – until we realised that Gavin was purposely trying to drive a wedge between us. He would find things for us to fight about and bring them to our individual attention, pitting us against each other. I knew that I was pushing Andries to his limits, and he knew he was doing the same to me. Eventually, we sat down to resolve our differences and find some middle ground, becoming lifelong friends in the process.

Back in the early 2000s, Bosasa's coffers were rarely bursting at the seams. In those years, Andries van Tonder and I would physically go out to our difficult clients' offices to collect outstanding payments. Either that or nobody in the company was getting paid. My favourite trick was to arrive at a client's offices, wearing my oldest, most worn-out pair of shoes, my socks clearly visible through the gaping holes in the leather, to demonstrate just how bad things were. I would sit down in the company's reception area, and wouldn't leave until a signed cheque was in my hands. Another trick was to order a delivery of the greasiest fast food we could lay our hands on while we were waiting. For some reason, this always accelerated the speed at which the cheques were issued.

I vividly remember one occasion when Andries and I were out collecting money from the Kebbles' offices. Their payment of R1.5-million was already three days overdue, and we had salaries and wages to pay. On that particular day, the Kebbles were holding a conference in their boardroom and, as luck would have it, there were international investors present. "There is nobody available to see you right now," the receptionist politely told us, looking us up and down. "That's not a problem," I replied. "We will sit here and wait until somebody is available." We sat back in the waiting area, and then, true to form, I placed an order for an extra-large double serving of Russians and deep-fried salt and vinegar chips.

With the reception area slowly filling up with the greasy haze of our early lunch, company employees began approaching us. "Can we help you?" they would ask. "Yes," Andries or I would answer, "we're just waiting for our money." I'll never forget Roger Kebble bursting out of the boardroom and blasting us for bringing their company into disrepute with our unprofessional conduct. "Wait till I speak to Ronnie Watson about this," he threatened. I doubt he ever did speak to Ronnie; somehow, the old man seemed to enjoy our tenacity.

Roger wrote out a cheque there and then, pointed us in the direction of the front door, and told us to leave the premises immediately.

CHAPTER 13

Nobody is Indispensable

"He found something that he wanted, had always wanted and always would want – not to be admired, as he had feared; not to be loved, as he had made himself believe; but to be necessary to people, to be indispensable ... very few things matter and nothing matters very much."
– F. Scott Fitzgerald, *This Side of Paradise*

With me in charge of operations and Andries van Tonder in charge of finances, the company slowly began to evolve into a more structured and stable entity. After years of having the banks viewing us with a healthy measure of scepticism, they were starting to take us seriously. Our clients began accepting us as a reputable service provider that offered good value for money. Profits were impressive – 45% was the norm when compared to the 20% that other companies in our industry were making at the time. Bosasa had the advantage of buying power, something that added to our competitive advantage from a price perspective. Our pricing and quality service played a significant role in igniting our growth.

Operationally, little fault could be found. I would go as far as saying that the business was impeccable when it came to delivery. Right until the bitter end, not once did we steal from anybody's plate. When we promised two hundred grams of beef, the client got two hundred grams of beef. If they ordered four hundred grams of pap[16] per person per day, that's exactly what we provided. In the three years that followed the name change, business shot through the roof. While Gavin ascribed the awarding of the Gold Fields, Sasol and Randfontein Estates contracts to his relationship with the National Union of Mineworkers and the BB-BEE[17] factor –

---

16 Maize porridge
17 Broad-Based Black Economic Empowerment

I think there was so much more to it than that. While in those early days I stood my ground and argued that our success was largely due to our operational prowess, the ISO 9001:2000 standards we had set for the industry, our expertise, and our people thinking out of the box, I eventually backed down. Gavin was never going to change his stance and if I continued to fight, even for a sliver of the limelight, I was going to drive myself insane.

Gavin Watson had a zero-tolerance policy – anyone who dared question him or stepped outside the line would be on the receiving end of his oft-repeated dismissive words – "Who pays your salary?"

In Kristin Williamson's book *Brothers to Us: The Story of a Remarkable Family's Fight Against Apartheid*, Gavin is described at age eight as refusing to share his toys with his brothers and his friends. Instead, he would hand them stones to play with. This modus operandi followed him into adulthood. He could never simply relax and enjoy life – he had to prove that he was better than everyone else. Life was a game, and he had to win it at all costs.

His attempts to swim upstream in an effort to remind people that they were not indispensable were often quite memorable, especially when they backfired. When the South African National Defence Force's (SANDF) catering contract came up for renewal later in the same year, everyone in the catering space wanted a piece of the pie. This was a prized contract – it was probably the largest government catering contract at the time.

Gavin decided that we were going to bid, but that I would be excluded from working on the tender. He was on a mission to prove to me that he had access to other people who were just as – or far more – competent than I was. He handed the bid to Lindie Gouws and Leon Snyman, paired them with a group of people employed by the SANDF who had been involved in previous tenders, and paid them to complete the documents.

With many years of experience at Molope Foods with similar tenders under my belt, I knew that there were two key elements on these tender documents that, if incorrectly completed, would lead to immediate disqualification. One was how you presented the tender, and the other was how well you presented the ration scale[18] that the client provided to the menus you suggested. Matching the ration scales to a menu was painstaking work and had to be done properly and accurately – one mistake and the tender would be thrown out.

"Gavin, let me get involved," I insisted. "You know I've done this before." He refused point-blank, insisting that I focus on the catering contracts we

---

18 A means for arriving at a reasonably priced, wholesome, dietary-balanced and nationally equable basis for the provisioning of food rations.

were opening at the mines at the time.

I watched from the sidelines and asked pertinent questions from time to time – especially when bringing up the subject of the ration scales – which frequently led to Lindie Gouws losing her cool. While I tried to put her mood swings and temper tantrums down to too many Red Bull energy drinks, Gavin always assured me that they had everything under control and that my services were not required.

After working on the tender for about six weeks, it was ready to be submitted. I asked Gavin and Lindie if I could give it a once-over, and again, they refused. Before leaving the room, I decided to add insult to injury and quote from the Scriptures. "Unless the Lord builds the house," I said, quoting Psalm 127:1, "those who build it labour in vain."

I later managed to get my hands on a copy of the document, only to discover that they had completely forgotten to add in the ration scales. I said nothing, and a few weeks later, a letter of decline emerged from the fax machine in my office. Bosasa had been disqualified due to a lack of competency. Again, my lips were sealed, but the fax eventually found its way into Gavin's hands.

When I asked him whether he had heard anything from the Defence Force about the tender, he told me he hadn't, and then added that it was probably better that it wasn't awarded to us because there was far too much politics involved.

Not long after, Gavin took me on in an open staff meeting. "What new business are we getting in?" he demanded.

"Well, Gavin," I said matter-of-factly, "the Defence Force contract would have been ours had you not stuffed it up."

I knew his ego was bruised, but I had no qualms about confronting him. He was often brazen with me, but I was happy to give as good as I got. I knew that he wasn't as sharp as he made himself out to be – and I think he knew it too. I had a feeling that he wanted to prove to me that he was better than me, that he could also go out and win a large contract. He would push, and he would bribe – he would do whatever it took to prove that he was not a failure.

After a few pleasurable weeks of ragging him about the Defence Force disaster, the Department of Correctional Services' catering tender was advertised in the press. This time, Gavin went all out to redeem himself. Although he had been dismissive about the Defence Force tender, he did not allow his ego to overtake reason. While he was still aiming to prove to the world that I was a whippersnapper, he needed all the help he could get in securing that tender. "We can do it this time, Angelo." he said, "We can do it." Of course, being Gavin, he was careful not to lead me to believe that I was of any value to the company.

We all knew that we were dispensable. I remember Gavin belittling an employee once by handing him a glass of water and instructing him to dip his finger into it.

"Now take it out," he said. The employee removed his finger from the glass. "See, nothing's different," he said. "I can get rid of you."

Sadly, it was that same hubris that led to Gavin's ultimate demise.

 Scan here to watch Gavin belittling staff at various company imbizos.

CHAPTER 14

Brothers, Let's Pray

"And when you pray, do not be like the hypocrites, for they love to pray standing in the synagogues and on the street corners to be seen by others. Truly I tell you, they have received their reward in full. But when you pray, go into your room, close the door and pray to your Father, who is unseen. Then your Father, who sees what is done in secret, will reward you. And when you pray, do not keep on babbling like pagans, for they think they will be heard because of their many words. Do not be like them, for your Father knows what you need before you ask him."
– Matthew 6:5-8

Back in the early days of Bosasa, Leon van Tonder – Andries's younger brother and the company's IT specialist – came up with the idea of having early morning prayer meetings in his office. Since I was at the office from 5 a.m. anyway, I thought it was a great idea. We would gather in his office just after six. Leon would begin by reading from the Scriptures, and then we would all pray until about 8 a.m. When Gavin found out about the prayer meetings, he decided to join us. When we moved to the new Bosasa office park, we moved the meetings to the boardroom.

Gavin refused to have an office of his own. His theory was that as long as he had a car, a key and a cell phone, he could work from anywhere. So, when he arrived at work around 5:30 a.m., he would saunter into my office, usually to "discuss business". Invariably, he had been out and about the night before hobnobbing with politicians, so the discussions usually centred around whom he'd met up with, what he wanted done, and who needed to go out and deal with whom.

At about 6:30 a.m., people would start filtering into the boardroom. The prayer meeting, usually attended by the directors and some of the company's senior leadership, was, for the most part, a continuation of Gavin's earlier revelations of the previous evening's antics. It was impossible for him to keep a secret, so unless there was a R1-million fine if he spoke (something I introduced after I realised he was sharing information about which I'd spoken to him in confidence), he would eagerly spill the beans to everyone present.

It wasn't long before a somewhat sinister element crept into these prayer meetings. Gavin would insist that everyone prayed out loud – but not all at the same time. Everyone had a turn to pray – be it about the business or something personal – so we all heard each other's prayers. Sometimes a "problematic" person would be targeted by name because everyone knew that Gavin would take action the following day, either by firing the person or belittling them in a public forum.

"Why is so-and-so working here?" he'd ask, walking into her office after her name was mentioned in one of the prayers. "Get rid of her! Fire her!"

While Andries and Leon van Tonder eventually refused to attend these prayer meetings – which they referred to as "a farce" – I made sure I was there so that I knew who was next in the firing line. Somebody had to be responsible for damage control.

While Gavin used any opportunity to suggest we pray – including when we had people visiting us – I took every opportunity to take the mickey out of him.

"Let's have a prayer about that," he'd say.

"Remember to hold their hands," I'd whisper, "just in case they try to steal from you while your eyes are closed."

CHAPTER 15
Self-obsessed Gavin

"The truth is, I've never fooled anyone. I've let people fool themselves. They didn't bother to find out who and what I was. Instead, they would invent a character for me. I wouldn't argue with them."
– Anon

Gavin Watson lived at The Palms, a small residential estate in Oribi Street in Constantia Kloof, Roodepoort. I purchased a corner house in Fairview Street, about one hundred and fifty meters from Gavin's home, without realising where he lived. It wasn't long before this became an issue, with Gavin pitching up at my front door at all hours of the day and night. With Gavin's wife and children living in Port Elizabeth, life was probably quite lonely for him, especially over weekends. He had no hobbies, other than working. As a result, we would often end up working or visiting the company's various sites on Saturdays and Sundays. When we weren't working, he would ask me to pick him up at his house, and we'd drive around visiting his family – Valence in particular – and the people he called his friends. Kevin Wakeford often made an appearance at these gatherings. The discussions were usually about business – Bosasa in particular – and Gavin would refer to me as the guy responsible for the company's unprecedented growth, making me feel like a million bucks every time. His acquaintances were mostly business contacts – his friendship circle did not extend beyond his working relationships with people. I found it quite sad that he did not know what it meant to have that one true friend, a blood brother in whom he could confide.

Gavin often imposed on my personal life. Once, I booked a trip to see the Grand Prix in Abu Dhabi. When Gavin found out about it, he insisted on coming along. On another occasion, Debbie arranged a trip with the

Ferrari Club to visit their headquarters in Italy. Again, Gavin invited himself. The trip was priced per couple, so he took one of the company's directors, Joe Gumede. Debbie was furious. She had planned the trip down to the last detail for just the two of us, but there was nothing we could do. This was Gavin, after all. Not only did he impose, but his behaviour while on the trip was embarrassing. The club members knew me, and they had only ever seen me treat people with respect and humility. They were now looking at me with raised eyebrows, and I felt guilty for bringing this obnoxious and arrogant person into the fold.

I quickly learned that, when it came to Gavin, everything was not always as it seemed. It was all about smoke and mirrors. While he played the confident, politically connected mover-and-shaker on the outside, he was a gullible hypochondriac on the inside. He was obsessed with his health and his looks. If somebody handed him a slimming tablet, he'd take it. He trained at the gym twice a day, every day. He spent a fortune on Botox injections, making him look significantly younger than he was.

Gavin was also always ready to try any new vitamin or treatment that came onto the market and, every time he wanted to try something new, he would insist that I go along with him. There is a clinic in Bryanston that sells SOLAL vitamins, but before they prescribe anything, they perform a full-body analysis. Gavin had been there before, and swore by it, insisting that I go for an analysis of my own. So off we went. The clinic was filled with machines. They could tell if your body was short of a vitamin or mineral simply by examining your fingernails. There was a device that could analyse your health simply by having you breathe into it. While I found it all a bit gimmicky, Gavin sat and waited patiently for me in the reception area. When I eventually emerged, I found him sitting there, holding two enormous bags. There must have been about forty bottles of tablets, mixtures and ointments inside. "Gavin, this is a load of hogwash," I laughed. "How can one human being possibly ingest so many tablets?" But Gavin was resolute. He told me that the tests had confirmed that his testosterone levels were elevated, and he had been given oestrogen cream to rub behind his knees. I knew he was going to binge on the stuff. If a drug could make him younger, all he needed was a glass of water and a free hand to throw the tablets down his throat.

One day, I altered some Myprodol anti-inflammatory capsules, emptying the powder out and placing the green caps on the green, and the red caps on the red. I told Gavin that it was a new brand of pain medication that not only relieved back pain but was also a mild sleeping tablet. "Really?" he asked. "Yes, really," I replied. He took one of the capsules home with him that night, and when he arrived at the office early the following morning, he said, "Angelo, I need more of those tablets. Can you get me more?" I gave him another four but warned him not to exceed the recommended daily dosage of one tablet. "It's unbelievable, Angelo," he would say every morning when he saw me. "Unbelievable. I'm sleeping like a baby."

On another occasion, many years later, I was called into a meeting. Sitting around the table were Gavin Watson, David Sadie, Danny Mansell, Vossie Vorster, and Danie van Tonder, who was responsible for the Youth Centres. "All the senior guys in the company are going for chelation therapy," I was told. I rolled my eyes. "Here we go again," I thought.

"And what exactly is chelation therapy?" I asked.

"Basically, they put you on a drip for two hours that gathers and removes all the heavy metals and compounds in your body," said Danie van Tonder. I decided to pay the doctor a visit before I signed up. I deliberately booked my consultation at lunchtime on a Wednesday when I knew all the staff members would be partaking in their joint two-hour therapy session. True to form, I arrived to find eight senior Bosasa management staff sitting there like chemotherapy patients, all attached to their respective drips. During my consultation, the doctor explained that chelation therapy was used during the Vietnam War to remove the side effects of heavy metals or shrapnel in the bodies of war veterans. "How much does it cost?" I asked, mostly out of curiosity. "Four thousand rands a shot," he replied, "but don't worry, Gavin's paying for it."

When I asked him whether it was FDA approved, he declined to respond. I made an appointment with my GP, who also happened to be Gavin's doctor, and he cautioned me against it. "Studies are showing that chelation therapy leeches essential vitamins and minerals from your body," he explained, "and the FDA has never approved it."

When I told Gavin that I wouldn't be partaking in the sessions because the therapy was not FDA approved, his immediate response was, "Who is the damn FDA anyway, and what do they know?"

I decided to pop in and visit my colleagues at the following Wednesday session. Doc Smith, Danny Mansell, Danie van Tonder, Leon Snyman, Gavin Watson, David Sadie, Vossie Vorster and Frans Vorster were all lined up, drips between them, receiving their infusions. I laughed at them and then turned around and walked out.

Their treatments continued every Wednesday until one Saturday morning, three weeks later, I received a call that Vossie Vorster had passed away. He had been out cycling and returned home for coffee and rusks. The family were unclear about what happened after that – he may have choked on a rusk, nobody knew, but within a matter of minutes, he was dead. It probably didn't have anything to do with the therapy but the following Wednesday, everybody was at the office, and that was the end of the chelation therapy. On another occasion, Gavin told me that I needed to go for something called Scan for Life at the Rosebank Hospital in Johannesburg. "Oh boy," I thought, "not again." Gavin explained that it involved a preventative 3D scan that screens for predispositions to heart disease, cancer and strokes. A colonoscopy would be thrown in for good measure. What a bonus! Gavin and I were to report to the hospital after completing a two-day fast – doctor's orders.

While in the consulting room, my stomach grumbling louder than a whale's mating call, Gavin and I were given a drink of iodine. Just as we were about to go in, the doctor appeared and apologetically announced that the machine had packed up and that we would have to return in two weeks. Gavin, equally ravenous, bought the largest slab of Toblerone he could lay his hands on, only to ask me to pull over to the side of the road halfway home to vomit it all up.

Two weeks later and by now starving to death, after having verified that the machine was in working order, we reported for duty once more. Gavin went in for his scan first, and I went in after him. We were told to return in two weeks for the results, which we duly did.

"Who would like to see their results first?" the doctor asked. I volunteered, and Gavin insisted on joining me in the doctor's room. "I want to see how healthy you are," he joked.

The doctor had both sets of results laid out on the table in front of him. "It's interesting," he said, "because if you look at your individual reports, they should actually be swapped around. "Angelo," he said, "your heart is like that of a baby, and your lungs – do you smoke?"

I told him I had quit smoking fifteen years earlier. "Well, it's almost impossible to tell," he said. "They're squeaky clean." I was obviously pleased with my clean bill of health, but I was curious about Gavin's results, knowing what a health nut he was. Gavin was the type of person who would order a pizza and dab all the oil off with a paper towel.

We often ate breakfast together, and I remember ordering my regular plate of bacon and eggs one morning. "Do you know how much fat is in bacon?" Gavin asked. I immediately raised my hand, summoned the waiter, and ordered a second portion. Over time, I think he realised it was useless trying to convert me to his ways. I once gave Gavin an article on the health benefits of olive oil, and it wasn't long before he began pouring generous lashings of it over his vegetables.

"Gavin," the doctor said, "you have a number of issues – you have a considerable amount of plaque in your arteries, on your heart and on your brain." Although these issues were not insurmountable and could be treated through diet and medication, Gavin was visibly angry and confused. People often thought I was older than Gavin, even though he was twenty years my senior. I'm clearly a large man. Gavin appeared to be a fit and trim gym bunny. We were polar opposites in terms of our physiques and our lifestyles, yet there he was, diagnosed as the unhealthy one. Needless to say, he was furious.

One winter's evening, I received an impromptu call from Gavin, inviting Debbie and me for dinner at Casalinga with some of the other senior management and their partners. Seated at the table with him were Lindie Gouws, Andries van Tonder, Danie van Tonder and his wife, Gayle.

While we waited for our starters to arrive, Gavin began to make small talk. At some point, he raised the topic of his snoring and said that he was planning on visiting a doctor to have a groundbreaking procedure performed. He announced that the surgery involved making an incision in his "clitoris".

I nearly climbed under the table, and the rest of the party giggled uncontrollably. Never one to be outdone, Gavin repeated himself. "No, seriously chaps, it's a quick and easy process – it's just a matter of making a few small incisions in the clitoris, and your snoring is cured for life."

By now, most of Casalinga had turned to listen to Gavin expounding on this revolutionary medical advancement. While everyone except Lindie Gouws was roaring with laughter, he was clearly perplexed. He opened his mouth to speak, but I stopped him before he could dig the hole any deeper.

"Gavin," I asked, "are you not referring to your *epiglottis*?"

The room fell silent. Debbie and I were in stitches all the way home, and could barely fall asleep that night without one of us bursting into an uncontrollable fit of laughter.

Not only was Gavin a health fanatic, but he was also extremely image-conscious. He was always impeccably dressed and would judge other people by the clothes they wore. He would often point people out and openly say things like, "That's a bloody dutchman[19] – look at the shoes he's wearing."

---

19 A derogatory term for an Afrikaner

For years, I purchased my suits from PK Outfitters at the Oriental Plaza in downtown Johannesburg. I liked them because they dressed the *Carte Blanche* presenters when the investigative TV series was first screened. On my recommendation, Gavin and his brothers began shopping there too. Gavin would buy up to fifteen suits at a time. At one point, a PK representative brought fabric samples to the company headquarters, so that Gavin could have a range of shirts tailor-made for him. He did the same for the directors, and the company clothing bill often reached as much as R400 000 a month. For Gavin, who had a penchant for Italian shoes, the regular Moreschi and Prada shoes were not good enough – instead, his shoes were custom-made in Italy. Either that or he would get me to order Church's shoes online. Gavin went as far as having extra cupboards fitted in his townhouse to accommodate his burgeoning wardrobe, most of which he never wore.

Despite Gavin's character flaws and failings, I was completely sold on him in those early days. Like most human beings, he had his good and his bad sides. I constantly chose to see his good. I saw how exceptionally loyal he was to the team, rarely hesitating to go the extra mile for the people close to him. From behind my rose-tinted specs, he was the epitome of a true leader, particularly when the company was struggling. In my naivety, I saw him as a brilliant entrepreneur with some seriously maverick ideas. Although there was often smoke and mirrors around his dealings, I never considered him to be a bad guy.

Gavin was extremely protective and supportive of the people closest to him. During that time, between 2003 and 2011, nothing was ever too much. He would refurbish our houses, set up companies for us, and even purchase properties for us – whatever it was that we needed, he would be there with the cash to make it happen. In hindsight – and knowing what I know now – it was all part of his strategy to keep us under his control. While we all believed that he was taking care of us, I remember saying to my colleague, Andries van Tonder, that this was too good to be true. And we all know that when something seems too good to be true, it probably is.

CHAPTER 16

"God, why hast thou forsaken me?"

"Two things are infinite: the universe and human stupidity – and I'm not sure about the universe."
– Albert Einstein

There are moments in my life that will always be imprinted on my memory. One of them was the 9th of July 2000. Debbie had taken Giancarlo and Natasha on a road trip to visit her family in Steytlerville in the Eastern Cape in our brand-new Pajero. Andries van Tonder and I were out collecting money again, this time from Randfontein Estates, when I received a call that made my blood run cold. It was Debbie's mother. There had been an accident. While driving on the sand road between Graaff-Reinet and Steytlerville, the car's front wheels had locked. Nobody was buckled in. The car rolled seven times and, somewhere in those terrifying split-seconds, Giancarlo, who was eight years old at the time, was thrown from the car and into a fence. His liver and spleen had ruptured, and he was fighting for his life. Debbie and Natasha were alive, but details were sketchy.

"Get me to the airport," I told Andries, my hands shaking.

Gavin, who was visiting his family at the time, was waiting to collect me in Port Elizabeth when I landed. Together, we rushed through to the hospital, only to be told that my critically injured family were still en route. There had been a delay because the only ambulance available between Graaff-Reinet and Jansenville had no wheels, and the paramedics on duty literally had to go and borrow some.

When the ambulance eventually arrived at the Port Elizabeth hospital, I could hardly believe my eyes. It was so old it might as well have been an ice-cream truck. When the doors opened, I stood back in horror. Giancarlo was lying on the floor between Debbie and Natasha. There was blood everywhere. Natasha's left leg was visibly broken, and Debbie's right arm was severely mangled. Debbie had landed under the wheels of the Pajero, and one of the mags had sliced off her elbow. Seeing my wife and children in this state sparked an explosive rage inside me. I couldn't understand why God had abandoned my family like this.

"Why are you doing this to us?" I asked Him, fighting back the tears, consumed with the fear that Giancarlo might slip away at any moment.

It was a turbulent time for me, having to fly in and out of Port Elizabeth, meeting with one doctor after another, each one's prognosis less hopeful than the next. Although things were touch-and-go, the doctors agreed on one thing – that it was a miracle that my family was alive and that it was God's grace that had carried them through. When Debbie and the children were out of the woods, the discussions began to centre on the recuperation process. The doctors had little hope of saving Debbie's arm – it was, unfortunately, beyond repair. Giancarlo had, however, made significant progress, and Natasha was out of any potential danger, with only severe scarring remaining to mark this traumatic ordeal in her young life.

After two weeks, permission was granted for Giancarlo and Natasha to see their mother for the first time since the accident. It was an emotional moment for all of us as the nurses wheeled the children into Debbie's ward. This broken and battered family could now begin to heal.

After eight arduous weeks in hospital, Giancarlo pulled through, Debbie was fitted with a prosthesis, and Natasha's leg began to heal – but something had changed inside me. I had always relied on God to guide me through the difficult times, but this time it was not God who carried me through – it was Gavin Watson. From the outset, he had been there for us. When I needed his help, he was there in an instant. He even went as far as sending his wife and children to visit my family in hospital. Throughout the ordeal, Gavin positioned himself as a saviour in my life. I moved my reliance away from God and onto this man. I decided to push myself even harder and prove to Gavin that I would do anything for him.

And Gavin, the calculating man that he was, knew exactly what he was doing. Because in the world of Gavin Watson, nothing ever came for free. I had fallen for his charismatic ways, and in so doing, my pact with the beast was made.

CHAPTER 17

When Miners Strike

"I am fundamentally an optimist. Whether that comes from nature or nurture, I cannot say. Part of being optimistic is keeping one's head pointed toward the sun, one's feet moving forward. There were many dark moments when my faith in humanity was sorely tested, but I would not and could not give myself up to despair. That way lays defeat and death."
– Nelson Mandela

David Sadie had been in mining hostels his entire life, having grown up in and around them, and eventually going on to run them. A short, exceptionally bright young Lebanese guy, he was the embodiment of human resources. He also had the typical A-type personality.

I'll never forget the morning of the 2001 Hartebeesfontein Gold Mine strike. Arriving home from church that Sunday morning, I found David pacing up and down my driveway. Solomon, our gardener, told me that David had been there since 8 a.m., and had probably worn through the soles of his shoes with all his pacing. There was a wage dispute brought by the facilities management staff at the mine. While their demands were high, we were in a catch-22 situation: the National Union of Mineworkers was our client, but they were also representing the masses, making them our direct opponent in this wage dispute. The staff had followed all the correct procedures – they had their CCMA Strike Notice certificate and planned to go on strike at midnight. The impact of not providing food and other basic services to the twelve thousand hostel dwellers meant risking underground sit-ins and riots. The mine was looking at losses of R1-million per hour if operations were put on hold. Mine management had been in contact with David, asking that he and I handle the strike in such a way that there was no disruption in services.

David had never handled a large-scale strike situation before. All he wanted to do was get to Hartebeesfontein in Klerksdorp as quickly as possible and settle the dispute. By the time we got there, Prince Monyela, the Bosasa Unit Leader, was already on site waiting for us. We had picked up Seef Wolmarans, the Operational Leader for the region, on the way. While driving out to the mine, David tapped away at his calculator. "It's going to cost us an additional R700 000 a month, Angelo," he said. "I reckon that if we can afford it, we must meet their demands." The net contribution from Hartebeesfontein was in excess of R1.3-million per month, so we had room to settle with the union – but the ramifications, if we made them an offer, would be far-reaching.

We both knew that Gavin wasn't going to budge – there was no way he was going to pay the unions a cent more than he was already paying. "Let them strike," he told us. Of course, he didn't have to worry if people weren't catered for or cleaned up after, or if the liquor stores weren't running. It was up to Seef, David and me to sort out the problem.

While I could see how flustered David was, I decided to let him sweat a bit. I had already decided on the strategy, but I wanted him to learn the hard way. Knowing how meticulous he was and how annoying his nagging would get if I let him in on the game plan, I thought it best that he spent his time fielding Gavin's calls. Other than the obvious entertainment factor, I was happy to allow him and Gavin to stew together while Seef and I did what we needed to do.

When we walked into the Hartebeesfontein Mine hostel, the union asked to see us immediately. Sitting around the boardroom table, I put on my best poker face and explained the rules of engagement.

"Gentlemen, we just need to iron out the strike rules. We are well aware that your intention to strike was issued on Friday. We are also aware that you are entitled to notify us of your strike action, as you have done. You are welcome to go on strike, but you must understand that we have planned accordingly."

The room was silent, barring a few nods and seat shuffles, so I proceeded to tell the union leaders a little white lie. "We have seven hundred people waiting in the wings to take over. They are currently on standby in a hall in Potchefstroom. All we're asking is that you handle this maturely and don't prevent the scab labour from coming in."

At that point, David left the room, and the union leaders began to speak among themselves. Unbeknown to me, David had gone off his rocker and called Gavin to tell him that I was encouraging the strike. I could hear my phone ringing in my pocket – I must have received about a dozen missed calls – but I ignored it. I allowed a few moments for the information to sink in. The union decided they were going ahead and issued us with the strike certificate, which we duly accepted. A disinformation campaign was immediately launched, with several company-loyal individuals chosen to deliver the fake news. Reports went out that they had found the location where Bosasa was housing the scab labour, and that it was clear from the contingent of buses and training teams on-site, that they were ready to move in at a moment's notice.

As the messages went out, so sources within the union echelons began giving us feedback. It was the day before payday, and suddenly it didn't seem like such a good idea to go on the offensive, especially since rumour had it that payments had been paused until the matter was resolved. Workers were also notified that advances and loans would be withdrawn from their wages with immediate effect.

And so, the house of cards began to fall.

Two hours later, the union leaders were back in the boardroom, asking for another meeting. I agreed, and we all sat down again. "We are asking to postpone the strike for a few days," said one of the union leaders, his earlier arrogance having subsided considerably.

Everything was going perfectly according to plan. I looked at him with the most professional poker face I could muster. "I'm sorry," I said, throwing my hands up in the air, "you've already handed me your certificate, so you have to go on strike. There's no turning back now – unless we offer a compromise and structure a two- or three-year agreement. I'll put it together in such a way that you look good in the eyes of your members."

It was clear that I had piqued his interest.

The union leaders asked that we allow them a few minutes to discuss the matter outside, and then promptly disappeared. Next thing, David burst into the office looking somewhat dishevelled – his tie halfway down his chest, and sweating profusely. "Angelo," he said, clearly flustered, "Gavin's looking for you. Everybody's looking for you. Can you please just answer your damn phone?"

"I'll phone them when I'm done," I said, and then proceeded to explain what had just transpired. "Are you out of your mind?" David shrieked, unravelling even further. "Listen, I know I'm your junior, but please, stop what you're doing! Gavin has already agreed to pay them what they want."

I sat back in my chair with arms folded. "I don't think you've thought this through," I said, "Remember, it's not just these guys – we have 3 200 staff, so whatever we decide today is going to have a ripple effect." I knew that if we made them an offer, we would be setting a precedent for every other facilities management staff member we employed across the group.

At 4 p.m., the union asked to see me again. This time, the four mine hostel managers from the different centres were present. "We want to withdraw the strike action," the union leader said.

I shook my head. "No," I said. "You may not."

David almost wet himself right there in the boardroom. Everybody was dumbfounded. My phone was still ringing in my pocket. I was ready to go home. It had been an exhausting day, and I wasn't looking forward to the two-hour drive back to Johannesburg.

Half an hour later, one of the union leaders entered the boardroom. He got down on his hands and knees and begged us to allow them to retract the strike action completely.

It was the first time the union had gone this route to have their demands met, but I was well-versed in these tactics. Ronnie Lousteau had trained me well. Sometimes you just had to put your foot down and say no. A two-year settlement agreement was subsequently entered into, with a notable eight percent increase in year one, and seven-and-a-half percent in year two. While the union declared victory, I smiled at Seef and Prince – we had done well.

Another strike that I always remember took place on the 3rd of December 2002, my thirty-fourth birthday. Unbeknown to me, Debbie had hired out a venue and spent months arranging a surprise party for me that evening.

At about 2 p.m., I received a call from Blyvooruitzicht Mine in Carletonville. The security staff had gone on a wildcat strike. The standard procedure with a strike of this nature was to give the workers three warnings to return to work, one hour apart, and to start with dismissals if they were not working by the third warning. They had already received their first two warnings – all that remained was for us to add water and stir well.

I called David Sadie and Joe Gumede, and we headed out to Carletonville to issue the third warning. We knew that our physical presence on-site generally had a positive and far-reaching effect. We called in the shop stewards. "This is the National Union of Mineworkers," I said. "What do you think you guys are doing?"

The shop stewards shook their heads. "We are on strike," they told us. The mineworkers had decided not to listen to the union leaders and were doing as they pleased, oblivious to the rules.

"What you're doing is illegal," I said. "You haven't followed due process, so now I'm going to issue the final ultimatum."

The National Union of Mineworkers leaders stood rooted to the spot, stunned. They knew they had a problem, but they had no idea how to deal with it. Needless to say, nobody returned to work. We told the shop stewards to bring their people in. One by one, we dismissed them. Of course, this was done with the intention of re-employing them, but I wanted to teach them a lesson they'd never forget.

In the meantime, hour upon hour was passing by. In between the dismissals, I kept receiving calls, asking where I was and when I was coming home. Even my personal assistant, Riana Mulder, called. My cell phone battery was going flat, so I switched it off. Next thing, David's phone is ringing. It's Debbie. It's Riana. Everyone wants to know where I am. I couldn't understand why everybody was so worried about me. Joe Gumede's phone was the last to ring. It was Gavin telling him to tell me that the strike had been resolved and I should leave immediately.

And then the penny dropped – something had been planned. I called Debbie. She told me she'd booked out an entire restaurant for my birthday and that everyone was there, including half of the Bosasa executive team, waiting for me to grace them with my presence.

"But I'm only going to be getting back at about eleven tonight," I said.

"But, Angelo, it's your birthday," she argued. "How can you still be working?"

"I'm sorry," I said. "You'll have to celebrate this one without me."

At that stage, there was nothing I could do. I had to follow through. A few hours after the strike was resolved, the perpetrators were charged in terms of the disciplinary code. Those who had blindly followed instructions were issued with final written warnings and lost their privilege to participate in any extra-mural activities for the next six months – something that was permissible at the time.

Strikes in those days rarely lasted more than a few hours. After all, the National Union of Mineworkers was our client, and Gavin had a good relationship with their different heads. Although the unions, for the most part, were committed and reasonable, they were visibly frustrated that their leadership had been compromised – and all over something as simple as a plate of food and who was in charge of cooking it.

CHAPTER 18

A Young White Boy and Equal Trade Foods

"Friends don't always make the best of business partners."
– Chris Campbell

By 2003, Bosasa had set the benchmark for the catering and facilities management sector. Other companies were now attempting to encroach on our space. An element within the National Union of Mineworkers, the union over which Gavin had reigned for four consecutive years, decided they wanted an alternative service provider. One of these companies was Equal Trade Foods, owned by my erstwhile colleague at Molope foods, Greg Lacon-Allin, an amenable chap who spoke Zulu as if it was his mother tongue.

Suddenly, we found ourselves thrust into a bidding war to win the union's favour. Although we were all eventually fed up with being played off against each other, Gavin refused to accept the fact that the war for union favour had to stop. He eventually sent Joe, Papa, Ishmael and some of the company's black managers out to the hostels to speak to the union leaders and rescue the contract from Equal Trade Foods. They returned with their tails between their legs, after being forced to stand on vegetable crates in front of the jeering hostel-dwellers. Their once-confident attitudes were somewhat diluted when they reported back to the team that there was no hope of rescuing the contract. This young white boy (as I liked to call Greg) with no political connections (as I enjoyed reminding Gavin) had succeeded in undermining the National Union of Mineworkers' long-standing loyalty to Bosasa.

While Gavin was convinced that this change of heart on the part of the unions had everything to do with our costings, what we failed to realise was that the unions had become divided.

With all this uncertainty, our regular Wednesday morning Operations meetings quickly became what I termed the Wednesday "Confessionals". The meetings usually began with discussions about Manchester United, Liverpool and Kaizer Chiefs, followed by a run-down of illicit employee affairs that Gavin had heard about that needed attending to, culminating in Gavin dragging people over the coals as each operational unit's financial costing was dissected. All the meetings served to do was to destroy people's morale. Of course, nobody had any clue as to whether the figures spat out by the company's so-called "Business Intelligence" (which Frans Vorster renamed "Bullshit Information") system and displayed on the overhead projector were anything close to the truth.

What had become glaringly evident to me was that the only thing Bosasa was being managed by was fear.

Greg Lacon-Allin eventually approached Gavin and offered to buy all the mining-related contracts over from Bosasa. Gavin liked the idea, and I was only too happy to wave goodbye to the problem. If the company's "Business Intelligence" system was anything to go by, we were only making in the region of half a million rands' profit a month off these contracts. By selling them off to Equal Trade Foods, we could rid ourselves of the one part of the company that was causing the most internal strife – not to mention that it was barely ticking over – and focus on growing other aspects of the business.

We signed a three-year restraint of trade agreement, moved one thousand two hundred people over to Equal Trade Foods, and kissed the Wednesday morning "Confessionals" goodbye. David Sadie, who by then was done with Gavin Watson and his narcissistic leadership style, also took the opportunity to leave Bosasa and take up a position with Greg and his team.

Having gone from a staff complement of three thousand people to one thousand eight hundred, and with our hands wiped clean of the mines, I was able to take a step back and turn my attention to developing Bosasa's security management model so that we could poise ourselves for future growth. At this stage, Bosasa represented the possibilities of great and glittering fortunes – "The Future". It felt like I was on the precipice of reaping the rewards for all the years of toil and sowing of seeds. In reality, I had become sucked into the acquisition of my own personal wealth, and so I refused to see the cracks in the house that Gavin Watson lorded over.

CHAPTER 19

Company Secretary Extraordinaire – Tony Perry

"If everyone were clothed with integrity, if every heart were just, frank, kindly, the other virtues would be well-nigh useless."
– Molière [Jean Baptiste Poquelin] – *Tartuffe*, V, i (1622-1673)

Tony Perry was brought into Bosasa as Company Secretary in 2002. The reason Gavin brought him on board was twofold. One, they had a long-standing relationship, and two, Gavin needed someone to help him structure the company and its insurances in such a way that he had full control of everything.

Firstly, the relationship. Danny Mansell and Gavin Watson's relationship extended back to when Danny worked for the SBDC.[20] At the time, Gavin was consulting to the organisation. When Gavin submitted his invoices, Tony Perry, who also worked for the SBDC, had to sign off the invoices before Danny could make payment. Secondly, Bosasa's structure and insurances required attending to. Tony happened to have a good relationship with Gavin's wife, Leigh-Ann. He also happened to be well-associated with a gentleman by the name of Philip Putziger who ran a leading insurance brokerage in Port Elizabeth.

I'm sure it was Tony's relationship with Leigh-Ann that made Gavin take extra-special care of him. Gavin spent time with Tony, looking out for him and making him feel good. He brought in a lady by the name of Natasha Olivier as Tony's PA.

Tony was the epitome of everything prim and proper. He was so straight down the line that we named him Mr Integrity.

---

20 Small Business Development Corporation

Tony and Doc Smith were extremely prudent with the company's finances and frowned upon unnecessary expenditure. One Friday afternoon I suggested that it was about time we bought a fleet of golf carts for the office park. One of the benefits would be saving the cleaning staff from having to walk the long distances between the different buildings, while another benefit was more personal. I was walking the campus three to four times a day and doing about twelve thousand steps in the process. I was certainly not training to compete in the next Ironman and, quite frankly, all that unnecessary exercise was killing me.

The two of them looked at me as if I had lost the plot – it was clear that neither would approve such a ludicrous idea.

Unbeknown to Tony and Doc, Frans Vorster and I had arranged for a top-of-the-range golf cart to be delivered to the offices the following Wednesday so that we could give it a test drive. When it arrived, I took great pride in unveiling it in the parking area adjacent to Tony's office. His subsequent outburst was probably amplified by the fact that we had just walked out of a strategic cost-cutting meeting that involved notifying nine hundred staff members of their impending retrenchments.

Thankfully, the retrenchments never went ahead, but what happened in the parking lot that afternoon was priceless. While Frans and I took turns doing doughnuts on the grass, Tony Perry looked on, his face turning crimson until he erupted into a fit of rage, hurling abuse at us with such eloquence that his office windowpanes all but started vibrating.

Perhaps my fondest Tony memory was the day I had to collect an out-of-town visitor from the Cedar Lodge in Krugersdorp early one morning, to accompany me to a meeting in Pretoria. I drove up the long road that led to the lodge and stopped in the main parking area outside the restaurant to wait for him. The eastern sky was filled with a blend of sandy yellows and rosy pinks, and the outlines of the lodge's buildings were slowly becoming clearer. While my car was idling, I spotted a gentleman up ahead, walking hand-in-hand with a woman. He looked vaguely familiar, but it was too dark for me to be sure. I turned my car's brights on so that I could see more clearly. It was none other than Tony Perry, and the woman whose hand he was holding was Elise Marais, our payroll administrator. They were both, much to my amusement, grinning like Cheshire cats.

Now, I knew that Tony was staying at the same lodge, but I certainly didn't expect to see him at that ghastly hour of the morning. The company driver would usually pick him up in the mornings and bring him through to the office, but it seemed a bit early for somebody else from the company to be collecting him.

I leaned out of the window. "Good morning, Tony," I called out. And then, "Good morning, Elise."

Tony walked straight past me. Elise, dressed in her company uniform, didn't know where to look. At that moment, the person I was collecting knocked on my passenger window, and, when I looked back again, Elise and Tony had disappeared. I chuckled to myself as I hit the open road to Pretoria. It felt quite surreal seeing "old" Tony with what seemed to be the love of his life.

After I left, my phone wouldn't stop ringing. There were at least fifteen missed calls from Tony every hour. Eventually, in between meetings, I answered one of his calls. "Please, Angelo – boetie,"[21] he said. Now, when someone from the Eastern Cape calls you "boet"[22] or "boetie", you must know that they are desperate for your help. "Please keep what you saw this morning confidential, boetie," he said. "I don't want anybody to know about Elise and me."

Here was this fifty-seven-year-old male divorcee in a normal relationship with a fifty-year-old female divorcee – hardly anything illicit or unusual – but I promised Tony I would keep what I had seen between the three of us.

On the first Saturday morning of March each year, the remuneration committee would meet to review wages and salaries for the different divisions and subsidiaries of the group. While the latter was more general and across the board, when it came to reviews for head office staff, each person was assessed individually. There must have been about fifteen of us there that day, over and above Gavin and the directors.

We sat down, and everyone was handed the list of names. Tony Perry was exceptionally fidgety. It was the middle of winter, but his face was pouring with perspiration. He looked quite ill.

I nudged him. "Are you okay, Tony?" He looked away and continued shuffling in his seat as if there were ants in his pants.

We moved on from the Accounts department to the Payroll department. I turned the page to see who was first on the list. It was Elise Marais. Before anyone else could flip the paper over, Tony stood up and threw his hands in the air.

---

21 Little brother
22 Brother

"I have to declare my interests," he blurted out. Everyone looked at him, wide-eyed in subtle amusement. And, right there and then, in front of everyone, Tony confessed that he and Elise were an item.

The meeting ended there and then. Nobody could focus after that. The rest of the staff simply had to be happy with an across-the-board seven percent salary increase.

Another memorable Tony Perry moment took place during a time when Bosasa was seriously short of cash, and I'd have to drive out to clients and wait there until they produced a cheque. When necessary, I would pull out my Russians and chips trick, because nothing smells worse than greasy Russians and vinegary chips, and nothing makes a receptionist move faster than offering her a taste.

Having just sold the catering division of the business to Equal Trade Food, monies needed to be paid out to them. Durban Roodepoort Deep (DRD) owed us their final R1.6-million, but payment was being held back because of a R20 000 water and lights dispute. As far as I was concerned, DRD could pay us for the difference in the meantime, and we'd sort out the utilities issue later.

It was a Friday afternoon, and I wanted my money, so I drove out there. I collected the cheque, sans grease, and gave it to Tony to bank. "We can't accept this," he said, pushing the cheque back into my hands.

"Why not?" I asked.

"Because if we bank it, we're admitting that this is the full and final settlement," he replied.

I wasn't in the mood for this, and he wanted me out of his office, so I stormed out and headed over to Andries van Tonder. "I'm going to teach this old man a lesson and show him who's who in the zoo," I said, waving the cheque in my hand.

Andries laughed nervously. He knew what I was capable of.

One of our high-end photocopy machines made perfect copies. I placed the cheque on the glass and hit the "copy" button. I stopped by at Reception and asked that they call Tony in a few minutes to tell him Equal Trade was there to collect their cheque.

Then I walked back over to Tony's office with the photocopied cheque and remittance advice in my hand and found Doc Smith sitting there with him. The two old ballies[23] would sit for hours chatting away. "Tony, this

23 Old fogies

112

cheque needs to be deposited," I said, with all the seriousness I could muster.

"Angelo, I told you – I'm not depositing it," he said. "Tony, I'm warning you," I said, putting the cheque down on his desk. "I didn't go and sit at DRD this morning for nothing."

Tony picked up the cheque and threw it back across the table at me. "I'm not doing it," he insisted. I picked up the cheque, tore it up, and threw it back at him. Tony's eyes nearly fell out of his head. At that point, the phone on his desk started ringing.

"Equal Trade is here to pick up their cheque," said the voice on the other end of the line. Barely able to contain my laughter, I thought it best to leave Tony's office immediately. The next minute, my phone was ringing. It was Gavin. "Now, Angelo, how do you plan to sort this out?"

"Gavin," I said, "the cheque is already in the bank. I arranged for somebody else to deposit it. I was just trying to teach the old man a lesson."

I don't think Tony ever forgave me for that.

PART 4

CHAPTER 20

Intelligent Security

"As we know,
There are known knowns.
There are things we know we know.
We also know
There are known unknowns.
That is to say
We know there are some things
We do not know.
But there are also unknown unknowns,
The ones we don't know
We don't know."
– Donald Rumsfeld, February 12, 2002, US Department of Defense
news briefing

Running any full facilities management contract usually entails offering basic security services to guard the site. From security that involved a man with a stick at the gate outside the hostels during the Dyambu days, it was in 2001 that Bosasa ventured into the private security sector on a more formal basis. "The future" looked bright when the company was awarded a five-year contract by the Airports Company of South Africa (ACSA), valued at R43.2-million, to guard their car parks at the then-Johannesburg International Airport.

Where we really made a name for ourselves was thanks to an ingenious invention that we came up with to assist in the prevention of tailgating and the theft of motor vehicles from the airport's multi-storey car parks. At the time, there were no access-controlled boom gates, and ACSA was losing up to thirty-six motor vehicles a month. They asked us to come up with a solution. I had enlisted a company to weld nails onto long chains that would be dragged across the car park exit points. The guard positioned at each point would be required to verify that each vehicle leaving the car park had its keys in the ignition, and only then would he pull the chain away. It was a cumbersome process, and in those early days the guards managed to flatten about twenty tyres (which we replaced), but after six months of using the spiked chains, only one vehicle was reported stolen. What I learned through this process is that as long as you apply your mind and keep things simple, you can make almost anything successful.

In 2002, we were awarded a three-year contract valued at R43.5-million for guarding services at the South African Post Office, which was extended by a further two years. We were responsible for rolling out the security for their pension pay-out points, which was later expanded to some of their mail-sorting hubs, like Witspos.

While the trend in much of the developed world was to form security intelligence databases and augment traditional guarding with technology and systems, this was a relatively new phenomenon in South Africa. South Africa's private security industry, born out of necessity, was, back in the early 2000s, comprised mainly of armed guards and their dogs – and a weapon of some shape or form.

While this industry was largely dominated (and regulated) by the Private Security Industry Regulatory Authority (PSIRA), I had always found this method of managing security antiquated. Guards are fallible, while technology, for the most part, is accurate and incorruptible.

After spending two weeks in Dubai attending conferences and trade shows, meeting with international industry leaders and researching the industry in general, it was clear to me that CCTV, biometrics and access control systems were most certainly the way of the future. To make a real difference to the security sector in South Africa, we were going to need to design a blueprint for success.

I returned to South Africa with two goals: one was to build a team of people who would develop and install CCTV, access control and specialised surveillance technology, and the other was to take security guards and turn them into intelligence officers – gathering intelligence from CCTV screens in control rooms and reporting back on it. Back then, an upskilled security guard doing the work of three security guards could go from earning R5 000 a month to R8 000 a month, while saving their employers thousands. To me, it was a no-brainer.

It didn't take long for us to discover that suggesting an overhaul to the traditional security model in South Africa would be met with resistance by the existing security cluster, but we pursued it anyway.

The Lindela Repatriation Centre became my test bench. Together with Dr Denise Bjorkman, who ran Bosasa's Wellness Clinic, I embarked on designing bespoke training on how to identify suspicious activities and unusual behaviour.

Once we had successfully rolled the training out at Lindela, we founded the Pan African Council of Surveillance Professionals and Technologists to train security officers in peacekeeping, law enforcement, counter-terrorism and anti-money-laundering techniques. This initiative was an important development in South Africa's security industry because it kick-started the formalisation of what was expected of trained guards.

Bosasa ran several Youth Centres, much like the original Meritum Youth Development Centre founded by Fanie van Zijl and Doc Smith in Mogale City. These centres had a footprint in various provinces across South Africa, accommodating youth who were in conflict with the law and awaiting trial. With our expansion into high-tech security, an opportunity arose to develop a centralised control system for these Youth Centres, with remote capabilities that would allow an authorised person to link up to any Youth Centre, anywhere in the country, from a smartphone or computer, to see what was happening on the ground.

Eighteen months later, the system was implemented. Then we found out that some of the older offender boys were watching soft porn late at night, thanks to one of the channels broadcasting this material. This was problematic, especially with younger boys living in the same room. We decided to link the individual televisions to our centralised system so that we could screen the content being viewed and block the offending channels remotely. This was a defining moment for our management teams who were now able to set the rules and parameters around these young offenders' viewing habits.

ACSA, who liked what they saw, signed a contract with Bosasa to upgrade their security systems. From day one, it became a well-known fact that if there was a crime incident in the car park, it wasn't on our watch. Rolling out technology-augmented guarding systems saw our bottom-line profits increase significantly. While we originally employed about seven hundred guards across the different airports, we were able to reduce the number of guards down to about five hundred. The beauty of it all was that we were paying people better salaries, which had a direct impact on motivation and productivity.

Bosasa's contracts with ACSA grew phenomenally. Eventually, we were awarded contracts – valued at just over R484-million – at the King Shaka, Cape Town, Bloemfontein, Kimberley, Port Elizabeth and East London airports. During peak season, our contracts were expanded to overseeing baggage handling to reduce pilfering.

During this time, we were also awarded a South African Post Office tender – valued at an estimated R120-million – to redefine and redevelop their CCTV and access control systems.

I employed Gordon Howes, an MBA graduate and General Electric specialist to look after the day-to-day management of the new business unit – which we called Sondolo IT – hoping that this would free me up to focus on the growth of the Bosasa group as a whole, instead of being bogged down with running one business unit. Gordon even wore his Tuks[24] tie as part of his Sondolo IT uniform.

In the meantime, Gavin Watson, ever the expansionist, decided it was time to re-enter the catering space – this time at the Department of Correctional Services.

---

24 University of Pretoria

CHAPTER 21

Patrick Gillingham, Linda Mti and the R800-million Prisons' Catering Contract

"It is rare indeed that people give. Most people guard and keep; they suppose that it is they themselves and what they identify with themselves that they are guarding and keeping, whereas what they are actually guarding and keeping is their system of reality and what they assume themselves to be."
– James Baldwin, *The Fire Next Time*

"Gillingham wants to know what he is getting out of this," said Danny.

It was 2004. Gavin was sitting with Danny Mansell in the boardroom. I was in the bathroom next door. The drywalling separating the two rooms was paper-thin, so I was able to follow the conversation word for word. Danny and his family had just returned from a weekend getaway with somebody by the name of Patrick Gillingham and his family. According to Danny, it had been a "successful" trip. I had no idea who this Patrick Gillingham was to whom Danny was referring, but what was clear was that Danny and Gavin had patched up their relationship and that Danny was back on board.

"Do whatever you have to do," said Gavin. "Mti is going to get him [Gillingham] into the position of CFO, and he's going to be key in getting us those contracts."

Linda Mti, unbeknown to me, was the National Commissioner for the Department of Correctional Services (DCS) at the time.

Linda Morris Mti and Gavin Watson's family were deeply intertwined, their roots set firmly in the Eastern Cape where they had first met. An exiled ANC military veteran who was detained by security police together with Steve Biko in 1977, Mti trained and studied in Russia before returning to South Africa in the early 1990s to chair the ANC in the Eastern Cape. During his time in exile, Mti became close friends with Gibson Njenje, who would later go on to become the Director of the domestic branch of the South African State Security Agency.

Although a trained laboratory technician in his youth, Mti took up employment at the Department of Correctional Services in Pretoria. Not only was Mti an old friend of Gavin's, but he was also involved in the adjudication of bids and tenders at the DCS.

I first met Mti at a DCS conference in September 2004. I was representing the company at one of their breakaway sessions when he came up to me and introduced himself. It would be two years before we would see each other again.

Patrick Gillingham, I later discovered, was the prison warder responsible for Nelson Mandela during his incarceration on Robben Island. On the day of Mandela's release from prison, it was Patrick who signed his exit forms. He was, at that stage, employed by the DCS as Chief Deputy Commissioner for one of the regions, and was primed to take over the role of CFO of that department.

A few days later, while on a site visit to the Lindela Repatriation Centre, I bumped into Gavin. Standing with him was a well-dressed gentleman, his military uniform decorated with gold stars and ribbons. He was introduced to me as Patrick Gillingham.

"You must work closely with Gillingham," Gavin whispered, pulling me aside. "Danny's coming back – he and Patrick go back years. Danny's going to be reporting directly to you, and we're going to be working with Corrections[25]."

I barely gave his comment a second thought. We were already working with the DCS because many of Lindela's offenders came directly from the prisons. I simply presumed that Gillingham would be the person assisting us with deporting people being released from the prisons out of the country in future.

What I was oblivious to was the fact that Danny Mansell seems to have been brought back on board to help Bosasa capture Patrick Gillingham, and in turn, the DCS.

What I had noticed, however, was a string of invoices from Riekele Construction, a construction company owned by a character by the name of Riaan Hoeksma, for two houses they were building – one in Savannah

---

25 Department of Correctional Services

Hills Estate in Midrand, and the other in Midstream Estate in Centurion. Bosasa was footing the bill, and it was costing the company dearly, but the recipients of those houses, up until 2009, were incognito.

A few days after meeting Patrick Gillingham, I received a call from Gavin. "Angelo, get your bags ready. Wear casual clothes. I want you to conduct a survey for me at Johannesburg Prison. They want a blueprint from us on how to improve efficiencies in the prisons. Find out where their faults are. Make notes. Draw up an action plan."

Our only previous dealings with the prisons (not counting Lindela) had been many years earlier when Boksburg Correctional Services, which fell under the Boksburg Management Area, had a small contract with Dyambu Meat Trading, one of our butcher shops, to supply them with small quantities of beef when they were unable to obtain it from their regular suppliers.

The DCS wanted to know how we could design a system that would allow them to feed thousands of people in under twenty minutes. They were interested in seeing our capabilities. At Lindela, we designed a kitchen that could cater for up to four thousand five hundred people. We could dish up food for all those people in fifteen minutes. I come from a background of large-scale catering operations at the mines, where I had catered for up to twelve thousand people a day. It was years of training, experience and expertise that put us on the map. We were primed to take over that contract.

There were six of us from Bosasa who marched into Johannesburg Prison that day. Gillingham was waiting for us inside. We were introduced to the Area Commissioner, Hento Davids, and then we were taken on a tour.

At that stage, all their catering was being done in-house and, in the two days we spent at the prison, I immediately picked up on some fundamentals that weren't in place. There was no sign that any form of stock management was taking place. Standard practice with any kitchen storeroom is that anything taken from the shelves is immediately recorded – it is the only way of tracking how many people are being catered for. Not only was their inventory not being managed, but the people running the kitchen appeared to have no idea how to record what they had taken from the stores. Added to this, they had none of the basic tools with which to measure or weigh a plate of food – there wasn't a ruler or scale in sight.

After running through various exercises and calculations, I discovered that while three plates of food should have been costing them a maximum of R7 per person per day, it was costing them almost R12.

Once I had completed the analysis, I prepared a report with my findings and my recommendations. I gave the report to Gavin and Danny, who, I believe, sent it on to the relevant people at the DCS. After being told how impressed everyone was, I was then asked to conduct the same study at Pollsmoor, St Albans, Patensie, North End and Westville prisons.

In my experience, it is an unfortunate reality that most tenders in South Africa – especially multimillion-rand projects requiring a single service provider – are pre-adjudicated. The tender advert is nothing more than a formality to prove that other companies were given a chance to bid before the tender was awarded. The tenders that Bosasa won were no different. Where we knew we had a definite "in", we helped the department write the specifications for that particular tender so that nobody else could enter and play in that space, something the media would later pick up on.

With the prisons, the specifications were based on a detailed understanding of the project's unique requirements. It involved countrywide site visits and extensive research on where the opportunities were. It often involved identifying shortcomings and proposing solutions. I looked at food security, stock control and equipment, and proposed, among other things, the hiring of mobile kitchens and specialised equipment for refrigeration. Each of these proposals formed the basis of the blueprint I created for the specifications of the final tender document.

Since Bosasa met all the requirements by default, we were subsequently awarded the tender to cater for all the DCS prisons, countrywide, for a period of three years. The contract was valued at R800-million.

In those early days, I truly believed, perhaps naively, that winning those contracts had everything to do with our capabilities and nothing to do with any cash changing hands. While there were allegations of the tender being rigged, many of our competitors had omitted critical documents – things like tax clearance certificates and guarantees – that led to them being disqualified. Pricing was also critical. While we were not the cheapest, we were certainly not the most expensive. Some of our competitors did not understand the magnitude of what a mobile kitchen was. When the prisons ask for a mobile kitchen, they're looking for one that is a thousand metres squared – not a little caravan. We went into minute detail, showing them schematics and drawing up project plans, right down to how the prisoners would be managed at mealtimes.

By then, Molope Foods had closed their doors but, had the other contenders applied their minds and followed the proper procedures, they too would have been able to get through the process.

It was important for us to impress that while we were a politically strong company, we were more than capable of delivering on our promises. When we presented our initial bid, it filled twenty-five lever arch files. Even though Bosasa was smaller than many of the other companies competing for the tender; for the prisons adjudication team, it was clear that we were far more credible (and capable) than our competitors.

Bosasa's greatest nemesis and ultimate undoing, however, was the way in which it chose to acquire its business in the years that followed – something that continues to haunt me to this day. Throwing caution to the wind, the company, under Gavin Watson's watchful eye – not to mention his burgeoning vaults – chose to slide deep into the cesspit of the country's political underbelly. I was blinded by my own greed. Caught up with chasing my once noble dreams of material success, I slowly began replacing the ambitions I'd always had for myself and my family with the aspirations of a beast, one lacking in morality and soul – an ever-hungry, ever-expanding machine of greed and corruption.

CHAPTER 22

Chicken or Beef – or Bosasa?

"Food brings people together on many different levels. It's nourishment of the soul and body – it's truly love."
– Giada De Laurentiis

If there is one thing a prisoner looks forward to every day, it's that plate of food. When we examined the meals that were being prepared in-house before Bosasa came on board, it might as well have been dog food. A regular evening meal was a plate of soya chunks cooked up without any spices. To expect any human being (criminal or not) to eat the rubbish they were serving up was nothing short of inhuman.

Before Bosasa was appointed to manage prison catering, prison management was fielding up to ten food-related court applications (by the inmates) per week, for substandard food. We were feeding 144 000 meals to prisoners in thirty-seven facilities countrywide, but hardly ever during our tenure were there complaints about our services – everybody ate the food, and nobody fell ill.

When we took over the contracts, most of the inmates weren't even eating off plates. They would queue up with their margarine tubs or their ice-cream containers. Many were using plastic bank cards as cutlery. We brought in proper army-type mess kits and worked with the US-based company, DuPont, to custom-design and manufacture pre-moulded spoons without shanks that couldn't be sharpened and that could withstand serious abuse.

Of the thirty to forty million rands a month we were charging the prisons, we were making ten to fifteen million rands in profit, so we had the money and the resources to improve the quality of the food. We did proper menu planning according to the Department's ration scale. We brought in qualified chefs to cook the meals, and invested R54-million in equipment to help retain the moisture, nutrients and taste of the food. We implemented systems so that we could see *exactly* what we were doing.

For the prisoners, the impact of our presence was immediate. When they lined up for their meals, there were people standing on the other side of the counters, clad in white and wearing head guards, masks and gloves. The quality of the food was a far cry from the pet food they had previously been served – the meals had colour and looked and tasted good. Plus, everyone had a spoon, a plate and a tray.

Our systems were working. We were measuring. We were counting. Nothing was going missing. Everybody was getting their plate of food. On the other hand, prison staff were pissed off. In the past, they were cooking two different sets of meals – one for the inmates, and another for themselves and the prison warders. They were even taking food home, often directly out of the storerooms. With Bosasa on board, this became a thing of the past, despite the internal grumblings.

CHAPTER 23

The Great Prison Heist

"Play by the rules, but be ferocious."
– Phil Knight – Founder, Nike

Once Johannesburg Prison was up and running, it was time to tackle the others. The plan was to open all the contracts countrywide on the same day. The DCS was concerned about our safety at Patensie, North End and St Albans Prisons in Port Elizabeth – and in fact advised us against opening contracts in those kitchens – but I knew that with the right people on the ground, we could pull this off.

"St Albans is the most dangerous," I was told. Not one to pass up a challenge, I decided I would tackle that prison personally, and then head over to North End and Patensie, just outside Port Elizabeth.

We utilised the existing prison staff, but we also put in our own people to manage and train them. I assembled my teams a month ahead of schedule to train and fine-tune these people at workshops and seminars across the country before the official openings.

I employed some incredible, salt-of-the-earth people – people who were used to finding themselves being rejected for employment elsewhere. I remember taking the most unlikely candidates and bringing out the best in them by pairing them up with existing employees. It was always a black person and a white person I knew would complement each other.

Kobus Theunissen was one of these people. He was slap bang in the middle of a nasty divorce, desperate for a mind-shift and passionate about his work. I appointed him as the Operational Manager for the KwaZulu-Natal region. Prince Monyela, whom I had worked with previously, joined Kobus in Durban.

And then there was Serf de Kok who I paired with Thabo Mabetha in

Pretoria. Serf was an old school principal, and while catering was not his forte, discipline most certainly was. Thabo, on the other hand, was a lay preacher. Although I found Thabo's negative remarks towards the company extremely annoying at the time, I must confess that his sentiments were, for the most part, wholly warranted – especially when it came to Gavin's integrity (or lack thereof) as a Christian.

Patrick Littler and I paired up. He had run the facilities management at Optimum Colliery for Molope Foods back in the day. Young, single and impressionable, I took him under my wing as his mentor, and he rose through the ranks at Molope. When I invited him to join me at Bosasa, he jumped at the opportunity, eventually becoming my 2IC. Patrick had a solid personality and strong leadership qualities but lacked the fundamental "screw you" attitude that he should have adopted towards some of the directors. The teams I put together all came from other operational units with similar areas of expertise, so I knew they would be able to do the work even if the training didn't pan out as planned. Carol Mkele, one of Bosasa's original "shareholders", was among the people Gavin asked me to train down in Port Elizabeth. Although she was employed as an administrator at the time, Gavin wanted her in charge of the catering operation at St Albans Correctional Facility. I paired her up with one of the newer employees, Ernest McDermott, a gentle giant who had been in catering since his days in the South African navy. With his background in industrial catering, I was confident that I wouldn't need to spend more than a few days with him before returning to Johannesburg.

On the first day of training, Gavin walked into the session with one of his brothers. Before I knew it, he had taken over the meeting. I sat back and allowed him to continue. He spent more time lecturing the trainees on adopting and embracing the local politics than he did on any form of training, and the sun had long since set when we left the venue that day. The following morning, I had to start from scratch and undo everything Gavin had done the day before.

Even though I was told that it would be impossible to open all the prison contracts on a single day, each one went ahead, from Westville to Pollsmoor to Witbank, without a hitch. By the end of the day, we were serving one hundred and fifty thousand meals like clockwork. I was proud.

Within our first year, not only had we improved the facilities, the food and the control mechanisms, but we had also saved the DCS between thirty and fifty million rands. By year two, we had saved them between fifteen and twenty-five million. By that stage, most of the prison warders loved what we were doing, from our service to the food to the training. One prison after another came on board. Westville Prison even extended their contract without going through the proper tender procedures.

Before long, the prisons were requesting value-adds – anything that would improve the offenders' living conditions and make the warders' jobs easier. Being an entrepreneur at heart, I readily jumped at those opportunities. We had faked it, but now we had made it. They wanted pest control – we delivered it on a silver platter. They wanted training and development, we developed SAQA[26] NQF[27]-aligned courses in-house on anything revolving around catering, the tourism industry and hotel management.[28]

And then, when the prisons were in the market for CCTV and access control, we offered to come to that party too. It was only many years later that I discovered that Gavin was having his own private parties with the people in charge.

If there was one thing Gavin should have been more vigilant about, it was not to leave a trail of evidence – no matter how miniscule – between Bosasa and the string of individuals he was taking care of every month, in exchange for the lucrative business opportunities that were being passed Bosasa's way.

In early 2005, I stepped out of a meeting with Gavin and Tony Perry to visit the adjacent bathroom with its paper-thin walls. The two men were bickering back and forth. Tony was questioning the legitimacy of something that Gavin was asking him to do, and Gavin was being his usual condescending, passive-aggressive self.

"Tony, just register Lianorah Investments and leave me to worry about the politicians. Your job is to do what I tell you to do, so just do it."

It was not long after this altercation that Tony resigned. His health was taking a pounding. He seemed depressed and suffered from various other ailments. I think he must have been swallowing about forty different tablets a day.[29]

Without him even realising it – and I fell into the same trap myself as the years wore on – Bosasa was surreptitiously sucking the life out of him. Bosasa's web of deception was pulling us all in so deeply that it began to fundamentally change our psychological DNA, destroying our moral fabric, while we blindly followed our cult leader like lambs to the slaughter.

---

26 South African Qualifications Authority
27 National Qualifications Framework
28 Over a period of eight years, Bosasa trained over sixty-two thousand offenders.
29 I met up with Tony and Elise in the months following my appearance at the Zondo Commission in 2019 and had the privilege of driving them around in what Elise fondly termed "her" car – my BMW 760Li. They had been together for over seventeen years, and were as infatuated with each other then as they were back at the Cedar Lodge when they stood together, holding hands like teenagers under the beams of my headlights. Tony looked twenty years younger and was tablet-free.

CHAPTER 24

Nepotism and Growing Pains

"Mistakes are the growing pains of wisdom."
– William George Jordan

Where food was involved, where family was involved, and where Bosasa was involved, one must assume that the rot ran deep. Gavin Watson practised unashamed nepotism at Bosasa, deciding whether people were overtly listed on the company payroll or not.

His sister, Sharon, was married to Mark Taverner. When Mark and Sharon arrived in Johannesburg from Port Elizabeth in 2003, Gavin asked me to give him some work. Having spent a large part of his career as a buyer for KFC, Mark was well-positioned to be appointed in a similar role at Bosasa, so I appointed him as a Procurement Manager in BEE Foods, the company's (commercialised) Procurement division.

Besides procurement, Mark was also involved in the training and development of senior DCS officials involved with the catering side of the prison operations. The course, which he developed with the help of Doc Smith and a former school principal by the name of Dr Louis Scholtz, was essentially a thumb-suck stock management course. I had no idea that they were even running the course until I was invited to the second intake's graduation ceremony.

The ceremony was held in early 2004 at the Krugersdorp Game Reserve, where the trainees had been accommodated for two weeks and trained onsite. I was quite surprised when I walked in to find senior Corrections officials like Patrick Gillingham in attendance. The company had spared no expense in putting on a magnificent spread. They had even hired a comedian for the evening, and Papa Leshabane was the Master of Ceremonies.

Lindie Gouws was (deliberately) not invited. When she found out, she threw her toys out of the cot. Poor Joe Gumede and Papa Leshabane were sent out to go and buy her flowers. I chuckled to myself, picturing these two black men carefully placing a gigantic bouquet in the back seat of their car to deliver to the white woman who was upset because she hadn't been invited to the function the night before.

As I would later testify before the Zondo Commission, Mark was also largely responsible for making sure the homes of certain DCS officials[30] were refurbished, furnished and decorated, courtesy of the Bosasa off-the-record prisons décor budget, along with all their individual travelling costs and family holidays.[31]

Mark Taverner later approached me and asked if he could buy BEE Foods, which we sold to him for R1.8-million. He moved into an old mining hostel in Randfontein and set up operations there, using the existing kitchen and facilities to warehouse his goods. He insisted that a clause be written into the conditions of sale that stipulated that he would have first right of refusal to supply Bosasa, which we agreed upon without guarantees, provided his prices remained constant and competitive.

While BEE Foods was awarded an initial contract to supply powdered soup, powdered milk and cold drink powders to Bosasa, Mark didn't hold up his end of the bargain. I had a go at him after bringing the other operational guys in to prove my case, which saw Mark running to the Watson brothers for help. I was told to "make it work for him".

In 2005, Sondolo IT was awarded a R237-million contract to install CCTV and access control systems in sixty-six prisons across the country.

I brought a gentleman on board, by the name of Johan Helmand, to manage, run and oversee the rollout of the contract – under Gordon Howes' supervision. During Johan's interview, he claimed that he had developed Fidelity Guards' control rooms and that he was head of their CCTV and access control systems. He came across as exceptionally knowledgeable and ticked all the right boxes. But perhaps I should have been paying more attention to two things – integrity and ability.

It was only much later, after meeting with Wahl Bartmann, Fidelity's CEO, that I learned that Johan was actually employed as one of their control room call centre agents. Wahl gently broke the news to Gavin that they had been trying to get rid of Johan for years and that I had done him a huge

---

30 Namely, Linda Mti and Patrick Gillingham.
31 In the 2009 SIU report, it emerged that Mark Taverner had been paying Patrick Gillingham a monthly salary of R65 000 (plus a company vehicle) through BEE Foods.

favour by taking him on.

In terms of what I expected, Johan's work proved to be substandard at best. He was more interested in researching and developing new products – and getting samples of products to test at home – than he was in doing the work he was employed to do. The only time I had available to inspect Johan's team's installations was over weekends, and, after receiving complaints from the DCS that the work wasn't up to scratch, I headed out to the different sites to see for myself. The trunking and cabling were skew, televisions were mounted at the wrong angles, and the cameras were either too low down or too high up. Clearly, Johan had no interest in maintaining the high standards I expected. When I confronted him and Gordon about what I had seen, Gordon sat there with a mouth full of teeth and Johan was openly stroppy, saying that he was under pressure and that he would "look at things later".

"But Johan," I said, "if you haven't got time to get it right the first time, when are you going to find the time to get it right later?"

Realising I was fighting a losing battle, I promptly told Johan to step aside and told the two of them that I'd employ a new project manager to oversee the work.

I had a gentleman by the name of Retief van der Merwe on the backburner. Introduced to me by Frans Vorster, Retief was a devout Christian who instantly found a deep connection with Bosasa after seeing the numerous Bibles and bible verses on display throughout the office park. A bright, young ex-police captain, I liked Retief's methodical approach to problem-solving and project management. He was, at the time, employed by Bosasa as a security coordinator at OR Tambo International Airport, but I started taking him with me to site visits over weekends and training him into Johan's position.

When I formally appointed Retief as Project Oversight Manager, Johan and Gordon were furious. Gordon stopped by my office, waving Johan's resignation letter in his hand.

"Angelo," he insisted, "you need to relook that decision you took. I can't afford to lose Johan."

"Really?" I said. "Hand me that resignation letter." Gordon passed it to me, and I quickly scanned it. I called Gina, my personal assistant, into the office. Signing Johan's resignation letter, I gave it to Gina and asked her to make two copies, one for me, and one for Gordon to give to Johan.

"Oh, and Gina," I said as she walked out of my office, "arrange with HR that Johan can leave right away."

Papa later fired Gordon for visiting a strip joint in Port Elizabeth with a colleague while wearing his company uniform.

Although the Sondolo IT implementation team endured more than their fair share of ridicule from DCS staff after Johan's abrupt departure, they quickly cleaned up his mess in an attempt to restore Bosasa's good name within the department.

However, Sondolo IT was a problem child from day one in terms of its people – there was continuous in-fighting, so we struggled to get the team to gel. I decided to bring in a few older fellows, thinking it might help bring the company's internal politics under control.

I eventually appointed Trevor Mathenjwa as the company's Managing Director after I was introduced to him by Joe Gumede. What I didn't know at the time was that Joe was married to Trevor's sister, making them brothers-in-law. Gavin's nepotism appeared to be rubbing off on the directors. I called Trevor the Romeo of the company. The directors thought I was being derogatory because I had a pet Capuchin monkey named Romeo, but that was not the case. The Romeo I was referring to was the one from the Shakespeare classic, *Romeo and Juliet*. Trevor was the type of guy who'd go out there and serenade the ladies. He wore his heart on his sleeve. Fortunately, this story did not erupt into bloodshed and suicide as it did in Shakespearean times, and he formed good relationships with the people of the Department of Justice, where Sondolo IT was also involved in installing CCTV and access control systems.

Unfortunately, strategic planning and implementation was not "Romeo's" forte, so we kept him busy with handling secondary issues and managing the staff, leaving Joe Gumede and the paler members of the management team to take over the strategic management of the business.

CHAPTER 25

Every Prison has a Story

"Prisons are built with stones of Law. Brothels with the bricks of religion."
– William Blake

The underground prison economy is a lucrative one when it comes to food, blades, cigarettes, alcohol and drugs, and it didn't take us long to figure out that our staff at the prisons were now susceptible to bribery. Our CCTV surveillance systems proved to be quite useful, not only for monitoring what our staff were getting up to, but also the prison officials.

The warders who had been reaping the benefits of being able to take food home before our teams moved in were feeling the pinch. While many were hell-bent on trying to sabotage Bosasa, none of them realised their after-hours antics were also being monitored. We caught them on camera going into the kitchens late at night and throwing bread all over the floor, forgetting that the camera systems were on and that we could not only see them but identify them too. When the warders presented photos of the far-flung bread to prison management the following day, we produced video footage of the actual events.

On another occasion, we caught prison officials smuggling boxes of frozen chicken out of the kitchen in the middle of the night. One of my favourite incidents was at Pollsmoor. A night warder had complained to the head of the prison that the night-shift security guard (employed by Bosasa) was sleeping on the job – and he had photos to prove it. We pulled the footage, only to find that it was the warder himself who was fast asleep. We watched him put two chairs together, spread out the blankets and lie down on his make-shift bed.

Of course, one had to be careful not to create enemies in that type of environment. When we took over St Albans, we discovered that we had to walk through about twelve different sections – all lined with overcrowded prison cells – to reach our facility. Each of these sections was divided by a solid-steel access-controlled door, which could only be opened by the warder or the official on duty. If that person didn't like you, they could make you wait behind one of those doors for up to an hour before they unlocked it. When that happened, there was nothing you could do but stand there, prisoners on either side of you, trying your damnedest to hide your fear. It took me about a month to grow accustomed to these walks of terror, and I quickly learned that the best approach was to be friendly. Having substantially improved the quality of their food, the prisoners eventually took a liking to us.

Every prison has its gangs, and the gangs, led by their generals, rule the prisons. At Pollsmoor, it's the Numbers gangs – the 26s, the 27s, and the 28s – the most dangerous and fearsome gangs in the Cape Town prison system.

I was down in Cape Town on business when I received a call that the prisoners at Pollsmoor had sent back all the bread – they were refusing to eat it. We had recently changed our bread supplier, but the difference in quality was barely noticeable – except to the inmates. They were threatening to go on strike or burn the prison to the ground if the bread was not replaced. Of course, I knew this was nothing more than the gangs flexing their muscles.

When I arrived at Pollsmoor, I met with the Area Commissioner who told me it was the 28s who had kicked up the fuss. I called one of the youngsters who worked for me at the prison and located the general of the 28s.

"You see that man over there? The one who works in our kitchen?" I said, pointing the general out to him. "He's the general of the 28s – he's the one we need to convince to take the bread."

I walked over to the general, shook his hand and made him feel important. "Hello," I said. "My name is Angelo Agrizzi."

"I know who you are," he said bluntly.

"I see you've got a problem here," I continued. "This is your place. You run the prison. How do we resolve this?"

Within a matter of minutes, he was back in the kitchen peeling carrots and potatoes, and making sure bread was being carried out to the different sections. I asked him if there was anything specific he needed.

"Lotion," he said. "Just lotion."

I made sure that every month, a two-litre bottle of lotion was delivered to the prison marked for his attention. I even ordered a few extra appliances for the kitchen for him, just to make his life a little easier.

CHAPTER 26

Establishing a Bid Office

"Innovators have to be open. They have to be able to imagine things that others cannot and be willing to challenge their own preconceptions. They also need to be conscientious."
– Malcolm Gladwell, *David & Goliath*

As the company grew, I decided to establish a formal bid office at the Bosasa Business Park that was completely separate from the rest of the company, to focus solely on tender and new venture applications. The department, comprised largely of teams of researchers and customer relationship managers and personnel, was named "Transactional Planning" because it was there that we planned tenders, from receiving the documents right through to the final rollout. We weren't simply handing in a bid – it was a full-on presentation. Our stance not only showed them what we had to offer but explained – in painstaking detail – how we were going to roll it out.

Whatever it was that we were bidding for, we made sure we had the right expertise on board to demonstrate our credibility – including people with doctorates. Whatever sector we were bidding on, we had a team researching that sector. We quoted statements made by industry leaders. Even with the occasional smokescreen, we showed the client that we had taken the time to aggregate business intelligence data, and that we had the management ability to identify trends in the marketplace and analyse them.

We used to have a lot of fun doing the tenders. People worked all hours of the night – they were motivated to get the job done. Julius Botha, our head designer, once went forty-eight hours without any sleep.

Just as we'd done with the prison's catering contract, we spent good money preparing the tender documents for submission. It wasn't uncommon for a presentation to cost in the region of R80 000 to R100 000.

The documents were encased in aluminium files with bespoke laser-etched tempered glass covers, unique to each tender. Once, when submitting a tender to USAASA[32] for e-learning at government schools, we embedded an iPad in the glass cover.

When government departments awarded us tenders, we added value in the form of CSI initiatives. Dr Denise Bjorkman from our Wellness Clinic started an initiative which we called the Job Centre Trust, which took youth between the ages of seventeen and thirty-five who were in conflict with the law through a process of personal development training and professional skills-building, and found employment for them. We set up computer centres with accredited e-learning systems at the Youth Centres, and employed counsellors to manage the holistic development of these youngsters. We trained promising offenders as chefs so that they could find employment once they were rehabilitated. We built butcheries and vegetable processing plants for those women whose husbands were in prison to earn money. We ran farms for DCS so that they could grow their own food, and we initiated feeding schemes for impoverished children. There was a great deal of good work that we did in return for the work we were given. I'd estimate that about 1% of what Bosasa made was ploughed back into communities. And of course, this was tax-deductible.

Tender offices require specific types of people who are prepared to put in the time and effort to tenaciously read, understand and work through the reams of documents. They need unique story-writing abilities to put something together that will stand out from the hundreds of other submissions. When complete, the documentation needs to be impeccable. Not everybody is cut out for this, and simple human error can mean the difference between winning and losing a bid.

There were times when the quality control mechanisms weren't as thorough as they should have been, and Bosasa fell short of meeting certain criteria because somebody neglected to check and verify the pack before submitting it. It was often something as simple as a missing BEE certificate, or a tax clearance certificate that was out of date.

Gavin alleged that he would receive a call in the middle of the night from the department in question when this kind of thing happened, informing him that our tender document had been received, but that something was missing. Whether this was true or not, we may never know, but the person

---

32 Universal Service and Access Agency of South Africa

calling would use the apparent oversight as an opportunity to elicit something out of Gavin in return for "sorting it out". There is no denying that the hand that fed us was deeply crooked, and we, being the veins of that appendage, were complicit.

CHAPTER 27

Who's Your Daddy? –
Papa Leshabane

"Any fool can criticise, complain, and condemn – and most fools do. But it takes character and self-control to be understanding and forgiving."
– Dale Carnegie, *How to Win Friends and Influence People*

Papa Leshabane, or Mr Flamboyance as I liked to call him, came from humble beginnings. While I don't know much about his father, he told me that his mother was a nurse and that she sang in a choir in his home town in the Limpopo Province.

Papa Leshabane was a Human Resources consultant for Telkom before he was appointed to the Bosasa board by David Sadie. My first encounter with Papa was at Libanon Mine. I was doing my rounds dealing with unhappy staff, and he happened to be there. I liked him instantly. He was well-spoken and impeccably dressed. One of my first thoughts about him was "this guy is going to go places". I remember calling David afterwards and telling him how impressed I was.

Working with Papa, however, proved to be quite a rude awakening. As charismatic as he was, him actually *doing* the work was another matter entirely. What he *was* good at was spin-doctoring and winning people over. I believed that for Papa, being seen with the right people in the right places was vital. He seemed to have connections everywhere. Certain staff went as far as nicknaming him "The Puppeteer".

An open credit card with an unlimited budget to buy stadium tickets, tickets to jazz festivals, or booze, was his magic wand – and I have the financials to prove it. A whiskey connoisseur of note, he had no problem blowing R100 000 in one night on the best single malts. On returning from an overseas trip, it was not uncommon to receive a cell phone bill of over R100 000. Papa would spend in the region of R200 000 a month on entertainment and booze. As it was not his money, he appeared to simply not care. This reckless spending created countless issues with the other directors who felt that Papa, having not been present during the company's initial rough periods, was living it up as if there were no end to the company's available resources.

While Papa was a big family man, he also loved travelling. He was the type of guy who chased Voyager points. I remember him asking me once why I had a platinum SAA Voyager card, and he didn't. He insisted that I make a special arrangement to get him one. If he saw somebody in the company with a platinum Amex card, he wanted one too.

In his early days as Bosasa's spokesperson and Human Resources Director, I suspected that he was virtually unknown in political circles. While he liked to believe he was politically savvy, people only started paying attention to him when he was dishing out money or tickets to rugby and soccer games. Papa was like the kid at the tuckshop who would buy sweets for all the other kids just so that he could have friends. By using Bosasa – and its associated cash – to grow his political stature, it wasn't long before he was hobnobbing with senior ANC politicians. Papa once managed to convince Gavin that Bosasa needed a box at every sports stadium across the country. In the end, there were five boxes. We paid in the region of R80 000 rental per box per month, excluding the tickets, the catering and the booze. Gavin didn't drink and was initially against stocking alcohol in the boxes, but Papa simply bypassed him and bought from the local liquor store. Eventually, Gavin gave in, knowing that the politicians Papa was supposedly entertaining were mostly big drinkers.

The boxes eventually became Papa's private entertainment venues. While we paid for them for three years, I believed it was primarily Papa's friends and family who used them. When there were roadblocks outside the stadiums, some of his connections were arrested for drinking and driving. The negative publicity elicited after being pulled over by the police after partying it up at one of the Bosasa boxes was problematic, and we eventually had to close the boxes down.

Besides the stadiums, the company – without my knowledge – had a long-term rental on a serviced suite at the Michelangelo Hotel in Sandton. I kicked against the idea when Papa first approached me about having a room there, but after reading about its existence in the newspapers many years later, I realised he must have pushed it through past Gavin. While Papa was in the background, at the expense of the Bosasa Group of companies, he was skillfully transforming himself from a non-descript human resources official into a (seemingly) knowledgeable political envoy. Before long, he was sharing stadium boxes with the likes of Multichoice CEO, Calvo Mawela, who later went on to marry Gwede Mantashe's daughter. Papa also loved women. While, for the most part, we tried to downplay the directors and their sexual pursuits, I could no longer keep my mouth shut when I discovered a number of them were openly using the guest lodge at the office park. This was sometimes done in full view of the cleaning staff who often lodged complaints with the Wellness team. Gavin reprimanded everyone about it except Papa – and only because of Papa's political "connections".

The more I watched Papa evolve, the more he took on the persona of Gavin Watson Number Two, becoming, as far as I was concerned, increasingly conceited and arrogant. If something wasn't his idea, he rubbished it. Papa abhorred competition in any form. I remember him finding fault with anyone who tried to get too close to Gavin, running them down and bad-mouthing them. When I appointed Dr Thembi Madungwa and Dr Denise Bjorkman to open the Wellness Clinic at Bosasa, while it was partly for good corporate governance, it was also an attempt to manage any underlying negativity among its four thousand employees and the associated high staff turnover. The only problem was that the Wellness Clinic fell under HR – Papa's domain. I got the impression that he didn't like the idea that if somebody was being victimised, as often happened at Bosasa, they could go and openly discuss the matter with somebody like Denise or Thembi. In fact, the Wellness Clinic was shut down shortly after I left the company.

Papa and I had an acrimonious relationship. I'm sure it was because I put my foot down every time he stretched his hand out. Eventually, he went out of his way to make life difficult for me. He would counter every argument I put forward and fight against every division within the group of companies that had my backing. Often it was quite minor, like withholding his signature on important documents that needed to go out or being late in submitting content for the company's newsletter – which sometimes went out without his input. Other times it was more public. Nothing gave him more pleasure than running these divisions down in board meetings.

Papa also enjoyed forming alliances. How it unfolded at Bosasa was remarkably like the hit TV series *Survivor*, minus the islands and physical challenges but complete with all the rewards and "tribal" councils, where people would be voted out if they were perceived to be a threat to the group. One such alliance began early on with none other than Lindie Gouws. I suspect Papa thought that, with Lindie on his side, Gavin could easily be swayed to his ideas and plans.

Gavin Watson, drawn to politics like a fly to manure, liked to consider himself something of a political guru. It was not unusual for him to leave home in the middle of the night to attend clandestine political meetings, not wanting to miss out on any of the action. Needless to say, if you were politically connected and politically knowledgeable, your future with Gavin was bound to be a financially lucrative one.

Sesinyi Seopela, the politically connected childhood friend of Papa Leshabane, was introduced to Gavin by Papa back in 2004 when he was brought on board as a consultant. I was first introduced to Seopela in 2005 at a breakfast meeting with Gavin, Danny Mansell and Papa at Tasha's in Hyde Park, Johannesburg, where it became clear that Gavin wanted to bring him on board as a full-time employee. I was told to issue Seopela with a company credit card and buy him a brand-new Audi S5 Coupé. At that stage, he was on the payroll for R100 000 a month. Gavin and Seopela worked well together. The two men not only took great pleasure in playing the game of politics, but they also spoke the same political language. Seopela and Gavin only ever had one major fall-out, when Gavin was discovered to have disseminated highly confidential political information.

"Commander", as I later nicknamed Seopela, was the former bodyguard of the late ANC Youth League President, Peter Mokaba. Perhaps the title I bestowed upon him was far too generous – never before had I come across a less-disciplined cadre, especially when it came to time-keeping, irrespective of who we were meeting. This was the root of many an altercation between us. He was, however, an intelligent man who understood the workings of the government engine well. Influential in government circles, he created the impression on me that he was well-connected to people at the National Prosecuting Authority (NPA), the Special Investigating Unit (SIU), and various other law enforcement agencies. I recall that he was friends with Fana Hlongwane, who also had alleged links to the Guptas. Seopela was also supposedly a close friend of the former National Director of Public Prosecutions, Menzi Simelane.

Seopela also worked with Siza Nxumani, an old political hustler and a Watson faithful who had formed a business relationship with Tokyo Sexwale, who wanted Siza to provide consulting services to his company,

Mvelaphanda. Siza's only problem was that he'd placed the horse before the cart. His company was not registered as a legal entity, nor did he have a business bank account. With Mvelaphanda waving a cheque under his nose and asking for an invoice before 4 p.m. that afternoon, Siza needed help – and fast.

After being locked in a meeting for almost three hours, Gavin and Siza emerged with a plan. Bosasa would handle the daunting task of finding a shelf company, and the company's marketing team would build a brand and create his marketing collateral. Obtaining a VAT registration number within a matter of hours was something an auditor and tax consultant by the name of Peet Venter would do. While he took over from Doc Smith when Doc fell ill, Peet was everything Doc Smith was not. His company handled everyone's income tax at Bosasa, including that of Linda Mti and Patrick Gillingham.

Through his connections, Peet Venter succeeded in getting a tax clearance certificate early that afternoon and, by 9 a.m. the following morning, Mvelaphanda's money was in Siza's account.

Siza would appear every now and then when he needed something, or if he had some "classified intelligence information" to offer Gavin. Gavin and I were so impressed with Seopela's knowledge of the political lay of the land – not to mention his astute approach to people – that we were both completely hopeless at discerning whether the people we were dealing with were credible or not.

Papa Leshabane, in the meantime – through a process of his own design – catapulted himself into a position where I believe that he hoodwinked Gavin into believing that he wielded a certain measure of control over the ANC-led government. During this time, Papa Leshabane's obsessive hold over his childhood friend seemed to deepen considerably. While Seopela appeared to me to be the more astute and intelligent of the two, Papa over-shadowed him significantly. Seopela was certainly no longer his own person.

CHAPTER 28

Moving Lindie to Greener Pastures

"Some people are so delusional that they believe it's disrespectful when you refuse to sit back and allow them to disrespect you."
– Anon

Lindie's acrimonious behaviour progressively worsened as the years wore on. She would go around shouting and screaming, sometimes even throwing her keys at people, asking them, "Do you know who I am?" on the back of Gavin's name. Gavin, seemingly beholden to her, allowed it to continue. There was one occasion that I overheard him on the phone to his pastor in Port Elizabeth, begging him to intervene and get Lindie to focus on her work in the ministry, but it went nowhere.

Lindie cost many people their jobs and damaged countless lives.

In 2001, I hired Riana Mulder as my personal assistant. Highly competent, she had trained with Standard Bank and was a top-class PA for their CEO. In 2003, Lindie asked if she could take Riana over, claiming that she needed a decent PA. I had no problem with training up a replacement and, knowing that Riana was the best we had in the group, I thought that perhaps, with the right tools and resources, Lindie might be able to make something work for a change. Eight months later, Lindie fired Riana, accusing her of theft and working against her.

One evening in 2004, while on a walk around the company's park, Gavin called me. I could hear Lindie in the background riling him up, saying, "You need to get rid of Andries Erasmus and Jacques van Zyl." The two men were working for her as accountants, and she wanted them fired without a disciplinary hearing.

When Allister Esau joined Bosasa in 2004, he had no idea what he was in for. Allister was the Executive Chef for Sun International and Protea Hotels as well as the Deputy President of the South African Chef's Association before Gavin brought him on board. We hit it off from the start because we shared the same passion for fast cars. At this stage, I owned a top of the range Audi A6, a Q7 and a Mitsubishi Pajero.

Allister's primary role was to arrange the catering and accommodation for the many ANC Siyanqoba rallies, lekgotlas[33], golf days and birthday parties that were proudly sponsored by Bosasa. These lavish functions, held in hired, air-conditioned marquees, usually tipped the scales at between R2-million and R3-million each.

One of his responsibilities in his later years with the company included training up chefs for then-President Jacob Zuma on-site at Nkandla. Allister was also instructed to be at the beck and call of Dudu Myeni, the Executive Chairperson of the Jacob G Zuma Foundation and SAA board Chairperson at the time.

I was out one Sunday when Gavin called. "It's Jacob Zuma's seventy-second birthday – you need to bake him a cake."

"What kind of cake?" I asked, my thoughts racing off in all directions.

"Any cake," he said. "Just make sure it's big."

There was only one person who would be willing to open his bakery and take on this mammoth task at such short notice, and that was Fritz from Café Mozart in Midrand. I drove through to meet with him to design, bake and decorate the bloody cake. It was about two metres long, two tiers high and included photos of Zuma, the ANC flag and the Youth Centres, with children holding hands around the sides of the cake – and, of course, the Bosasa logo.

Allister also had to cater for numerous private funerals – at Bosasa's expense – held for family members of Nomvula Mokonyane, the-then Gauteng Premier and later Minister of Water Affairs and Sanitation. In 2013, after one of her visits to Bosasa's offices, Gavin instructed me to arrange a party for about 150 people at the Victorian Guest House in Krugersdorp for her 40th birthday. The theme of the function was "break a leg" – something the owner of the guest lodge probably wanted to do after having to clean up the mess after the extravagant event.

Often, we had to come up with menus and meals at extremely short notice. I remember Gavin once receiving a call from Sandy Thomas, Nomvula Mokonyane's PA, at 6 p.m. one evening, requesting that five thousand lunch packs be delivered to the University of Johannesburg (UJ) by 7 a.m.

---

33 A meeting to decide what to do, especially one that involves public officials.

the following morning. Allister always came through for us, and I knew I could trust him to get the job done professionally and within budget. For orders like this, we used our kitchens at Lindela, where we could cook four thousand pieces of chicken in forty-five minutes. We had enough equipment, and the kitchen staff were on-site 24/7. Because these kinds of requests came through quite regularly, I always made sure that the Lindela storerooms were well-stocked for such eventualities.

The UJ experience turned out to be a hair-raising one. We were at the Auckland Park campus, five thousand lunch packs waiting to be offloaded when Gavin received a call from Sandy.

"Where are your people?" she asked. It just so happened that we were on the wrong campus and that the lunch packs were supposed to be delivered to the UJ Soweto campus.

Lindie Gouws occasionally got involved in setting up these functions with Allister. During one particular function hosted abroad, Allister called me up in a flat spin.

"Angelo, I'm resigning," he said, clearly flustered. "I'm getting on a plane and flying back to South Africa. I cannot spend another minute with that woman."

I calmed him down and convinced him to stay on for the remaining four days but, by the time he landed on South African soil, he was exhausted. I had to give him a week's leave just to recover from his ordeal.

By 2005, while the company had grown exponentially and was performing well, staff morale was at an all-time low – and everyone knew its main source. None of the directors or senior management had the guts to stand up to Gavin about the toll Gavin and Lindie's relationship, whatever its nature, was taking on employees.

Dr Denise Bjorkman was the first of many Bosasa staff members to come out and state that Gavin was compromised. I was tired of the politicking and disruption, as was the rest of the team, but I was the only one prepared to take the matter on. I called Gavin, Lindie and Joe Gumede into a meeting and laid my cards on the table.

"Gavin," I said, "we cannot work with this woman anymore. She's creating havoc."

Gavin sat with his head in his hands. "I can't be everything to everybody. I can't please everybody," he said.

"You don't have to please anybody, Gavin," I said. "You have a company to run." I looked Lindie in the eyes and delivered my ultimatum. "Lindie, the company has outgrown you. Gavin needs to make a choice – it's either you or me."

I knew what Gavin's obvious choice would be. The company was in the middle of a growth spurt, and it would have been foolish of him to let me go, after everything I had already achieved within the Group. And so it was agreed – albeit far from amicably – that Lindie would unofficially exit the company.

Gavin decided to keep her busy by starting a publication for her called *My World Ministries*. She continued to work from the company's offices, under strict conditions that she neither intermingled nor interfered with anybody within the organisation. Bosasa coughed up in excess of R700 000 a month to subsidise the publication's production and distribution. The publication, a large coffee-table style book, printed in China, was a collage of plants, swaddled babies and the occasional pretty woman, strung together with inspirational quotes from the Scriptures, but it never quite made it out of the starting blocks. The magazine lacked substance, with sales dependent on the odd auntie who received a sudden revelation from God whilst crocheting beanies on a Sunday afternoon.

I remember walking through the office park with Gavin one day, and we ended up in one of the empty offices on the mezzanine level of the building. It was packed with boxes containing in excess of three thousand copies of the doomed publication.

My World Ministries eventually became nothing more than a deep and hungry pit and was subsequently shut down. Lindie took over *Joy!* magazine in 2005 but it was closed after just six months.

Several years later, Lindie decided to host a trip to Israel, predominantly for Bosasa employees. She invited Thandi Makoko and Carol Mkele to join her. One night at midnight, Lindie apparently went into Carol and Thandi's rooms and woke them up, telling them that she'd "had enough of this ministry crap" and that she wanted to return to Bosasa "where she belonged".

Thandi Makoko, on her return, immediately called me and Jackie Leyds, one of the Executive Directors, into her office. After shutting the door behind us, she related the story of Lindie's midnight antics to us in glaring detail. She told us, in no uncertain terms, to use whatever means necessary to avert the catastrophe that would be caused if we allowed Lindie back into the business.

Unfortunately, Lindie was never fully out of the picture at Bosasa. While she couldn't be found on the premises during office hours, she was frequently spotted working there at night. Exactly what she was doing, nobody knows.

CHAPTER 29

The Web of Corruption Expands

"When one gets in bed with government, one must expect the diseases it spreads."
– Ron Paul

Corruption is not a black or a white thing. Corruption is colour blind. In many instances, it permeates the very being of a person and consumes them. At Bosasa, everyone – in some way – became corrupted.

After meeting Kevin Wakeford, the former CEO of state-owned arms procurement agency, Armscor, I quickly learnt that all is not always as it appears. Kevin, a well-respected man in his day, worked with author Barry Sergeant on a book, *The Assault on the Rand*[34] where Sergeant documented Kevin's findings regarding Deutsche Bank's involvement in the devaluation – and subsequent collapse – of the South African rand in 2001.

But Kevin Wakeford is also a typical example of one of many individuals who moved around the Bosasa periphery. While he did his fair share of running around for the Watsons, in my opinion, he was also in it for himself. He would bring influential people to the Bosasa office park and show them around – but, I believe, always with the intention of showing them what he could do for them *through* Bosasa.

It wasn't long before he started making requests of the company. As I would later tell the Zondo Commission, one such request involved delivering cement to a certain George Papadakis, a well-known consultant to the South African Revenue Service (SARS) at the time. Papadakis was in the process of building a house in Meyersdal, south of Johannesburg. Gavin issued the instruction to Frans Vorster, and Papadakis got his cement – loads

---

34 Sergeant, Barry (2013). *The Assault on the Rand: Kevin Wakeford and the Battle to Save a Currency*. South Africa: Zebra Press.

of it.[35] In return, Papadakis promised to do Kevin a favour and quell one of Bosasa's SARS headaches – an audit inquiry. He told Kevin what to write, how to write it, and when to write it. Kevin sometimes went as far as authorising similar letters on behalf of Bosasa. Any action SARS took to counter us was a pointless exercise on their part because we were always one step ahead of them – thanks to our friend George Papadakis and a few truck-loads of wet and dry cement.

As I would later explain at the Zondo Commission, Gavin paid Kevin a tidy sum of R100 000 for enlisting Papadakis's help. In a press statement released by Wakeford, he would deny this, saying the allegations were "malicious, a gross fabrication and the fabric of lies". The last time I heard from my attorneys, Kevin had applied to the Commission to cross-examine me. Thinking back to this time when I was at the company, the rot of bribery and corruption was quickly becoming a pandemic that indiscriminately eroded what remained of the morally incorruptible, sweeping through the corridors of government and the offices of Bosasa with reckless abandon.

When Nosiviwe Mapisa-Nqakula, one of the original Dyambu trustees who was extremely close to the Watsons, left Dyambu to join the ANC-led government in 1994, Gavin was always hot on her heels. Kevin Wakeford was no different – when Nosiviwe moved to the Department of Defence, Kevin would soon move there too. During Nosiviwe's tenure as Minister of Home Affairs[36] (she was later appointed as Minister of Correctional Services), Kevin was her special advisor and trusted confidant. He ticked all the boxes – not only was he good-looking, but he spoke fluent Xhosa, was well educated and had access to seemingly endless funding. He even helped transport the meat from hunts her husband Charles[37] participated in on Ronnie Watson's farm to the various Nqakula family homes.

One issue that arose at the time was a discussion centred around the Lindela Repatriation Centre and what Bosasa was charging the Department of Home Affairs to run it. The department wanted to renegotiate Bosasa's contract in an effort to reduce costs.

Fever Tree Consultants were the consultants responsible for managing

35 Approximately R600 000 worth of wet and dry cement was delivered to Papadakis's property in Meyersdal. To my knowledge, Papadakis has remained silent regarding these allegations.
36 Nosiviwe Mapisa-Nqakula was Minister of Home Affairs from 2004 to 2009, and Minister of Correctional Services from 2009 to 2012.
37 Nosiviwe Mapisa-Nqakula's husband, Charles Nqakula (former Minister of Safety and Security, and Minister of Defence from 2008 to 2009), was a long-term friend to Ronnie Watson.

the department's negotiations. Fever Tree outsourced the consulting for this particular project to a small treasury-approved company called Akhile Management and Consulting. Given the fact that the contract was valued at R110-million, I was shocked to find that instead of working with a sizeable team of consultants from Akhile, I would only be working with a gentleman by the name of Aneel Radhakrishna.

As I would tell the Zondo Commission, I was present at a meeting with Kevin and Gavin where it was agreed that Radhakrishna could be "managed". I was later informed by Radhakrishna that payment of an amount of R7-million – payable to him – had been discussed, presumably with Kevin or Gavin.

What I was unaware of was that Gavin and Kevin had promised Aneel R7-million in consulting fees for a successful renegotiation with the department.

I presented Aneel with a slightly different model to the existing one at Lindela, which provided a guarantee that the financial wellbeing of our side of the contract would not be adversely affected. After a thorough – and at times acrimonious – negotiation, Aneel and I settled on an agreement that was beneficial to Bosasa.[38]

With the negotiations successfully concluded, Aneel put in an immediate claim for payment. My jaw nearly dropped to the floor when I added up all the zeros. When I confronted Gavin and Kevin about the amount, they agreed that it was excessive and suggested that, to manage expectations, we spread the payment out over a period of time.

I stifled a smile and left the room. "And guess who has to manage those expectations?" I muttered under my breath. I felt sick to the core of my being. By now, I was inextricably entwined with the Bosasa web of lies and corruption. I had less and less energy to fight for what I knew was right.

When I did question processes and the effectiveness of making use of consultants or advisors, like Aneel, it deeply annoyed Kevin. We frequently found ourselves wrapped up in what I termed "The Debates" over our differences of opinion on the subject. To me, it made no sense paying exorbitant fees to consultants, some legitimate, others less so, who used the company's resources to tell us what we already knew – and who then charged us a fortune to repair it, despite the fact that we could have done

---

38 Had Bosasa remained in business, they would have received a monthly payment of R8.4-million in 2019, irrespective of the number of people detained at Lindela. The average cost per detainee worked out to about R15 000 per month. During the COVID-19 pandemic of 2020, the Lindela Repatriation facility, on instruction from President Ramaphosa, instigated a mass repatriation of Mozambican and Zimbabwean nationals after thirty-seven detainees escaped. The total number of detainees during that period dropped to five hundred people.

the repair-work ourselves. I felt that many of the so-called consultants that Kevin brought to Bosasa added little or no value – people like Stephen Laufer – who would supposedly handle Bosasa's persecution by the press; Barry Sergeant – who would assist in changing the public's perception of the Bosasa group of companies; and then Aneel Radhakrishna – to attend to the Lindela renegotiations. Kevin disagreed. One such character was the liberal SWAPO[39] activist and independent political and socio-economic analyst and columnist, Udo Froese, who authors a controversial blog entitled "Afrika: The Other Side of the Coin". He admired and supported Winnie Mandela, and worked extensively with her (recently deceased) daughter, Zindzi Mandela. I always wondered why it was that Udo never made a success of himself politically, or took up a position as a lecturer at a university.

Udo would arrange various visits and meetings, and after a few beers, the stories would start flowing, and he would provide detailed political overviews of the country. Unfortunately, all of the deals he brought to the table failed dismally. Many – because they were mired in controversy and conspiracy theory – did not even make it out of the starting blocks.

As much as we knew what was going on, in general, it was pointless questioning the source of any incoming or outgoing funds – it was Gavin's company, it was Gavin's money, and he did with it as he pleased.

---

39 The South West Africa People's Organisation

CHAPTER 30

From Ford to Ferrari – Joe Gumede

"The world will not be destroyed by those who do evil, but by those who watch them without doing anything."
– Albert Einstein

I was first introduced to Joe Gumede in 1999. Joe was quiet and reserved, well-read, and exceptionally knowledgeable across a wide range of topics. An HR clerk at the time, he drove around in a little Ford Focus – his pride and joy.

I remember the day we discovered we were both petrol heads. Joe had just returned from a CCMA hearing and was visibly upset. When he left the CCMA building that day, he discovered, with horror, that his car was missing. While commiserating, we got onto the subject of cars – which became the foundation of our relationship going forward. We'd spend hours talking about anything with four wheels. His family and mine spent a wonderful weekend together in Clarens in the Free State, and Joe often came to dinner at my home. I taught him how to drive on a track, and we'd drive up and down, racing against each other. I'd often let him drive one of my Ferraris when we were out on the road together. At the height of my success, I owned a Ferrari F12 and a 360 Modena that I built from scrap.

One of Joe's travel highlights was a specially arranged tour of Italy where we visited Modena (the home of Ferrari), the Ducati factory, and Maserati. We topped off the trip with a dramatic F1 showdown at Monza. It was a scorcher of a day, and the seats were by far the most uncomfortable I'd ever sat on, but the die-hards were there, supporting the brand with vigour. The day, much to our disappointment, ended abruptly with a breakdown on turn six – the exact spot at which we were seated on the podium.

Joe Gumede was by no means a fool. He was astute and, with his strong people skills, identified problematic situations early on. We would often find ourselves deep in discussion about how Gavin treated his people, and how, inevitably, his sins would catch up with him.

When Gavin got wind that people were disillusioned and were questioning his intentions, he promptly scheduled meetings to proactively attend to them. Videos of a particular meeting held at Silverstar Casino started doing the rounds. Staff, more dejected than ever, were once again terrified of being called up and ridiculed in front of their peers.

"You cannot treat people like dogs and expect them to be faithful when the chips are down," Joe said. "People will eventually revolt." While he agreed that the manner in which Bosasa conducted business would eventually lead to its demise, Joe openly admitted that, like me, he lacked the energy to turn things around.

"What makes or breaks Gavin Watson?" I asked, hoping for a plausible answer. "Is it a desire for power and sex? Is it money? Is it because he grew up with nothing on a humble farming outpost? Why else would he and his brothers adopt an attitude of 'go big or go home'?"

Joe looked at me with a grin on his face. "My friend," he said, "I don't think you fully understand the beast you have saddled. All you can do is manage Gavin Watson as best as you can."

CHAPTER 31

A Thorn in Gavin's side –
Ishmael Dikane

"The black sheep are the ones you want to get to know."
– Marty Rubin

Ishmael Dikane started out life as Ishmael Themba Mncwaba. While I'm not entirely sure why he changed his name, Ishmael and Gavin got to know each other while Ishmael was working as a cook at Buffelspoort Mine in Krugersdorp, west of Johannesburg. I suspect it was Ishmael's arrogance and forthrightness that made him so likeable to Gavin, and why Gavin decided to make him a director.

Ishmael, in his role as Director of Operations, fell under my department. I spent about a year out on the road with him during the early days with DCS in 2004. During this time, I mentored, trained and developed him but – not for any lack of trying on my part – got nowhere. Still, we worked closely for the better part of twelve years and, while he was initially apprehensive, he learned to trust me over time.

Ishmael had a penchant for saying awkward things. Some meetings had many of us wishing that a hole would open up under his chair and suck him in. He was the type of guy who would crack inappropriate jokes at a client meeting or, being soccer-mad, discuss soccer uniforms for the staff at a large EXCO meeting. Sometimes external people – banks or auditors – would be in attendance, and Ishmael would pipe up and ask an arbitrary question like, "How much are we spending on teaching kids?"

While it was embarrassing, people were initially reluctant to make him feel bad by telling him to stop talking rubbish and just listen. It eventually reached a point where either Joe or Papa would have to speak to him before a meeting and sensitise him to the implications of raising irrelevant issues.

Ishmael was the proverbial black sheep of the company, and he was often in trouble. His timekeeping, for instance, left much to be desired. We caught many flights together, and the arrangement was that he would pick me up and drive us to the airport. The problem was that he was generally at least forty-five minutes late. Our house was situated on a driveway with a seventy-five-degree incline, so I would walk down and wait for him on the road. It was an excellent opportunity to meet all the neighbours while they were out walking their dogs. Often, one of them would wave at me and say, "Hi Angelo! Are you waiting for Ishmael again?"

I eventually lost count of the number of flights I missed when Ishmael was involved and decided to get to the airport under my own steam instead. Either he would miss the flight, or not arrive at all, but there was always an excuse.

At one stage, Gavin allowed the directors to utilise company resources to perform minor repairs or renovations to their homes. All they had to do was to call on one of the maintenance teams. When Ishmael cottoned on to this company perk, he immediately embarked on extensive renovations to the tune of R900 000 on his R1.8-million house in Rant-en-Dal, Krugersdorp. I know this because I signed it off myself.

During one of our road trips together, Ishmael brought up the subject of Gavin and Lindie's relationship. He was dead scared of Gavin and was terrified to verbalise his feelings about the relationship and how wrong it was.

Fast-forward three months, and Ishmael was caught making out with a colleague in one of the offices. Gavin, upon hearing the news, was furious and called an urgent meeting with the directors. The female directors were instructed to deal harshly with Ishmael's love interest, as Gavin fumed, "There is no way I'm allowing this kind of thing to happen in my company." The male directors were sent out to deal with Ishmael in an equally punitive manner.

They returned later after having confronted the two offenders and assured Gavin that they had roughed Ishmael up good and solid and that he would never do it again.

Ishmael was the one person who often commented on Gavin's gullibility and his inability to instil discipline within people. This concerned Ishmael because he knew how many of the directors got away with murder after spinning a good story. He himself, however, couldn't spin a story if he tried. He was too straightforward and too damn tactless.

While Ishmael, in my opinion, may not have been the sharpest, he understood Gavin's game plan. He knew Gavin would abandon the company at some point. "Be careful," he would say to me, "Gavin's going to drop you guys – he's going to drop all of us and worry only about himself."

He was also a staunch employee advocate, which annoyed Gavin. Towards the end, he became a real thorn in Gavin's side, challenging him for all the right reasons. His questions were born from genuine concern. "Where is the employees' trust?" he once asked. "You promised the employees a 22% share in this business. Where are the trust shares? When are the employees getting their shares?" Gavin would quickly put his foot down and pay the other directors a bonus of R100 000 each in cash to pull Ishmael into line.

At one of the board meetings, Ishmael asked a pertinent question. "Gavin, you keep telling us about the company's other shareholders. Who are they exactly?"

Gavin baulked at the question. Everybody in the room knew that Gavin was the only shareholder. It was only Gavin who didn't know that we knew. The meeting wound down to a close at about 11 p.m., and when Ishmael left, Gavin went off at everybody. "You had better call him back here and give him a talking-to," he snapped. "And if he ever asks a question like that again, he'll get himself fired."

Half an hour later, Ishmael was called back to the office, and Joe Gumede was tasked with telling him off. I remember Ishmael standing on a patch of grass next to a fire hydrant while Joe spent fifteen minutes telling him his fortune. Of course, Joe knew Ishmael was right, but what choice did he have?

We later named that patch of grass in Ishmael's honour.

PART 5

CHAPTER 32

Prison Fences – The Big Swindle

"He moves in darkness as it seems to me,
Not of woods only and the shade of trees.
He will not go behind his father's saying,
And he likes having thought of it so well
He says again, 'Good fences make good neighbors.'"
– Robert Frost, *Mending Wall*

I was working at the office one Saturday morning in 2005, getting my admin up to date, when through my window, I spotted a truck delivering three-metre-long panels of 458 wire mesh – I must have counted about fifty of them. Next thing, Danny Mansell and his sons Gwilym and Jarred arrived at the office. The three of them sat down with Hennie Viljoen, Bosasa's maintenance man, who also happened to be working that day. I left them to their own devices and continued with my admin, not wanting to get caught up in anything involving the Mansell sons.

"What is all this fencing for?" I asked Danny after his sons had left. "Word is out that DCS is looking for a company to make climb-resistant fences for the prisons," he told me. "So we're going to see if we can design one and put a sample up here on our premises. Hennie is going to set it up in the area adjacent to the control room."

Curious about the type of fences DCS was looking for, Danny told me that a sample of the prototype had already been erected at Pretoria Central Prison. I decided to drive out there and take a look for myself. One of the guards directed me to the sample fence. I noticed that the material was identical to the material that had been delivered to Bosasa's offices.

Danny and his sons, unbeknown to me at the time, had purchased an electronic, GPS-enabled theodolite which they were using, with full permission from the DCS, to plot distances and produce topographical maps at the prisons, presumably as research for putting up the fences.

One Sunday morning, two weeks later, Gavin called me to tell me that he was sitting in Cape Town with Tony Perry, Danny Mansell, and the Betafence guys. He wanted to know if I had any ideas about taking the prototype fence at Pretoria Central Prison and making it unique to us. I scratched my head and told him I'd call him back in half an hour. I took out a sheet of paper and sketched the prototype that I had seen two weeks earlier. It was structured in such a way that it bowed inwards on itself, making it difficult for a prisoner to climb. One thing the fence was lacking was rigidity. I added in an additional length of wire on the inside which would not only serve to reinforce the fence, but if a prisoner tried to cut through the fence, it would take significantly longer.

I called Gavin back and explained my idea. He told me he'd discuss it with the Betafence guys. Not long afterwards, my phone was buzzing. They loved the idea. "But what are we going to call the bloody fence now?" Gavin asked.

It just so happened that I was sitting on the floor with my nephews who were playing with their Duplo building blocks when he called. "Let's call it a Duplo Fence," I suggested.

A week later, Gavin invited me for dinner at Casalinga. Seated at the table were Gavin Watson, Danny Mansell and three of the Betafence guys. Gavin announced that he was pleased to note that Bosasa "now has a 26% shareholding in Betafence".

While everybody was talking amongst themselves, I leaned into Gavin.

"How the hell are you paying for this shit?" I asked. "This isn't a small company, you know."

"We're not paying for our shares," he said. "We're doing it as a swap."

"A swap?" I asked. "What do you mean, a *swap*?"

"We're going to provide them with the business equivalent of what we would have purchased those shares for," he explained, before adding, "Danny has the details."

The following day, shareholders' agreements were flying up and down the office. Danny explained to me that two black empowerment entities, Mpako and Nzunzo, which were controlled by Bosasa, would be taking up the shareholding. I decided to put the question to Danny; "Tell me, Danny, how is this paying for itself?"

"Well," he said. "Correctional Services has agreed to put out a tender in which they will specify the Duplo Fence [which Betafence had since patented] as the only fence that companies can bid on."

My blood ran cold. "Danny, do you realise how dangerous this is? The Duplo Fence is proprietary. The Competition Commission will eat us alive when they find out that we are the only company that has tendered."

Danny laughed. "Relax," he said. "Betafence is going to offer the fence to everybody, but they're going to give Bosasa a 45% discount, and we'll win on pricing."

"And who exactly is 'everybody'?" I asked.

"We're going to invite all these fencing companies to come and sit at Bosasa's offices to complete their tenders."

"What about the other manufacturers in the sector?" I was worried.

"Angelo, don't worry, we're working on that," said Danny.

Only years later, at a meeting with Bruce Cochrane (the founder and owner of Cochrane Steel) and his son Lex, did I find out that Danny Mansell approached Bruce with a R40-million proposal to give up 26% of his company in exchange for a BEE shareholding by a Bosasa-owned company.

Cochrane Steel was, at the time, manufacturing the competition's mesh fences. Gavin and Danny had not, at that stage, approached Betafence with a proposal. Being a technical engineer by trade, Bruce needed the proposal to be explained to him in far more detail than Danny was able to. He was willing to participate, but he wanted it to be on his terms and according to his action plan, not Danny's.

According to Bruce, it was not the approach or the concept that riled him up, but the arrogance with which Danny Mansell came across – it was Danny's way or the highway. Danny eventually became quite threatening, insisting that Bruce accept his offer. But Bruce refused to back down, and as a result, Cochrane Steel did not do business during this time with us. Lex told me that to this day, the hair on Bruce's neck still rises if anybody mentions the name Bosasa.

"And you don't think that somebody at DCS is going to raise their eyebrows when they see that another huge contract has been awarded to a Bosasa company?" I asked Danny.

"We've already got that covered," Danny told me. "The contract won't be awarded to us – it will be given to Phezulu Fencing, who will do the installations."

This was becoming more complicated and more intricate by the second.

"As soon as Phezulu is awarded the tender, Bosasa is going to buy the business from them," Danny explained.

Being awarded the tender was one thing, but delivering on it was another. Although we had access to hundreds of millions of rands, I was acutely aware of the fact that, as a company, we did not have enough time or spare bodies available to roll out and coordinate a project of this magnitude.

It wasn't long before the different fencing providers, excluding Cochrane Steel, were sitting around Bosasa's boardroom table. Danny explained to the different companies that Bosasa would be tendering through Phezulu Fencing. He also explained that while everyone was going to submit their bids, Phezulu would ultimately win the tender. Before anybody could raise their hand in objection, he went on to explain that 25% of the total business would be outsourced to each company, so that everyone could have a slice of the pie.

Although Gavin appointed Carol Mkele[40] and Joe Gumede as directors in Betafence, he refused to allow them to attend any of that company's board meetings alone. Soon I was boarding flights to Cape Town, Belgium and Italy, not only to manage the board meetings but to set down proposals in terms of what Bosasa wanted out of each deal. It seemed clear, judging from Betafence's continuous requests for feedback on the "second round of fencing tenders", that Gavin and Danny had led the company to believe that the DCS had a further pipeline of fencing contracts. I spent almost every board meeting skirting the topic, knowing that, in all likelihood, there would be no second phase, and that it was probably this "phase" that had given Bosasa their 26% gratis share in Betafence in the first place.

As if things were not already complicated enough at the time, Gavin took it upon himself to employ the senior management team of a company called HSA, a specialist fleet management and e-fuel management service provider whose primary client was Transnet. By taking over the team, Gavin appeared to be hopeful that HSA would implode, allowing Bosasa the opportunity to take over a lucrative Transnet e-fuel and fleet management contract. The expected implosion didn't take place as expected, and Bosasa ended up saddled with a team of ten highly overpaid individuals. Fortunately, the HSA team was able to add some value back to the Phezulu Fencing contract, freeing me up to focus on other areas.

When the contract was eventually awarded to Phezulu Fencing, Gavin managed to secure R500-million in upfront payments from the DCS. There was a clause in the tender that allowed for 90% of the contract price to be paid as soon as the raw materials were delivered to the various sites. To my mind, this was in full transgression of the rules of the Public Finance Management Act at the time, which stipulated that payment could only be made once the work had been completed.

While I was under the impression that the funds would be placed in an

---

40 Carol later changed her name to Muneira Oliveria.

escrow account, it was not to be. Sitting on this large sum of cash, Gavin decided that instead of using the R500-million to purchase fencing material, he was going to buy a stake in South Africa's largest mining group, Simmers & Jack.

Vulisango, run by Valence Watson, already had a minority share in Simmers, but Gavin's contribution would help take things up a notch. Simmers was sitting on untold reserves of cash and assets at the time, and the Watsons knew that if they wanted to get their hands on those reserves and profit off them, they would need a majority shareholding.

No sooner had the DCS down payment landed in Phezulu Fencing's account than Andries van Tonder was instructed to transfer it out to Simmers & Jack. Between Vulisango – made up of Valence; his sons Jared, Daniel and Nkosi (Valence Junior); Kevin Wakeford and Baba Njenje – and Gavin, the Watsons now held majority shares in the group.

CHAPTER 33

Acquisitions, Liquidations, Shady Deals and Bad Decisions

"If you must break the law, do it to seize power. In all other cases, observe it."
– Julius Caesar (100 BC - 44 BC)

Between 2004 and 2009, Gavin went on a massive acquisition spree, using the company's profits to invest in (often) shady deals or buy up other businesses. Because many of the entities were purchased without performing any due diligence, a significant number of them were liquidated as quickly as they were acquired. I was never involved in any of the acquisitions, and Gavin insisted on building his own teams to manage these businesses, along with each company's original staff. Each business continued operating from its original premises, with their people only visiting Bosasa's offices when they required funding or loans.

Gavin was frequently approached by people who wanted to form joint ventures. Two such people were Brian Gwebu and Itu Moraba, who ran Wesbank's fleet management contracts through their company, Kgwerano Financial Services. They wanted Bosasa on board so that they could secure a ten-year tender – valued in the region of R14.5-million a month – to provide fleet management services to the Department of Transport for vehicles procured for senior government officials. At that stage, the contract was to fully maintain and service in the region of fifteen thousand vehicles. Eventually, Bosasa acquired Kgwerano from Brian and Itu for R25-million, and Papa Leshabane was appointed as Chairman of the company.

Of the more notable acquisitions were F&R Phakisa and its subsidiary, Vanco, a company that built bodies for trucks. Gavin took an 80% share in the business, formerly named F&R Diesel and owned by Hein Späth.

The company had a contract to perform maintenance on Telkom's armadillo-body-type maintenance vehicles, and one of their divisions built armoured vehicles for Fidelity Security (now Fidelity ADT). Gavin bought his shares in the business for about R42-million, and Hein came along as part of the deal. One of the arrangements was that F&R Phakisa would service the fifteen-thousand-odd vehicles in Kgwerano's fleet.

Gavin then went out and purchased a crane company called Bowman Cranes and a steel-cutting company called Cutting Edge Technologies. Each was operating from their own premises, but Gavin wanted to consolidate the companies at the Bosasa office park. This proved to be impossible because Vanco was out in Witbank, Bowman Cranes was in Alrode, Cutting Edge Technologies was in Durban, and F&R Phakisa was in Randburg – and none of them was prepared to move. With no due diligence done and many of these companies a fair distance away, everybody was pretty much left to their own devices.

While working in my office one Saturday morning in 2006, I couldn't help but overhear an argument filtering through from the boardroom. Upon closer inspection, I realised it was Gavin and Hein. Hein marched out of the boardroom with Gavin in hot pursuit, begging him to come back. At that stage, I had no idea what the argument was about, but I was later to discover that in the two-year period that Hein was left in charge of F&R Phakisa, there appeared to be money missing from the business.

The only reason I found this out was that I decided to get involved – but without Gavin's knowledge. I called on a retired actuary by the name of David Janks and asked him to work with Bosasa's accountant, Carlos Bonifacio, and dig into the accounting records of F&R Phakisa.

I first met Carlos when he was the Financial Manager for a contractor that operated at the Blyvooruitzicht mines. Way back then, it was already a battle to get money out of the somewhat tight-fisted Carlos. After a chance encounter with Doc Smith at the bank one day, Carlos eventually joined Bosasa to head up the group's Accounts department at the ripe old age of fifty-four. Carlos Bonifacio was not only an exceptional Chartered Accountant but an outstanding coach and mentor towards his people. He was also somewhat paranoid. Carlos was the embodiment of Chicken Little, spending much of his time worrying that the sky was about to come crashing down on his head. I used to joke that Carlos was so negative that if we locked him in the office, closed all the blinds and turned off all the lights, he would start developing photographs.

Carlos was the kind of person who planned his life to a tee and managed his money down to the last cent. He knew how much he had to spend, how much he needed to save, and how many Bitcoin he needed to have stashed away just in case inflation headed south. Carlos always made sound investment decisions, and his life appeared to be under control. That is, until his wife, who was fifty at the time, fell pregnant.

I'll never forget the deep anxiety this pregnancy caused him, but I couldn't help but laugh at him. First-time parents and all he kept saying was, "I never budgeted for this. How am I going to pay school fees when I'm sixty?" While I laughed at him, I secretly thanked God that I wasn't in his position, especially having maintained for years that the only new diapers in my house would be for my personal use.

With Carlos' help, I discovered that, for two years, F&R appeared to have charged Kgwerano a retainer of R1 250 per month per fleet vehicle, but had never performed a single service, purely because the original vehicle manufacturers were servicing these vehicles under their original three-year maintenance plans that came standard with each purchase. All that had to be provided in that three-year period was a set of replacement tyres. Whatever money was left over should have been transferred into a provision account for the latter lifespan of each vehicle. Despite the fact that Bosasa was an 80% shareholder in F&R, I don't think we ever saw a cent of that money. I also discovered that Hein was transferring money out of the company's bank account to fund a macadamia nut farm in Mpumalanga.[41]

I immediately went to Gavin and told him what was going on, but he did nothing about it. Knowing how much he liked his "second opinions", I went to the directors and explained the situation, and they agreed that I should confront Gavin again. Three months later, I went back to him with enough evidence to put forward a business case, including the fact that I had already consulted with the directors.

"Do what you have to do, Angelo," said Gavin.

We immediately took control of F&R Phakisa's bank account and transferred R23-million from their account into Bosasa's. Next up was taking control of the business itself and replacing Hein and his people.

It did, however, emerge that some kind of agreement had been reached between Gavin and Hein over the macadamia nut farm, with Hein insisting that he had express permission from Gavin to take whatever money he needed to fund the venture. I wasn't about to debate this with Gavin, fearing that the arrangement would be confirmed, and so I decided to let it go. None of these "agreements" were ever captured in writing, which is exactly how Gavin liked it. The fewer documents on which his signature appeared, the happier he was. As far as I was aware – and despite my many

41   Hein later told me that this was done with Gavin's permission.

warnings to Gavin – no complete forensic investigation was ever commissioned, nor were any further legal steps taken.

In 2008, Gavin made a particularly disastrous investment in a company called Dealstream. While nobody had heard of the company, other than the fact that it was owned by a certain Russell Leigh, Gavin told us that he had it on good authority (from his twenty-something-year-old nephew, Daniel) that we would be crazy not to invest in the CFDs that Dealstream had on offer. I was incredulous at how the Watson nieces and nephews appeared to be able to dictate to their parents where to invest and in whom to trust.

Gavin planned to sink a staggering R68-million in these CFDs. Andries van Tonder and I did a brief risk test on the company. We called in Carlos Bonifacio and David Janks. They both shook their heads, saying there was no way we should proceed with the transaction.

Gavin was furious. "You will do it," he said, before adding, "In fact, I'll sign it off myself." Which he did.

Over the course of two months, Dealstream leeched a total of R68-million out of Bosasa. One Thursday morning, Russell Leigh phoned Andries van Tonder asking for a further R10-million payment. Instead of transferring the cash, Andries decided to take a trip to Russell's offices, only to discover that Russell was on a one-way trip to Israel. The JSE later declared Dealstream in default of its future clearing agreement, and the company went belly-up. All the investors took losses in the Dealstream debacle – including Gavin's wife, Kevin Wakeford, Valence Watson, other Watson family members and even Lindie Gouws – and were required to pay in on the taxes, but it was Bosasa that ultimately paid for those losses.

Due to the easy availability of cash, these schemes and deals were never tested or verified. Had somebody taken the time to calculate the actual values and feasibility of these deals, ninety percent of them would probably never have gone ahead. But R68-million wasn't big money for Gavin. He wasn't interested in the day-to-day amounts that were floating around in the company's coffers. He always had a bigger picture in mind. Unfortunately, it was this big-picture thinking that put a serious strain on the company's finances on more than one occasion.

Some of the trading was so reckless that we were forced to extend our payment terms to suppliers – something that we were always dead set against doing. When things were tight, particularly in 2011, Andries van

Tonder and I bonded our houses to raise cash to pay salaries and wages, giving the company breathing room until the following month when our cash flow would be freed up again.

CHAPTER 34

I Won't Share my Shares

"Give a man a fish, and you feed him for a day. Teach a man to fish, and you feed him for a lifetime. Steal a fish from one guy and give it to another – and keep doing that on a daily basis – and you'll make the first guy pissed off, but you'll make the second guy lazy and dependent on you."
– Larken Rose

The first thing that struck me about Sabelo Macingwane[42] was that while he didn't appear to have two cents to rub together at our initial meeting, he seemed like someone who could make a plan. In meetings and negotiations, he was like a pit bull. He would sit there and wouldn't leave until he got what he wanted.

In 2004, Sabelo, together with his business partner Smuts Ngonyama[43], approached Gavin to come on board as a third shareholder in a consortium they founded called Nkonjane Economic Prospecting and Investment. The plan was that, through their individual investments, each would have a 33.3% share in the consortium. Sabelo had his eye on a mine near Hotazel in the Northern Cape called Tshipi é Ntle Manganese Mine. Ntsimbintle Mining owned 50.1% of Tshipi Mine, and Nkonjane had an 11% shareholding in Ntsimbintle. This same mine went on to become the largest manganese exporter in South Africa.

Gavin liked the idea and signed on the dotted line. I doubt Sabelo and Smuts understood what they were getting themselves into. The three men named themselves "The Elders" and set about creating the company and

---

42 Sabelo Macingwane is the current President of NAFCOC - National African Federated Chamber of Commerce.
43 Smuts Ngonyama was advisor to former President Thabo Mbeki and went on to take up the position of Ambassador to Spain, and later Ambassador to Japan.

its branding. I remember the logo was a copper swallow, purely because I was the one responsible for compiling the company profile. I often found myself driving around in the middle of the bloody night to drop these profiles off every time there was a meeting.

Gavin then got a bee in his bonnet after meeting with "some people in mining" who told him that Nkonjane's bid for Ntsimbintle was flawed because Nkonjane "was not broad-based enough".[44] A light went on in Gavin's head, and he proposed to Sabelo and Smuts that the only way to make the company more broad-based was to allocate some of their shares to the youth. By "youth", Gavin was referring to Bosasa's Youth Development Foundation. All the three men had to do was dilute their individual shareholdings in Nkonjane from 33.3% down to 25%, giving the Youth Development Foundation a 25% share; thereby fulfilling the company's Broad-Based Black Economic Empowerment commitments.

Of course, neither Smuts nor Sabelo realised that the Youth Development Foundation was a profit-based business or that the sole shareholder in Bosasa Youth Development Centre (Pty) Ltd was none other than Gavin Watson. I suspect they failed to understand that by handing over 16% of their shares, Gavin now held 50% of Nkonjane's shares. While I'm certain that Gavin knew exactly what he had done, he assured the men that "this would only be a temporary arrangement". The only way he could win them over was through compensation – especially to Sabelo, who didn't take long to figure out that something was rotten in the state of Denmark.

"Gavin," I said, "you're stealing their shares right from under them. What you're doing is dirty."

"But Angelo," he smiled, "they agreed to it."

Circa 2009, Sabelo was appointed Executive Chairman of Ntsimbintle. Gavin couldn't read an income statement or a balance sheet, so he sent Joe Gumede to attend all the meetings at the mine. At the same time, dividends started flowing, and Gavin, of course, was entitled to his 50%. I happened to see the dividend for that year, which amounted to about R2-million. I remember there was a heated argument in the office about signing off the pay-out. Sabelo was furious. Smuts refused to sign. "Either you pay me my full dividend, or I'm not taking a cent," Sabelo said.

Gavin grew agitated – it was clear the three men had reached a stalemate, and nothing was going to happen without everyone's signatures. I believe this was the tipping point that saw Gavin, after much deliberation,

---

44 In terms of Broad-Based Black Economic Empowerment (BB-BEE) legislation at the time.

deciding that the only way to resolve the matter would be to take the two men head-on, liquidate Nkonjane, and allow everyone to go their separate ways. Gavin would receive his 50% of the proceeds, while Smuts and Sabelo would each receive their 25%. Although the decision did not go down well with Smuts and Sabelo, Gavin went ahead and arranged for the liquidation papers to be filed.

Around that time, Smuts had moved from the ANC to COPE[45] and, in Gavin's eyes, no longer held influence. Every time the two men requested a meeting of The Elders, Gavin refused to take their calls. When Sabelo called, Gavin would hand his phone to somebody else to answer. It escalated to a point where I had to intervene on instruction from my boss and tell Sabelo to stop phoning Gavin. In fact, the matter degenerated to such an extent that I requested that Brian Biebuyck send Sabelo a letter stating that if he continued harassing Gavin, an interdict would be filed against him.

"What you're doing is wrong," I said to Gavin, knowing that his actions were punitive and unethical. "Give them what's rightfully theirs – 33.3% each."

"You're daft," Gavin smirked. "This is not what I've worked for."

"We've all worked for this, Gavin," I argued, "but what's fair is fair. This is going to come back and bite you if you're not careful."

I tried to explain to him that he would not be losing any real money because he had already substantially reaped the benefits of the dividends from as far back as 2006. I repeatedly tried to make him see reason, but my words fell on deaf ears. All I succeeded in doing was watching Gavin dig his heels in deeper.

While the liquidation action was going ahead, Gavin cleared out the Nkonjane bank accounts, transferring whatever cash was available over to Bosasa. Sabelo, on discovering Gavin's guileful move, filed a complaint of theft with the Specialised Commercial Crimes Unit, challenging the removal of the R2.5-million from the Nkonjane account. Smuts and Sabelo wanted Gavin arrested, but Gavin appeared to be unperturbed.

Gavin decided to fire back and take Sabelo to court to force him to pay back his shareholder "loan account". A comprehensive affidavit, including numerous documents and spreadsheets, was prepared by Doc Smith that would show the existence of loan accounts between Sabelo Macingwane and Nkonjane with the Bosasa Group. The night before Gavin was to appear in court, Ronnie Watson told me that Gavin wouldn't last more than a few minutes in the dock when being cross-questioned. Gavin, although visibly upset at the suggestion, immediately felt compelled to disprove the notion.

An over-confident Gavin Watson led the way to the North Gauteng

---

45 Congress of the People

High Court in Pretoria the following morning. The team – together with Bosasa's attorney, Brian Biebuyck, and Advocate Etienne Theron – assembled at a coffee shop adjacent to the court that seemed to be frequented by anyone appearing in court that day.

Doc Smith was up first. He was required to give testimony for a loan taken from the company by Sabelo Macingwane for seed capital for Nkonjane. Even though Gavin was a shareholder in Nkonjane, he had told Doc to allocate the funds to Sabelo's loan account. Despite Sabelo's Senior Counsel, Advocate Dumisa Ntsebeza, hammering Doc with questions and statements, little appeared to disrupt Doc's state of mind. He had kept impeccable records, and methodically explained that the loan had at that stage risen to an estimated R3.82-million.

Gavin was up next. With Sabelo maintaining that no definite repayment terms had been established, Gavin had to explain why Sabelo needed to pay the loan back immediately. We were all looking forward to watching Gavin teach counsel a "lesson".

Taking the affirmation instead of the oath, I watched Brian Biebuyck sit up straight in his chair in alarm.

"Comrade Skalie," Advocate Dumisa Ntsebeza said, looking directly at Gavin, "you don't mind me calling you by your clan name, do you, my friend?" Gavin smiled and nodded his head.

"Now, Comrade Skalie," Ntsebeza continued, "tell me, do you consider me a friend – perhaps even a brother?"

"Of course, brother," Gavin smiled. "We fought together in the trenches."[46]

Gavin's ego immediately took centre stage and, with each skillful question posed by Advocate Ntsebeza, Gavin slowly sunk himself and his credibility. Advocate Ntsebeza was a past master in his field. A few minutes in the dock was enough to neutralise Gavin.

"Would you do business with Mr Macingwane in the future?" Ntsebeza posed, knowing full well that Gavin had stated unequivocally in the court documents that he in no way trusted Sabelo.

"Without a doubt," Gavin declared.

Brian Biebuyck shook his head in dismay. Advocate Etienne Theron was discerning enough not to offer a rebuttal, which would only have been in vain. Gavin couldn't understand why everyone was so upset. The judge ruled in Sabelo's favour, who was not forced to pay back the loan. As Ishmael Dikane put it so succinctly later that day, "Gavin scored an own goal."

Sabelo called me shortly afterwards and asked if he could meet me at my

---

46 Referring to the rugby the Watson brothers played in the black townships during the era of white minority rule, when inter-racial sport was banned.

house. When he arrived, he told me that while he didn't feel comfortable with the animosity that had been created between him and Gavin, he felt that Gavin had betrayed him and Smuts, and he still wanted his money back.

"I'll get it back for you, Sabelo," I promised.

I met with Gavin and again tried to persuade him to do the right thing and return the unpaid dividends to the two men. Gavin laughed me off, and so the rift between us began to deepen.

In 2015 the Bloemfontein Supreme Court of Appeal granted Thunder Cats Investments 92 (Pty) Ltd (Smuts' company) and Turquoise Moon Trading 8 (Pty) Ltd (Sabelo's company) leave to appeal against the order to liquidate Nkonjane. Gavin, however, refused to comply with the order.

By the time July 2016 drew to a close, I had grown sick and tired of Gavin's procrastinating and doubted that he was ever going to pay what was due to these two men. Having watched him behave unethically on numerous other occasions, my loyalty, commitment and respect towards him had entirely diminished.

On the 7th of August 2016, I resigned from Bosasa.

In June 2019, justice was finally served in the Johannesburg High Court when Judge Fayeeza Kathree-Setiloane found Gavin guilty of material misrepresentation and ordered that he pay back the 550 shares in Ntsimbintle Mining as well as the shortfall in dividends from 2006 to 2015, with interest – a figure, as reported in the media, that ran into hundreds of millions of rands.

In the judgment, Judge Fayeeza Kathree-Setiloane noted that "Mr Watson acted dishonestly and reprehensibly by taking benefits allocated by the parties under the agreement to a Broad-Based Black Economic Empowerment entity and appropriating them to himself and his family."

As far as I know, the money owed is part of an ongoing liquidation claim against Gavin's estate.

CHAPTER 35

Archie Mkele, the Inferno and the Fronting

"There is no more dangerous menace to civilisation than a government of incompetent, corrupt, or vile men."
– Ludwig von Mises

In my experience, if a BEE deal was going down and Gavin Watson was involved, it invariably meant that something fishy was going on. By using certain members of political society to lay claim to some or other skewed Broad-Based Black Economic Empowerment deal, Gavin Watson became the master of BEE fronting in South Africa. While a company's shareholding and directorship may have appeared to be representative of the country's previously disempowered, disenfranchised and disadvantaged demographic, in reality, the shareholders often owned nothing, and the directors were appointed for everything *but* their business prowess. Veiled in contorted, elaborate (and encumbered) share structures, together with handsome salaries and other benefits, there was very little true empowerment.

Take husband and wife team, Carol and Archie Mkele, for example. Valence and Gavin called Archie "the fifth brother". The Mkele name is synonymous with the Watson name, and it involved a rather large favour. You see, the Watsons often owed *someone* a favour.

In late 1985, the Watson family home, described in the press as a fourteen-room cliffside mansion in Port Elizabeth, burnt down. Archie Mkele – a black rugby legend and childhood friend of the Watson brothers – and Geoffrey Nocanda happened to be on the property at the time and were severely burned in the blaze.

While the Watsons claimed it was a politically motivated bombing, the investigating officers believed the house was deliberately razed to the ground after being doused with petrol. The State reportedly discovered that the brothers' business was heavily in debt. While Archie confessed to the police that he had been paid to torch the house so that his friends, the Watsons, could claim against the property's insurance, his confession later appeared to have been made under duress.

While Valence, Cheeky and Ronnie denied the charges of fraud and arson that were levelled against them, Valence was later found guilty – a charge that was subsequently overturned.

During the trial, it reportedly emerged that Archie had smuggled notes to his wife, Carol Mkele, from prison, telling her that he had been tortured into making his confession.

On the day of the appeal in August 1987, the case was overturned, and the brothers were literally carried down the street in celebration by their ANC comrades who had packed the courtroom that day.

Although Archie and Carol subsequently divorced, Archie was presented as being central to Continental Tyres (part of the Vulisango Group, and owned by Valence Watson), and Carol was presented as Bosasa's majority shareholder. Favour repaid, it seemed, but the question remained whether Carol and Archie genuinely owned their shares, or whether it was simply an elaborate plan to make the Mkele family think they were important.

While Carol believed she was a bona fide shareholder, I believe that Gavin employed a similar tactic to the one he used with people like Hilda Ndude and the ANCWL ladies at Dyambu, successfully pulling the wool over her eyes and leaving her none the wiser. While she was allocated her 22% shares, those shares were encumbered. The shares reflected on the company's balance sheet, but they would only become hers when she paid for them. Any company perks she received over and above her salary – things like clothing, travel, entertainment, and even the car she drove – were credited to her shareholder's loan account (instead of as operational expenses), and all, I believe, without her knowledge. The loan account was Gavin's insurance for the day she questioned the value of her shareholding. Years later, with a loan account sitting in the millions, it would be no skin off his back to insist she first repay her loan account if she ever questioned him about her shares. And until she paid back her loan account, her shares belonged to nobody but him.

The intricate structure of the myriad of different trusts that made up Global Holdings (the main holding company of all the other companies that made up the Bosasa Group) was so complicated and so detailed that nobody was ever really able to understand it, let alone unwind it. Carol's shareholding was split across all these different trusts. In Global Holdings, the directors were listed as Gavin Watson, Carol Mkele, Ishmael Dikane, Papa Leshabane, Jackie Leyds, Joe Gumede and Thandi Makoko.

Although Carol had a 22% share in the consortium, she didn't even have a company credit card. She drove a Toyota Fortuner, while I drove a 7-series BMW. She was paid R80 000 a month, compared to Gavin's R5.2-million monthly earnings. Things just didn't add up. She may have been a director and a shareholder on paper, but she had little to show for it.

It was a catch-22 situation. Because of her burgeoning loan account and her encumbered shares, she couldn't just pack her bags, cash in her shares, and leave – even if she wanted to. Gavin, in terms of the shareholder's agreement, had first right of refusal on her shares anyway, so, even if she wanted out, there was nothing she could do except stay quiet and keep going.

While she was supposedly in charge of the catering operation at St Albans Correctional Facility, not once did she make any decisions regarding the management of that operation – she simply continued capturing invoices as before. It was either Ernest McDermott (and later, Gallie Stoltz) – or me – who took all the decisions. I found it sad that while she was a shareholder and a director, she didn't even have the authority to credit ten boxes of chicken.

Gavin Watson portrayed a different image of Carol to the one I saw and experienced. She was feisty when she needed to be, but she was also a true friend. She had two children, Abigail and Samuel, whom she spoke of fondly every time she collected me from the airport in Port Elizabeth. And then there was her grandchild, the light of her life.

Compared to the rest of us, Carol really struggled. A majority shareholder in a multibillion-rand company, she lived in a modest house in Walmer, Port Elizabeth. Whenever she needed something, I would have to motivate it for her.

Perhaps it was her blind loyalty that allowed her to be so completely enraptured by Gavin. Whatever it was, and as well-meaning as Carol was, she neglected to consider her fiduciary duties, not only as a director but as a majority shareholder.

Having spent the better part of fifteen years with Carol, not once did she discuss the 1985 inferno with me. She did, however, tell me – time and time again – that she "sacrificed a lot" for the Watsons.

Carol eventually succumbed to cancer early in 2020. Gallie Stoltz had been in constant contact with me, updating me as to her progress, but her health continued to deteriorate. She was eventually too tired to speak to me over the phone, and then, before I had time to say goodbye, she was gone. Perhaps it was a saving grace that she left this world. Had she pulled through, she would have had to answer for being complicit in Gavin Watson's illicit dealings. Of all people, she deserved so much better than that.

Gavin played the same game with Joe Gumede's 14% shareholding when he appointed Joe as company Chairperson. Although on paper, Joe was an owner and decision-maker in the company, I doubt he ever checked the share certificates to confirm that he was a bona fide shareholder. If he did, he would have realised that his shares had never been transferred into his name. Either way, I don't think Joe really cared. He was receiving a R150 000 pay cheque every month.

But I knew that Gavin was using Joe to further his own agenda, and one day I decided to point this out to Joe. While taken aback, Joe realised that there was some truth in the matter. He had done so much for Gavin but had nothing to show for it.

Joe promptly went to Gavin and demanded that Gavin look after him financially. This did not go down well with Gavin, who later approached me and said that we must look at ways of "getting rid" of Joe.

"Gavin," I said, referring to several dubious incidents that took place at the Lindela Repatriation Centre, "Joe is one hundred percent right. How many times have you taken a back seat so that Joe could go out and take the fall for you?"

Lindela, while being paid a whopping R9.5-million per month by the Department of Home Affairs (DHA), was also responsible for numerous (and often unexplained) deaths, mainly due to unsanitary living conditions and a lack of medical treatment. One of the deaths that allegedly took place at Lindela was that of four-year-old Sinoxolo Hlabanzana, the son of a Congolese detainee, who died after being hospitalised with severe diarrhoea. According to his father, Sinoxolo was left untreated for fourteen days before he passed away. In 2005 alone, twenty-one detainees died in the space of eight months.

The truth of the matter was that Lindela's DHA funding never quite made it to the upkeep of the detainees. Instead, the money ended up in Bosasa's coffers.

"Gavin," I said, "you need to look after Joe."

Shortly after that discussion, Gavin called a directors' meeting at Avianto, a hotel in Muldersdrift. It was there that he decided to give Joe R2.5-million as a lump-sum bonus. Although Joe was initially invited to air his concerns, the bonus was announced privately. None of the other directors were aware of the payment.

In terms of the company's shareholding, when it was time to update Bo-sasa's annual BEE certificate, all this lily-white-over-the-age-of-fifty-owned company needed to do to claim the right amount of points was appoint a corrupt verifications agent and pay them R20 000 for every level they wanted the company raised by. One has to wonder who checks on the people on the ground who issue these verification certificates. I am almost certain that up to 75% of white-owned companies are doing exactly what Bosasa did to raise their BEE ratings – and it appears that it's easier for government to look the other way than to do any digging of their own.

CHAPTER 36

The 6 800 TVs

"When another blames you or hates you, or people voice similar criticisms, go to their souls, penetrate inside and see what sort of people they are. You will realise that there is no need to be racked with anxiety that they should hold any particular opinion about you."
– Marcus Aurelius, *Meditations*

In early 2005, Patrick Gillingham sat down with Danny Mansell. He casually mentioned that the DCS had surplus funds to use up and that he thought the prisons should invest in a TV management system that would control the prisoner's viewing habits. At the time, prisoners were able to flick through channels and watch whatever caught their attention. Gillingham was looking for something more draconian and paternalistic where the head of the prison would be able to control and customise what the prisoners could watch, when they could watch it, and at what volume – and all from one centrally-controlled system. He also wanted a feature that would allow the prison heads to interrupt viewing and stream announcements to the prisoners. Taking it one step further, DCS-related broadcasts could be disseminated to prisons in the various provinces and regions directly from the DCS headquarters in Pretoria. The regions could then stream the broadcasts to the individual prisons, who would then stream them into the individual cells.

I quite liked the idea and even threw in a suggestion of my own that if the occupants of a particular cell behaved themselves, they would get to watch a movie, and, conversely, if they misbehaved, they would be forced to watch educational documentaries or have their television turned off.

Of course, all existing television sets would need to be removed and upgraded with specialised waterproof and vandal-resistant sets that could plug into the central system. Having TVs in the prison cells suited the DCS since offenders frequently hired television sets from Early Bird or Master Rentals. Despite the fact that these hired TVs were not the property of the individual offenders, the prisoners kicked up a storm over ownership rights when the prison officials came to remove them.

To develop a system like this was not going to be cheap, but I knew we could do it. "How many televisions are we talking about?" I asked. "We're looking at about 6 800 of them, right around the country," said Gillingham.

Using a local electronics engineer to assist us, we based the concept design on the typical Emirates ICE Entertainment system. The end result was a truly world-class South African solution.

Because all government contracts above R200 000 are subject to public tender procedures, this particular project had to go out to tender. Had this not been the case, Sondolo IT would have probably received an official purchase order and begun installing the system the following week. Gillingham handed Danny and Gavin his proposed design proforma of the process to follow, and I was told to draw up the specifications. These specifications formed the body of the DCS tender that would be advertised in mid-October 2005. Respondents were given three weeks in which to submit their bids. This shortened response time deviated from the standard response time by two weeks, which raised a few eyebrows within the department. But, with Bosasa's connections within the DCS, we knew any raised voices would be swiftly muffled.

As I would later testify at the Zondo Commission, it was around this time that Carlos Bonifacio received an instruction from Gavin to assist Frans Vorster with purchasing a vehicle – a Mercedes-Benz – for Patrick Gillingham's son. Gavin was annoyed because it was usually Danny Mansell who attended to matters of this nature, but Gillingham had called him directly. Because Gavin was never confrontational with outsiders – and he had an image to uphold – he had to oblige.

"Get this guy a vehicle, and get it now," Gavin growled. With Gavin, everything had to be done immediately. "The guy [Gillingham] has been good to us," I assured Carlos, noticing his raised eyebrows. "Now go and see Doc Smith and get the damn thing sorted."

Because transactions of this nature were never above board, the money had to go through a few channels before it reached the vehicle dealership. The arrangement was that Doc Smith would transfer the money to me in the form of a bi-annual bonus, which I would then "loan" to Frans Vorster so that he could purchase the vehicle.

There was, however, one inconvenient problem – the payment needed to show in the dealership's account the same day. Mercedes banked with Nedbank, but Frans banked with Standard Bank, meaning there would be a delay. Carlos innocently offered to pay the dealership directly from his Nedbank account so that the payment would clear immediately.

And so, because people like Gavin didn't want to wait, people like Carlos Bonifacio became part of the ever-darkening line that was being drawn between the dots linking Bosasa to their underhanded dealings with the Department of Correctional Services.

From late 2005 onwards, as I explained at the Zondo Commission, I was put in charge of Linda Mti's travel arrangements. I received many a late-night call from Gavin asking me to book Mti on a flight to Cape Town the following morning and arrange car hire. Sometimes the bookings were just for Mti, other times they were for his wife and children too. "He's going down to meet somebody," or "He's doing some work for me," were some of Gavin's reasons for covering the costs of these trips. It was difficult for me to question their legitimacy. Eventually, Mti would phone Bosasa's travel agent (Blake's Travel) directly to book his trips.

Unbeknown to me, Gavin also insisted that Bosasa security guards be posted outside Mti's house.

CHAPTER 37

Sondolo Wins the TV Tender

"Good name in man and woman, dear my lord,
Is the immediate jewel of their souls:
Who steals my purse steals trash; 'tis something, nothing;
'twas mine, 'tis his, and has been slave to thousands;
But he that filches from me my good name
Robs me of that which not enriches him,
And makes me poor indeed."
– William Shakespeare, *Othello*

Submitting a tender was a serious affair. Most of the tenders we worked on were valued at hundreds of millions of rands, so we could scarcely afford to have anything go wrong. There were always two vehicles involved when a tender was en route to the bid office – one driving behind the other, just in case the brown stuff hit the fan along the way.

Before we instituted the two-vehicle rule, an incident took place that I will never forget. Because I knew I would be out of town at the time, I left the prepared tender document for the 6 800 televisions in the hands of my colleague, Dave Wiggett, a few days before it was due to be handed in at the DCS bid office. He promised to deposit it into the tender box on the due date.

Dave was a typical accountant, but he was exceptionally skittish. I reckoned that as long as I checked in with him, he'd get the tender in on time.

I called him up the morning before it was due. "Dave," I said, "remember you have to submit the tender tomorrow at 2 p.m. Is it with you?" Dave immediately went and locked the tender documents in the boot of his car. And then, lo and behold, his car was stolen that same afternoon.

When I heard what had happened, I went through the roof. All that trouble to put the tender together had come to nought. Dave seemed to think the police might find his car before the following morning, but this was South Africa, and the chances of that happening were close to zero. Fortunately, Gina, my P.A., had a scanned copy of the completed tender, so she printed it out, and we submitted that.

Because none of the other companies that tendered were able to put a solution on the table in line with the specifications I had drawn up, Sondolo IT was awarded the tender on the 3rd of March 2006. The initial contract value was R224-million.

Before we had even switched the television sets on, Bosasa's name was rippling through parliament. As explained in his 2019 book, *Blessed by Bosasa*, Adriaan Basson, a straight-down-the-line news reporter from *Beeld* who had been investigating Bosasa for a number of years, received a call from his colleague, Carien du Plessis, a journalist working for *Die Burger* who happened to be listening in on that particular parliamentary discussion. According to Adriaan, Carien told him that the televisions were priced at R26 500 each. He worked with Carien, determined to draw a line between the admittedly suspicious series of dots that linked Bosasa to the Department of Correctional Services.

It wasn't long before the story was splashed all over the media with the focus being on the cost of the TVs rather than the system behind it and, of course, that Bosasa had been awarded yet *another* multimillion-rand prison tender.

I'll never forget the call I received the morning that the news broke. It was 7.30 a.m. and, with a packed car, we were off to the airport to take a well-deserved family vacation in Zanzibar. It was Lynn Burger, our administrator in Cape Town. "Angelo," she said, "I'm driving to the office, and the news headlines along all the major routes are saying that Bosasa has been awarded a R200-million tender to supply prisoners with TVs costing R28 000 a TV. Is this true?"

I immediately got on the phone to Gavin, who was attending a diamond-cutting exhibition in Switzerland with Sabelo Macingwane. "Don't stress, Angelo," he said. "Somebody's probably jealous. Now go and enjoy your break."

"That's easier said than done," I thought. My head was in a spin. All I wanted to do was turn around and head straight to the office. I turned to look at my family, who were all staring at me with expectant faces. I knew they would have been devastated had I chosen Bosasa over them – again. The deep furrows in my forehead were not deep enough to channel the sweat that was pouring down my face. I couldn't let them down.

Arriving at the airport, I decided to call Papa Leshabane. "What do you think, Papa?" I asked. "Angelo, it's just a flash in the pan. I really wouldn't stress," he said.

By now the bus was transporting us to the awaiting plane. I felt uneasy. "Why don't you just go sort it out and catch up later?" Debbie suggested. "You're not going to relax until it's resolved – and you know that." I glanced over at my daughter Natasha, who I could see had been praying for some kind of intervention that would allow her Daddy to spend some quality time with her.

"Not this time girl," I said, looking into Natasha's eyes. "Not this time."

After what felt like the longest flight I'd ever taken, a surprisingly supportive message was waiting for me when I landed. It was from Papa. "No need to worry – the problem has been resolved."

I should have known better than to take Papa's word as gospel. Within twenty-four hours, Adriaan's digging hit gold – he had stumbled across the missing link he'd been searching for and joined the Linda Mti dot to the Bosasa dot. Using CIPC's[47] records, he had discovered that Linda Mti had used Bosasa's accountant, Tony Perry, to register his business, Lianorah Investments. It was all he needed to connect Bosasa with the DCS, and he went out with guns blazing. Somebody's house of cards was about to come tumbling down.

Dennis Bloem[48] of COPE voiced his discontent in Parliament for allowing statutes and systems to be compromised and proper procedures to be ignored for the sake of BB-BEE compliance in what he knew was a department plagued by corruption. No amount of explaining could change the fact that Bosasa had been part of the tender specifications team from the outset and, with Mti in charge, no amount of spinning could change the fact that Bosasa was pushed to the front of the line when it came to the tender being awarded.

Eventually, the brothers – Gavin, Ronnie, and Valence – called Andries van Tonder and me in, demanding to know who "this young whipper-snapper thinks he is to write such defamatory stories about the company". Tasked with handling the press, my first port of call was to meet with Brian Biebuyck. Brian had worked with Cheeky Watson on rugby-related issues in the past, and the brothers felt that he would be the right person to help us take on the media.

I'd always made use of non-descript attorneys who wouldn't even offer you a cup of coffee when visiting their offices. Brian Biebuyck, whose

---

47 Companies and Intellectual Property Commission
48 Before joining the Congress of the People (COPE) as their spokesperson, Bloem chaired Parliament's Correctional Services committee as a legislator for the ANC.

offices were situated in a prime location on Fredman Drive in downtown Sandton, made for a pleasant surprise. When I walked in, everything was prim and proper – I was even offered a newspaper while I waited to meet with him. I remember spotting a pile of branded notepads and pens on one of their tables, which I shovelled into my briefcase in front of everybody. I wanted to make sure we got our money's worth.

Sitting in the firm's impressive boardroom, I was introduced to Brian and his team of three candidate attorneys and two chartered accountants. He certainly seemed to be on top of issues and told me that we were going to put in an application with the Press Ombudsman questioning Adriaan Basson's reports, in the hope that Adriaan would be forced to retract certain of his statements.

Brian's work ethic was impeccable. He was a stickler for detail, and everything he put out was meticulously researched. If I sent him a letter today, it was back with me – complete – by the following morning.

In his complaint to the Ombudsman, Brian stated that there was no pending litigation between Bosasa and any State department, that Bosasa had never been listed as a tender defaulter, and that Bosasa was in no way involved in any irregularities in any way. He referred to the media's "persistent, misleading and inaccurate campaign of vilification" against Bosasa, telling them to publish at their peril, and that Bosasa would sue anyone who wrote or spoke negatively about the company for defamation – including Adriaan Basson.[49] While the Ombudsman eventually ruled in Adriaan's favour, I liked Brian and rated him as one of the best litigators in the country – I still do.

Gavin continued to dig his heels in and, I suspect, went as far as employing people to level telephonic death threats against these journalists. About twenty-five cheap cell phones were purchased and handed out to staff members, including the company's security guards. They were instructed to make anonymous calls to both Adriaan Basson and Carien du Plessis and lambaste them for potentially costing them their jobs. Apparently, Adriaan and Carien also received some calls from landlines, possibly from within the Bosasa offices.

Gavin – who by that stage had realised it was time to tighten the sails and batten down the hatches – called a meeting at Valence's house in Morningside and announced that we – Gavin, his brothers Ronnie and Valence, Andries van Tonder, Kevin Wakeford and me – were going to enter into an unbreakable pact. The agreement was that nobody would rat on each

---

49 Bosasa subsequently lodged an application against the Mail & Guardian (M&G) and Adriaan Basson, demanding that M&G disclose their sources. Bosasa lost the application, withdrew their action, and paid M&G's costs.

other when the Special Investigating Unit (SIU) came sniffing, that we would all sing from the same hymn sheet, and that there would be severe consequences for anybody who broke the pact. He called it "The Watson Pact". It was also agreed that from that day forward, I would handle the legal and operational side of the business, Gavin and his brothers would handle the political side, and Andries would handle the banks and anything related to Bosasa's finances, with Kevin Wakeford acting as support.

Adriaan Basson called and scheduled a visit at Bosasa's offices. Now, the first thing you do when Adriaan asks to come by is remove all the shovels and spades from your tool shed and any earth-moving equipment from your premises. Because when Adriaan Basson comes to visit, he's not only coming to dig – he's coming to excavate.

Adriaan arrived carrying a little backpack. I offered him a cup of coffee, but he declined. I decided to take him on a tour of the office park and show him around. It took me about three hours on an average day to walk from one end of the park to the other, but I decided to take him on an extra-long walk and tire him out a bit. Four-and-a-half hours later, he had a reasonably good idea of Bosasa's immense capabilities.

"And so?" I asked. "What do you think?"

"It's impressive," he said, "but I'm not here to write a good story about Bosasa. It's not what I'm paid to do."

The penny dropped so loudly that I'm sure it could be heard clanging on the concrete from miles away. If the press has a story, they're going to follow it until they find what they're looking for – and when they find it, they're going to blow it out of the water. No journalist is going to bend the rules just because you're friendly and generous with your time.

Mti and I conversed regularly during the height of Adriaan's investigation of Bosasa, which felt to us like a full-on attack. He refused to speak to Adriaan because he had made up his mind that he wanted nothing to do with the man. I was beginning to realise that Mti had more enemies than friends. Not only did he create many enemies within the DCS, but within the press too. He maintained that he was guilty of no wrongdoing. I suspect that, as far as he was concerned, he, as an ANC "comrade", was entitled to a better life.

Gavin came up with elaborate conspiracy theories illustrated through convoluted spidergrams to explain how the company's good work was being undermined by the media, and that there was no merit in their attacks. He, quite literally, made shit up. I was tasked with drawing up his spidergrams to motivate the conspiracy theories that he'd feed out in news articles to the media. I would sit with him and take notes while he told me who was linked to whom and what and why. It was absolute hogwash from start to finish. His main thrust was that Bosasa was part of the struggle and played an integral role in building the nation economically while supporting the ANC-led government.

Without ever producing any evidence to back up what appeared to be nothing more than conspiracy theories, Gavin would say things like: "This attack on us was fuelled by Trevor Manuel and Pravin Gordhan because [Linda] Mti was part of the exiled ANC group and they [Manuel and Gordhan] weren't, and everyone knows there is a strained dynamic between the two groups." Or: "Half of SARS[50] is pro-Bosasa, and the other half is against us. The side that's against us is attacking us because they see us as being the ANC[51]."

He would separate people out according to the faction they supported and label them as either good guys or bad guys. He was sure there was a politically fuelled motive behind every attack on Bosasa and the people associated with it. While I thought his theories were laughable, he was sold on them. I didn't have the will or energy at this stage to tell him what rubbish he was talking.

As time went on, we realised that some proper reputation management was required if Bosasa was to save face against the media's increasingly scathing attacks. Kevin Wakeford introduced us to who I believed was a highly regarded former journalist by the name of Stephen Laufer. Laufer had reportedly worked as a spin doctor for companies implicated in the multibillion-rand arms deal scandal of the late 1990s. He was going to head up the company's arsenal of writers responsible for counteracting the growing negative press.

Stephen told us that the only way to deal with the media was not only to engage with them but to mollycoddle them. This made perfect sense to me. Fighting the press with their barrels of ink was going to get us nowhere.

I didn't like the press, nor did I want to deal with them, so I took the opportunity to retract myself and hand Stephen over to Papa. Stephen's first task was to roll out a campaign where senior editors and journalists would be invited to a Bosasa-sponsored monthly press conference in Cape Town. While sitting around the dinner table, he gave them the opportunity to ask questions while briefing them on the company's activities during the past month. Stephen also arranged that Bosasa bought a prime slot on eTV just before the evening news, where we had our own five-minute weekly documentary that waxed lyrical about the good work the company was

---

50 South African Revenue Service
51 African National Congress

doing out in the community.

Papa also brought his own people on board. One of them was Benedicta Dube, a former journalist who had worked for the SABC, the *Financial Mail* and eTV. Papa employed a private investigator to dig up dirt on Adriaan, and tasked Benedicta with creating a dossier that would be used to discredit him. One night, Benedicta apparently called Adriaan up, told him how brave he was, and then spilt the beans on what she was working on. Ferial Haffajee, Adriaan's editor at the *Mail & Guardian* at the time, proceeded to call me up, asking that we please lay off "the young man".

After about two months with Stephen Laufer on board, we asked him to leave. He was costing the company a small fortune and had made little impact on the media that was now hell-bent on destroying any remaining shred of Bosasa's reputation. Not one article presenting Bosasa in a positive light ever emerged from his press briefing dinners.

And then Lindie Gouws decided to get involved on the sidelines. Her plan was to run with *Truth Online* and *WATSOnline*, which was supposed to be Gavin's daily blog. Her idea was that the only way to bring down Google's ratings on negative articles in the media was to counteract them with positive articles. Now, common sense will tell you that Google's algorithms don't work that way. If an article is attracting attention from various sources, its ranking is going to climb. Writing four or five positive articles wasn't going to dent Google's rankings unless they were attracting a similar number of views. And nobody was Googling good stories on Bosasa.

The more the company's media teams tried to explain this to Lindie, the more she dug her heels in and insisted that she understood the media better than anybody else. She would call Gavin over and type the words "Gavin Watson Good Boy" into Google to prove to him that all the positive articles were working – and Gavin would believe her. Eventually, the media team, who were working day and night to optimise Bosasa's various websites to keep them from slipping too far down the page, lost all interest. Typing "Bosasa" into the search bar yielded a flurry of negative news articles, populating the first few pages of Google's search results, with Bosasa's website relegated to the virtual graveyard reserved for companies with tarnished reputations and other has-beens.

Adriaan Basson reminded me of a fearless lion cub on the prowl, willing to take on anything. Throughout his investigation into Bosasa, he was precise, he stuck to his facts, and he refused to let go.

After watching him receive the Taco Kuiper award for investigative journalism later that year, (which he shared with Carien du Plessis), I made a comment to the directors that didn't go down well at all. "Chaps," I said, "let's face it – Adriaan kept us on our toes and worked us good and solid. He deserves the award and, quite frankly, his prize money should be doubled."

 Scan here to view the elaborate spidergram that Gavin Watson drew up to describe the coordinated attack on the Presidency and Bosasa.

PART 6

CHAPTER 38

The SIU Comes Sniffing

"If we elect the same corrupt politicians every time; that's a very clear message that we don't want a change."
– Sukant Ratnakar

In November 2007, then-President Thabo Mbeki signed a proclamation authorising the Special Investigating Unit (SIU) to proceed with an investigation into the four major contracts that the DCS had awarded to Bosasa between 2003 and 2006.

The four contracts encompassed the prisons catering contract, the access control and CCTV contract, the televisions in the prison cells contract, and finally, the Phezulu fencing contract. The main allegations centred around the irregular relationship between Bosasa, the DCS and its officials – with special reference to Linda Mti and Patrick Gillingham; the unlawful benefits that Mti and Gillingham were alleged to have received for awarding these tenders to Bosasa; the irregular extension of two of the four tenders; and, finally, that it was Bosasa that had drafted the complex bid specifications for these tenders, and not the DCS. The proclamation further stated that Gillingham was instrumental in the developing and awarding of these tenders.

One other tender that the SIU planned to investigate was for mobile x-ray scanning machines that would be used to scan prisoners and their belongings (including their mattresses) for contraband.

Shortly after the proclamation was signed, we received a notice from the SIU that they were planning to investigate Bosasa and that they intended to mirror our server's hard drives. We immediately called up Brian Biebuyck, who suggested that we schedule a meeting with well-known criminal advocate and Senior Counsel, Laurance Hodes. Gavin, preferring to distance himself from anything confrontational, decided he didn't want to get involved with the legal side of things, so he sent me, Andries van Tonder, Leon van Tonder, and Brian Biebuyck to attend the meeting instead. At that first meeting, Laurance voiced his apprehension about dealing with us, so I called Gavin and told him to get in his car and join us immediately.

By the end of the meeting, we were all firm friends, and Laurance agreed to represent us.

We were advised to take an offensive stance against the SIU. Our first step would be to respond to the SIU immediately, offering to tender our assistance. That way, the SIU could do nothing but convene a meeting with us to tell us what they wanted from us. While there was a risk that they would request access to our servers and computers to gather information, Laurance and Brian advised against fiddling with any of our data.

On our way down to the basement parking lot, Gavin pulled Brian to one side and told him that, in terms of the SIU report, he would be dealing directly with me – and only me. After Brian Biebuyck had left, and just as we were all about to get into our cars, Gavin called an impromptu meeting. "They're my servers and my data," he said, "and I can do with them as I please."

I would later make a statement to the Zondo Commission, describing how Gavin had instructed Leon van Tonder to search our servers for documents containing the keywords "specification; tender specification; fencing and catering" – aka incriminating information – and destroy them, under the guise of performing routine system maintenance.

Leon had the foresight to copy these files onto two hard drives before hitting the delete button. In excess of thirty-five thousand documents were deleted using a computer program called Erasure. Documents were deleted in a haphazard manner, which resulted in some employees losing critical work. While it upset the company's workflow, Leon had no choice but to rush the process because Gavin wanted it done quickly. When all the files had been removed, we secretly moved the backups to a farm in Mooinooi, near Marikana in the North West Province, without Gavin knowing.

The SIU's planned meeting went ahead, but any further investigations came to an almost grinding halt – thanks to Gavin paying his political connections to put a stay on the investigation. We knew that the report was being compiled, but we had no idea what information would be revealed or when it would be released to the public. We were also pretty certain that whoever was implicated in the report would face arrest.

CHAPTER 39

Burgeoning Bribes

"For any politician who didn't enter office a wealthy man, nothing says 'I take bribes' like a Rolex watch."
– Timothy Noah

In 2008, after Mti left the DCS to take up a position with Danny Jordaan as the National Head of Security for the 2010 FIFA World Cup Local Organising Committee, it became a free-for-all. With Mti's departure having created a void, Ishmael and Papa proposed to Gavin that other role players within the Correctional Services engine needed to be lubricated – and by that, they were referring to people in middle management. With Mti no longer there to decide who was awarded what, these guys were going to be integral in the final decision-making processes. Gavin continued paying Mti his monthly bribe money – firstly so that Mti didn't open his mouth, and secondly because the arrangement was that he would receive his monthly stipend for as long as Bosasa held the DCS contract.

Soon enough, bags containing between ten and twenty thousand rands were being dished out to the key players every month. Both middle and top management were on board, as were the guys at the bottom – and the unions had Gavin wrapped around their fingers. The total amount going out to Correctional Services staff in those years must have been in the region of R3-million a month. And the contracts continued to roll in.

Various directors would go to Gavin every month with a list of names and amounts. Some months, the amounts were higher than others – especially when I wasn't around to check up on them – and Gavin wasn't one to ask questions. Some directors would come into the office in the morning, saying things like: "I need my parcels," – referring to the R30 000 they would be handing over at their meeting later that day – and Gavin would pack it up and send them on their way. Or another director would stick his head in and say, "I need R15 000 for this and R10 000 for that."

Eventually, it became a daily occurrence, and I was battling to keep track of all the disbursements. Not only that, but the system was open to abuse, so I asked Gavin if I could keep some kind of record of these transactions. I suggested a little black book with codes instead of names, and he agreed, with the proviso that the books resided in the vaults and never left the Bosasa premises. The arrangement was that Gavin would decide who would receive what, I would prepare a series of codes to match the recipient to the payment, and Jacques van Zyl would pack the cash. The cash would only leave the building once I had verified the payments. The codes – for example, SST45AXACS – would indicate the ultimate recipient's name (SST = Simon Simelane Tule[52]), the amount of cash in thousands (45 = R45 000), and where the money was being dropped off (AXACS = Oliver Tambo Airport, on the international side). The final letters could also indicate who was handling the drop-off. For example, AA might refer to Angelo Agrizzi. Sometimes, instead of using a person's initials, I'd use a defining characteristic about the person. For example, the code GLS might refer to an official who wore glasses. I made sure that the codes were changed frequently so that it would be difficult for anyone to associate a code with a particular person. We must have had about eighty different individuals receiving monthly cash parcels from us, making the coding quite an intricate and tedious process.

Each month, while sitting down with the directors responsible for disbursing cash payments to the various government officials and writing down the names of each recipient, I often wondered if the cash was actually reaching its intended destination and how much was being pocketed. I once suggested to Gavin that the directors ask the recipients to sign for their payments so that we knew that the cash was reaching its intended recipients, but he burst out laughing.

"Angelo, how can you expect them to do that?" he scoffed. "That would be like admitting guilt."

"How are we going to prove it then?" I asked. Gavin shrugged his shoulders. "We have to work on trust."

While testifying at the Zondo Commission in 2019, I explained that between 2008 and 2016, Sesinyi Seopela handed out monthly cash bribes of half a million rands to a middleman at the DCS, who would then distribute the monies to various officials. When Tom Moyane was appointed as

---

52 This person's name is for illustrative purposes only and bears no reference to anyone who actually received a payment.

the new National Commissioner in 2010, the monthly amount jumped to R750 000.[53]

Seopela insisted on receiving a 2.5% commission on all new contracts he brought to the table, and I eventually began referring to him as the "2.5% man".

There was a total of eight vaults on the Bosasa premises. The two safes in the bid office were originally used to store firearms until Gavin converted them into drop safes. Gavin's vault in the Company Secretary's office was referred to as "The Oven" – the money would rise until there was enough to feed the hungry officials. With the millions being removed from the vaults, my little black book system came in handy as I knew it was only a matter of time before Gavin would get a bee in his bonnet and demand to know where the rest of the money had disappeared to. I began to reconcile the amounts daily. That way, I'd know exactly what was in each vault when I went in the following morning, provided nobody went in there afterwards. There were always two books in rotation, so the final figures usually only denoted half of what was in the vaults at any one time. Eventually, Andries van Tonder or Lindsay Watson did the initial reconciliations, and I performed a second round, before handing everything over to Gavin for safekeeping.

Between R4-million and R6-million moved out of Gavin's vault each month, but since I could only ever account for about R2.5-million of it, I could only assume that somebody was moving money off-site when nobody was around. Where to and for what purpose, only the people who moved the cash knew. Without fail, by the middle of the month, that safe was empty.

Money meant everything and nothing to Gavin. "My job is to spend it," he'd say – and he was often quite careless with it. He would leave money lying around in the open or forget that he'd left tens of thousands of rands in his briefcase after a trip out of town. The vaults were usually a mess after he'd been inside. I remember once deciding to tidy one of the vaults after walking in to find papers and plastic bags all over the floor. I picked up one of the large dustbin bags that was lying there and looked inside – in between the rubbish was about R70 000 in crisp one-hundred-rand denominations.

"It's bloody Monopoly money," he'd often joke while counting it out and zipping the bags closed. "Monopoly money" was a phrase he frequently bandied about. Money had no real value to Gavin unless it could be used to gain control over people so that deals could be secured, or contracts extended.

53 Tom Moyane has, to date, remained silent on these allegations.

CHAPTER 40

Who Got What, and How

"It used to be said 'Build it, and they will come', now it is 'Build it and bribe them in.'"
– Bangambiki Habyarimana, *Pearls of Eternity*

It is human nature to elevate one's standard of living according to the quality – and quantity – of one's incoming funds. Gavin had it all worked out – pay a man a once-off bribe, and he'll say thank you, do what he can to sway the powers that be, and move on. But pay that man a bribe every month, and he is beholden to you for life. Gavin used the power of money to play the role of master puppeteer, not only with the politicians and certain government officials but also with his devoted cult members back on his home turf.

While I believed that politicians should handle politics and that there was absolutely no need to offer a bribe in return for a contract, Gavin would brush off my concerns and remind me that this practice was not unique to South Africa and that "even the Americans are doing it". He was always blasé about it – "I'm helping you as a friend," he'd say, handing over a bulging envelope.

People knew that if they approached him for money, he would be the last person to turn them away. If there was a funeral, Gavin would be the first to assist. If there was a birthday, he'd arrange an elaborate spread. If a child needed a car, he clicked his fingers and transformed Cinderella's pumpkin into a Mercedes-Benz. Luxury items that Gavin purchased on his AMEX or Diner's Club cards – a R150 000 set of golf clubs, or a R20 000 Louis Vuitton handbag – were recorded in the company's accounts as "expenses".

"Write me a motivation," he'd say, and I'd type up a letter, stating that the item in question was a prize for a golf day or an awards ceremony

– knowing full well that it was a gift for an official or a politician who had paved the way for Bosasa to be moved to the top of the heap, or who had ensured that a tender was renewed for another three years. Nothing was too large or too small when the trade-off was lifelong dependence, in return for an endless supply of lucrative tenders.

And besides, he'd say, they weren't bribes – they were "deals". The modus operandi usually went along the lines of: "We've made a deal with this guy, so go and drop this package off for him." Or it would be a request to book a flight for a politician and his family, with hotel accommodation and car hire thrown in. We would simply follow instructions and do as Gavin asked – there was no point in questioning his motives because we already knew what they were. Increasingly, it felt like I was just a puppet on Gavin's ever-expanding tangle of strings. I have deep roots in Christianity. I knew it was wrong, and it shamed me deeply, but Gavin often used biblical scriptures to back up his decisions – and so I continued to do his bidding. Inside I was slowly rotting.

We were no different from the politicians he was bribing. The multi-million-rand contracts handed to us afforded us a lifestyle that was well beyond the reach of the average white-collar worker. And so I was torn. Walking away from all the deceit and deception would mean forsaking the incredible wealth that working for Gavin Watson afforded me – the Ferraris, the designer clothing, the international travel to exotic locations, and the bulging bank balances.

Gavin was always the final deciding factor when it came to who received what. If he felt a person was worth R100 000 a month, he'd pay him that, but if that person's value to him was only R10 000 a month, they wouldn't receive a cent more than that. If problems started brewing, Gavin would throw in a substantial increase, topping payments up by tens of thousands of rands at the drop of a hat. The more he increased a person's standard of living, the more they were indebted to him – and the more likely they were to keep their lips sealed. Patrick Gillingham started out at R40 000 a month, but when eyebrows were raised over irregularities in the renewal of the catering contract, Gavin doubled the amount. When Gillingham lost his job at Corrections, Gavin increased his monthly stipend to R110 000, even after Bosasa's contract was cancelled.

As I would later testify to the Zondo Commission, Dudu Myeni received R300 000 a month for the "Jacob Zuma Foundation", but she refused to have the money transferred by EFT – it had to be cash. Either Joe Gumede, Trevor Mathenjwa or Gavin Watson himself handed it over. There was never a formal letter requesting this donation or thanking Bosasa for it afterwards. I often wondered whether these cash payments were ever legitimately for the Foundation.[54]

 Scan here to watch Angelo Agrizzi implicate Dudu Myeni at the Zondo Commission on 28 January 2019.

I'll never forget one particular bribe-handover meeting that Gavin and I had with a senior DCS official. We were sitting opposite him at the Michelangelo Hotel, having breakfast. Gavin had the cash in his briefcase but had forgotten to bring along an envelope, so he decided to put the money inside a newspaper and pass it across the table. The guy opened the newspaper as it was handed over, and the money fluttered out, all over the floor. There must have been R100 000 scattered everywhere – some of it loose and some of it in packs. It was quite a sight, the three of us scrambling to pick it all up before anybody noticed.

Vincent Smith was a classic example of how – no matter how incorruptible a person might be – money and greed can skew any seemingly infallible moral compass.

Vincent, who always wore a leather jacket, held multiple roles, including that of Head of the Portfolio Committee on Finance for SCOPA[55] and Correctional Services. An upstanding, straight-down-the-line guy, Vincent was anti-Bosasa for many years, but I suspect Gavin knew that Vincent could be instrumental in neutralising any Bosasa-related negativity that might arise during Parliamentary Portfolio Committee meetings – if only he could get Vincent on his side.

Enter Sesinyi Seopela, who – as I explained during my testimony at the Zondo Commission – was instrumental in introducing Bosasa to ANC MP Vincent Smith via Cedric Frolick, a senior ANC MP.

Cedric Frolick served as National Assembly House Chairperson for Committees, Oversight and ICT – a position referred to as the "Chairman

---

54 Dudu Myeni has publicly denied all allegations of receiving bribes from Bosasa.
55 Standing Committee on Public Accounts

of Chairs" in Parliament – so Gavin decided to get his claws into Cedric first. He flew Cedric up to Johannesburg, together with ANC MP, Buti Komphela, whom Gavin felt had enough clout to convince other ANC politicians that Bosasa was a credible partner to work with. Gavin even arranged for a golf cart to be made available to transport Buti around Bosasa's office park since he was physically disabled and unable to do the four-hour walking tour of the facilities.

After a lengthy discussion in the boardroom, Gavin excused himself from the meeting and collected a security bag filled with cash from his vault. I watched Gavin open Cedric's jacket and drop it into an inner pocket. Cedric assured us that he was "100% on board" and would set up a meeting with Vincent Smith as soon as possible. My understanding – to which I testified at the Zondo Commission – was that Cedric would be receiving R40 000 a month for his efforts.[56]

Sure enough, I was instructed to accompany Gibson Njenje (Bosasa's Chairperson at the time) to meet with Vincent Smith in Cape Town the following week. We stayed in the same hotel used by parliamentary officials and drove through to Parliament the following morning, where we were greeted by Cedric Frolick. Cedric took us on a brief tour of the parliamentary offices, and then took us through to meet with Vincent Smith. Well, the introductory meeting didn't pan out quite as planned. Vincent was clearly not expecting us. He was abrupt and visibly irritated by our presence and told us he did not wish to meet with us. I left him with our company brochures, and Cedric whisked us out of the building. We boarded our flight that afternoon, our tails between our legs, with no idea how we were going to break the bad news to Gavin.

Imagine my surprise some months later when I walked into a meeting at a hotel on Rivonia Road, Johannesburg, to find Vincent Smith, Sesinyi Seopela, and Gavin sitting together, chatting up a storm as if they were lifelong friends. Caught up in the bribes – like many others of his former moral standing who were, at some point or another, anti-Bosasa – Vincent (as I later testified) went as far as accepting Gavin's offer to have Bosasa pay for his daughter's education at Aberystwyth University in Wales, over and above his R40 000 monthly stipend.[57]

Countless others received bags of money from Gavin every month, but I don't have documented proof of every transaction – especially when it came to the cash that was removed from Gavin's vault without being recorded in one of the little black books, or where I was merely witness to

56 Cedric Frolick has, to date, denied all accusations of receiving these monthly bribes.
57 Vincent Smith has publicly stated that, to his knowledge, the funds were privately loaned to him by me in my personal capacity, and not by Bosasa.

the handover. I suspect that certain ministers received R50 000 a month from Gavin, but I can't prove it. At the Zondo commission, I testified that Nomvula Mokonyane received R50 000 a month, although it wasn't documented.[58] I can prove two months' payments to Cedric Frolick, but I don't know if further payments followed.

 Scan here to watch Angelo Agrizzi testifying at the Zondo Commission that he packed R50 000 a month for Minister Nomvula Mokonyane.

58 Nomvula Mokonyane, in her testimony at the Zondo Commission in July 2020, denied all claims of receiving monthly bribe money from Bosasa.

CHAPTER 41

Defrauding the Government

"Don't steal – the government hates competition."
– Ron Paul

Gavin had no problem helping his connections defraud the government, especially when it could be disguised as something as intangible as software. A classic example – as I would later testify – was when a certain Syvion Dlamini, the Director of Bosasa's Mogale Youth Development Centres, was asked by a colleague from the ruling party in Rustenburg in the North West Province to help raise funds for electioneering. Since there was money to be made, Gavin was coming to the party. Bosasa invoiced the Department of Social Development for software upgrades for the youth centres at an over-inflated price of R5.2-million. The Department authorised the payment, the youth centres received their R5.2-million, the politicians in the North West were handed R1.8-million in cash to fund their election campaign, and Bosasa retained the balance as a "handling fee". Of course, the supposed upgrades never took place – there was no way of checking since the software was already "installed".

Defrauding the government – and the taxpayer – in this manner was a frequent occurrence, but only the most astute of auditors would have smelled a rat. Everything was reflected in Bosasa's accounts as an "expense", and the amounts were small when compared to the R88-million the youth centres were turning over at the time. The profit margins looked good, so there was no need for the Department to question their return on investment.

Another trick was to register a company (without a VAT number), raise an invoice to Bosasa for a fictitious product or service, and have Bosasa pay this invoice by means of a cash cheque. The fake invoices would go through Bosasa's accounts as "expenses" and were, therefore, tax-deductible. The modus operandi was to form a company, pay that company, and close it down. By the time these companies were liquidated (usually after about a year), nobody – not even SARS – was any the wiser.

It was this precise tactic that Gavin used to claim R92-million against my name for payments made to companies that Peet Venter set up and later liquidated – companies that both Andries van Tonder and I were members of. Gavin didn't want the black directors knowing that Andries and I were earning more than them, so he used these entities to remunerate us for the excessive hours we worked.

This process would, in 2019, be identified by Bosasa's liquidators as fraudulent – Gavin had no right to authorise moving funds into those entities.

Gavin used all possible ways and means to filter money out of the company while still claiming back tax on the transactions. Money was paid out to hundreds of different companies – some were legally registered businesses, but deliberate over-billing was involved, while others were entirely fictitious entities.

Money laundering was a popular pastime. One of Gavin's arrangements (when he needed to top up the vaults) was with a gentleman by the name of Riaan Hoeksema who owned a company in Randfontein called Riekele Construction. Riaan had a good relationship with a large wholesale liquor outlet up the road called Jumbo Liquor Wholesalers.

Millions of rands in cash would pass through their doors on any given day, but it was expensive to bank. So, what Jumbo would do is hand the weekend's takings – which were usually in the region of R4-million – over to Riaan Hoeksema, usually in batches of about R1.2-million at a time. Jumbo Liquor Wholesalers would invoice Bosasa for liquor and soft drinks to the same value. Riaan would drop the cash off at Bosasa, Jacques van Zyl would capture the R4.2-million invoice into their system, and the same amount would be electronically transferred to Jumbo Liquor Wholesalers. No stock ever changed hands – not even a drop of communion wine – and Riaan Hoeksema received between 5% and 7.5% commission for his efforts.

Scan here to watch video footage of cash being dropped off at Bosasa's offices.

After some time, these large purchases from Jumbo Liquor Wholesalers started raising eyebrows amongst Bosasa's accounting staff, so another enterprising scheme was thought up – this time involving chicken. This arrangement was with Greg Lacon-Allin's Equal Trade Foods, which was already supplying large quantities of frozen chicken to Bosasa's thirty-seven catering operations.

Once a week, Greg would text Andries and ask him how much "chicken" Bosasa needed for the week. As Andries van Tonder later testified at the Zondo Commission, a purchase order would then be drawn up and sent to Equal Trade Foods (with the pricing in line with the buying manual), the "chicken" would be delivered and deposited into Jacques van Zyl's office vault, Equal Trade's invoice would be captured, and payment would be electronically transferred. Equal Trade Foods took between 12% and 15% commission for these transactions, while saving substantially on the bank's hefty cash deposit fees. While an average of two hundred and ten tons of (actual) chicken was ordered every month, we paid an IT specialist R20 000 a month to manipulate the chicken stock levels in our system so that nothing appeared untoward.

Joe Gumede and I walked into the vault once to find what appeared to be notes in Jacques van Zyl's handwriting, stipulating who had requested cash payments, with corresponding dates. Joe had a sneaking suspicion that Jacques was keeping records to use as evidence. Gavin immediately took the task away from Jacques and said that all future cash deliveries would go into the Company Secretary's[59] vault to be reconciled, after which they would be transferred to the drop-safe inside his personal vault.

The same cash exchange method was used for a petrol station that F&R Phakisa owned in Belfast, Witbank. Bosasa would collect the cash paid by motorists for fuel, F&R Phakisa would invoice Bosasa for the "fuel", and Bosasa would pay the money back to them via EFT.

Another practice involved writing out a cash cheque (in the region of R700 000) and cashing it at the bank, under the guise of paying construction workers who were working as casual labour. While there was building work going on, there were only ever about ten labourers being paid. The other ninety were ghost workers. (We stopped this practice at the end of 2003 when the Unemployment Insurance Fund changed their rules and insisted that UIF contributions were required on casual labour.)

Because the value of the bribes would increase over the Christmas period, cash would be drawn, disguised either as purchases from non-VAT BEE suppliers or as additional expenses for casual labourers working over public holidays.

---

59 Natasha Olivier

Before the mining contracts were sold to Equal Trade Foods, we used to take in hundreds of thousands of rands in cash from the canteens at the various mining hostels and Lindela. This cash was offset as payments for groceries, with only 10% to 15% of the sales declared as revenue.

One particular practice, which really does not sit well with me to this day, involved fraudulent activities around death claims. At one stage, we must have employed in the region of six thousand people, but at the same time, people were losing family members at a staggering rate and would continuously approach the company for financial assistance to cover funerals and other costs. I decided to approach Metropolitan Life to provide each staff member with a Death Benefit Fund that would cover up to R20 000 in funeral costs if the main member passed away, and about half of that if the deceased was a child or a parent. This was all completely above board, and the employees were grateful for the company's generosity. The untoward practice, as I later testified at the Zondo Commission, took shape after employees started claiming from the fund. Basically, Metropolitan Life wouldn't pay out a cent without an official death certificate – and death certificates were always notoriously delayed – so we would advance the employee the full amount so that they could bury their loved ones while waiting to recover the monies from Metropolitan Life.

While the employee was always under the impression that the payment was from Metropolitan, these advances were offset in the company's records as cash donations to these families and claimed as an expense. When Metropolitan eventually paid out, instead of returning the money to the employee, Bosasa drew the cash and retained it as a means of generating cash for bribes. Sometimes these amounts were as high as R300 000 a month.

Do the maths, and the millions in annual tax evasion are glaringly obvious.

Scan here to watch Angelo Agrizzi at the Zondo Commission explaining how death benefits were abused at Bosasa.

CHAPTER 42

The Ten Ton Tender

"You get the best effort from others not by lighting a fire beneath them, but by building a fire within."
– Bob Nelson

Nosiviwe Mapisa-Nqakula was wary of us. Not wanting to be compromised over her connection with the Watsons, she never directly gave Bosasa any business. When she was appointed Minister of Correctional Services in 2009, prisons across the country were running at over 220% occupancy, and prisoners were being forced to sleep in shifts. The overcrowding created a significant amount of tension which often spilt over into large-scale gang wars – all for power and an extra piece of the bed.

The only solution was for the DCS to put out a tender to reduce the massive overcrowding across the country by developing a new best-of-breed prison system that would meet every standard set. It was, by far, the largest PPP[60] tender ever contemplated by the South African government – and Bosasa wanted in.

Bringing the right team of people together to design, build and operate five new prisons from scratch would be no mean feat, and coordinating a bid of this size would take some serious doing. We estimated that the bidding process would take two to three years to complete, with the budgeted cost to prepare, compile and deliver the bid sitting at an estimated R48-million. It eventually came out at R60-million, with the construction of each prison being worth an estimated R1.8-billion.

We assembled a construction team that included the industry's crème de la crème – Group 5, WBHO, Rainbow Construction and Motheo

---

60 Public-private partnership – where public companies enter into a consortium to provide long-term funding to government. In this particular PPP, the contract was for twenty years.

Construction. The team of specialised architects and designers worked under the supervision of the operational teams of Bosasa Operations, and a US-based company that we joint ventured with called MTC (Management and Training Corporation). The legal and finance team was comprised of fifteen attorneys, two actuaries and four Chartered Accountants. We needed black representation too, so I brought in Ishmael Dikane because he was operationally minded.

We named the consortium Umtya Nethunga, which, translated from Tswana, means "strongly bound partners". It was amazing how the team gelled together. I chaired all the meetings over that two-year period. The teams would meet at 9 a.m. and often only finish up at 11 p.m. We did everything, from the design of the locks to the grade of the cement, right through to how the prison management team would be structured. We designed the sports fields and brought in specialists to help us plan the sewerage plants. The inter-connected toilets were designed with a hand-washing basin positioned over each toilet so that they could self-clean, and chemicals could be run through the entire system with one flush.

We were a formidable group, and, despite the fact that we were competing against other industry giants like G4S Solutions and multinationals like Sodexo, I was certain that we were leading the race to win the bid.

When the bid was complete, it weighed in at ten tons. Before we could deliver it, we had to make arrangements to perform a weight-load test on the seventeenth floor of the building to which the bid was being delivered. We had to obtain an engineer's report stating that the elevators could take the weight of the seven hundred lever arch files in their carefully prepared cages, together with large-scale models of what the prisons would look like. We even included mannequins dressed in prison uniforms. It was the largest and most impressive bid ever put together for DCS. We had to block off Church Street in Pretoria to accommodate the five-ton and seven-ton trucks that we hired to offload it. DCS was impressed, and justifiably so.

While our consortium was one of three short-listed companies, by the time the DCS reached the second phase of their adjudication, they announced that they were changing the terms and conditions of the PPP. Nosiviwe had called for a fundamental change to the Department's operational standards, insisting that the Department manage the staff and detainees at all times, instead of the appointed contractors. This was not well-received by the other two bidders, and the radios crackled into the early hours of the morning as various arguments were passed on and questions raised. One such question was around holding offenders (and the DCS) liable if the prisoners initiated a strike and broke (for instance) a glass countertop. I sensed that the Department was testing to see which companies would be prepared to compromise, and, if so, where they would be prepared to cut back.

After drafting a letter to Minister Nqakula confirming Umtya Nethunga's commitment to adhering to government's changes, we eventually got word that the other two companies were not prepared to comply. This effectively left the Department with only one fully compliant bidder, of which Bosasa was a part. Shortly thereafter, we received a cancellation notice on the tender. There was no explanation or justification. A twenty-year contract with returns of about R60-million per annum, two years in the making, with R60-million down the drain – what a waste.

I started with my enquiries, determined to find out why the tender had been cancelled, but a source quickly called me to stop me in my tracks. "Don't go there, Angelo," he warned me. "You were fully compliant, but you were also the only bidder remaining. Can you imagine the field day the opposition and the media would have had if Umtya Nethunga was awarded the contract?"

And so the lights went on. Minister Nosiviwe Mapisa-Nqakula had withdrawn the tender because she was afraid of being compromised if she awarded it to a Bosasa-linked consortium. In retrospect, I respect the Minister for her foresight. We had no recourse, and the consortium was shut down.

Political associations in business often create more havoc than they are worth.

PART 7

CHAPTER 43

The SIU Report

"An unbelieved truth can hurt a man much more than a lie. It takes great courage to back truth unacceptable to our times. There's a punishment for it, and it's usually crucifixion."
– John Steinbeck, *East of Eden*

Things simmered along on the back-burner between 2007 and 2008, while we waited for the SIU's report to rear its head. Through Bosasa's network of contacts, we were assured that the investigation could be controlled. We were constantly updated with information that Person A would be liaising with Person Y, or that Person C would be meeting with Gavin at an undisclosed location to update him on matters. It was all cloak-and-dagger. The fact that Bosasa always seemed to be one step ahead of the investigation must have frustrated the SIU to no end.

In 2009, Gavin got wind from one of his contacts in government that the report was resurfacing and, on the spur of the moment, he insisted that the three of us – him, Andries, and me – take a trip to France and Italy to strategise and plan the business's way forward. He instructed Debbie to book the holiday. He wanted no expense spared. He told me to draw R300 000 worth of forex in Euros and US Dollars, and to top all the company credit cards up with R200 000 each. He told Tony Perry to monitor the cards daily and to pump more money into them if funds ran low. In the end, the trip must have cost the company in the region of R1.5-million.

When we arrived in Rome, Gavin took us on a lavish shopping spree. I remember walking into a boutique and buying twenty-five shirts – and they weren't cheap either at between €250 and €550 each. On another spree, we purchased eleven pairs of expensive Italian shoes between the three of us – two pairs each for Andries and me, and seven pairs for Gavin.

Gavin booked us into one of the top hotels in Rome. I noticed when checking in that Debbie had booked Gavin on the eighth floor, where an A-list Hollywood actress just happened to be staying.

"Look," I whispered, pointing to the register, "guess whose room is right next door to yours?" Gavin was like a little kid. "No way!" he squealed.

"Just be careful," the concierge warned, handing him his access card, "Nobody is allowed on the eighth floor without special permission."

The following afternoon, while on our way to grab a cup of coffee, who happened to be walking down the passage but the very pretty actress, her small kids, her mother, and their bodyguard.

"Look, guys!" exclaimed Gavin. "It's Pretty Woman." It was embarrassing.

"Shhh," I said, turning to Gavin, "Don't speak so loudly – you're going to look like you come from Randfontein."

Eventually, our paths crossed with the actress and Gavin immediately walked over as if to greet her. Andries and I were quietly cringing in the background. Gavin was immediately on the phone to tell everyone back home that not only had he just met this top-notch actress but that she was sleeping in the room next door to him.

Returning from our coffees, Gavin noticed that she had placed her room service tray and her shoes outside her room to be cleaned. He bent down and picked up her shoes to check the brand – they were Ferragamos – and he then went through her tray to see what she had eaten. He also discovered what time she went down for breakfast, so he asked us to meet him in the dining area the following morning at 7 a.m. sharp for an early breakfast.

Unfortunately, the actress wouldn't allow anyone near her, but Gavin made sure that when she walked up to the buffet, he was directly behind her. I remember him lambasting us for not taking pictures.

Gavin arranged for a sought-after tour guide to take us around and show us the sights, but it was clear that he was uneasy about something, that something was brewing. He was suddenly obsessed with getting his hands on South African news articles and subscribing to different news channels. While he usually spoke freely on his phone in front of us, now he walked away when his phone rang.

We then flew to Paris and checked into another top-class hotel, near the Arc de Triomphe, complete with a Michelin-starred restaurant – it was the whole works, and then some.

The following morning, while in the taxi on our way to the Louvre with our tour guide, I received a call from our attorney, Brian Biebuyck, to inform me that he had a copy of the SIU report. Not wanting to put a damper on the holiday, I decided not to mention anything to Gavin or Andries.

Instead, I asked Brian to email the report to me. Within a few minutes, the report had come through. The more I scrolled, the more shocked I was at what I was reading.

"Gavin," I said, "I've got the SIU report here on my phone." He was visibly shocked – not about the report coming out (I suspect that, behind the scenes, he was fully aware that its release was imminent) – but that I had a copy of it.

I read through the document quickly, but there were things that made no sense. It was as if someone had drawn back a curtain to expose a myriad of events of which I had, up to that point, been completely unaware. "Gavin, they've listed all the flights that you told me to book for Mti and Gillingham," I said.

I continued reading. "And hang on," I said, shocked, "I didn't know you built them houses and bought them cars? It says here that Mark Taverner furnished the places. And that Waldo Nagel did the interior decorating? They even specify someone called Zietsman as the architect, and Riaan Hoeksma as the building contractor."

"No," said Gavin. "It can't be. I said it was to be done via Danny and Jarred Mansell."

"Evidently not," I replied. "A few people are implicated – some of them I've never even heard of – but it looks like the SIU has done a thorough investigation." A nasty bout of car sickness began to set in, forcing me to stop reading.

Patrick Gillingham's name, along with that of Linda Mti, Danny Mansell, Carlos Bonifacio, Andries van Tonder, Frans Vorster, and mine, all appeared on the SIU's draft 2010 charge sheet. Gavin's name didn't feature at all because he never signed anything off – that's what he paid the rest of us puppets to do.

Danny Mansell was to be charged with colluding with Gillingham and writing the tender specs. I was charged with being the conduit for Mti's flight and accommodation bookings. Carlos, Andries, Frans and I were being charged with the R180 000 bonus money I received via Andries van Tonder that I transferred to Carlos Bonifacio so that he could pay Frans Vorster to buy a Mercedes-Benz for Gillingham's daughter – all on Gavin's instruction, but with Gavin's instructions nowhere to be found. Mti was accused of contravening the Public Finance Management Act (PFMA) for failing to follow the correct procurement processes in his dealings with Bosasa in terms of the billions of rands' worth of tenders that he had a hand in awarding us over the duration of our fifteen-year relationship.

"Turn the taxi around," I told the driver. "Take us back to the hotel, now." I arranged to get the thing printed. It must have been about one hundred pages. We sat in Gavin's room, going through the report, page by page.

I turned over one of the pages and there it was, in black and white – Angelo Agrizzi, CEO. I could feel the blood draining from my body. "But Gavin," I said. "You know that's not true. I'm a damn operations person, nothing less and nothing more. Why would they list me as the CEO and not you?"

"Don't worry about that," Gavin said, brushing me off. "Just leave it. I have it under control." And then it dawned on me that I was the only person they had been dealing with. Whenever the SIU had questions, they would be directed to me.

We continued going through the report. Golf clubs purchased. University fees paid for. Sound systems. Curtains. A whole lot of furniture from Wetherleys. The list went on and on. "Gavin," I said, "when were you planning on telling us about all of this?"

"They've got it all wrong," Gavin protested.

"Gavin, how do you expect us to work together when you keep secrets from us?" I asked.

Eventually, Gavin agreed that what had happened was wrong. "We can't let this report get out," he said.

"But Gavin," I said, waving the document around, "the report is out! The story's out. What are we going to do?"

"Well," said Gavin, "we've just got to find a way around it. From now on, we stick together, and we work together. We have to make a pact. Angelo, you handle the attorneys. Andries, you handle the finances. I'll handle the politics."

Before we could get a word in edgeways, he added – "I will make a plan, so don't worry. When I get back, I'm going to sit with Peet Venter and Doc Smith and structure something so that you guys will be taken care of. Don't allow what has happened to destroy what God has put us together for."

He immediately got on the phone to Brian Biebuyck to set up a meeting. This was war.

While I knew there were bribes and I was aware of the corruption, I had no idea – until that moment – of the extent to which Danny Mansell had gone in terms of building Gillingham and Mti's houses, or that Gavin had involved his sister and his brother-in-law in the furnishing and decoration of the houses.

⚜

We arranged to fly back to South Africa the following day. That evening, looking for something to ease the stress, we decided to go for a two-and-a-half-hour massage at the Health Centre downstairs. We donned our white hotel-room gowns and tiny slippers and took the elevator down to the basement. My gown was a size medium, and I could barely get it to close. Fortunately, I had my boxer shorts on underneath.

When we reached what we thought was the basement, the elevator doors opened onto a large audience listening to someone playing a Baby Grand piano. Everybody turned to look at us, standing there like idiots in the elevator. Three Dutchmen from Randfontein (dressed only in white gowns) and a Baby Grand – what a pitiful sight. I frantically tried to close the door, but nothing was happening. And then it dawned on me – I had to use my card. Suddenly the doors closed, and we were whisked back up to the ground floor.

After that, nothing really mattered.

On the flight back to South Africa, it dawned on me that Gavin knew full well that the report was coming out and that he was privy to its contents. He thought he could win our confidence by taking us on a fancy holiday overseas, and he did, to some extent. But nothing could have prepared me for what that damning report unveiled – and the fact that I was the apparent kingpin behind it all.

When we arrived back home, Willie Hofmeyr – Deputy National Director of Public Prosecutions – was discussing the SIU report in parliament. While he did not mention the name of the company implicated, it wasn't difficult for anyone in the know to connect the dots. Gavin frantically called Brian Biebuyck to ask him to launch an application stopping the report from being discussed.

Not long afterwards, I arrived at work at 5 a.m. one Monday morning to find Danny Mansell pacing up and down outside my office. He looked terrible. I could see he hadn't slept. "I've been set up by Gavin," he said. "He's done it again – he has used and abused me. I'm not going to shut up this time. I'm going to the SIU to clear my name and apply for amnesty before the whole world finds out about this."

Danny was right. Gavin had distanced himself by making Danny set up and register different companies (in Danny's name) through which the monthly payments to Gillingham and Mti would be made. One such company was Grande Four Trust, which was also the vehicle through which Gillingham and Mti's houses were purchased, renovated and decorated. It was also used to buy Mti and the Gillinghams their upmarket cars.

Danny told me that Gavin wasn't taking his calls. He honestly believed he was going to be Gavin's fall guy because it was his name on the charge sheet and not Gavin's.

I tried Gavin's mobile phone. He answered. "Gavin," I said, "you had better get over here now. I've got Danny with me. He's threatening to go to the SIU and tell them everything."

Gavin drove through to the offices immediately. "Danny," he said, "relax. You're not going to apply for amnesty. We're going to get you out of this mess, out of the crap, and out of the country. I will arrange that you're paid an incentive for the rest of your life.

"Angelo," Gavin said, turning to me, "do whatever Danny wants. Make sure we pay for everything – just clear it with me first." Right there and then, Gavin decided that was how we would solve Danny's problem. He called Andries van Tonder to arrange that he escort Danny out of the country with his family. Andries would fly with Danny to his new home in Wichita, Texas under the premise that they were going to visit a shrimp manufacturing company over there.

In the space of about three weeks, flights were booked and paid for. Gavin told me to book return flights but to cancel them once they were on the plane "so that they don't come back". Danny's furniture was put into storage at Bosasa's offices. The Mansells told their friends and family that they were emigrating to set up a new business for Sondolo IT. Shares were either sold or transferred, and some of the businesses and other operations under his name were shut down.

The Mansells set up a company in Texas called Safe as Fences, registered it in Danny's name, and Bosasa paid that company $7,000 a month for Danny's upkeep. Gavin asked me to sign off Danny's application for a Green Card and residency in America under the authority of Bosasa Operations, stating that we were sponsoring this new business that he was starting up over there.

The family left first, followed later by Danny and Andries van Tonder.

A few weeks later, our nemesis Adriaan Basson published several new articles about Bosasa in the *Mail & Guardian* after getting his hands on a series of leaked documents from Blakes Travel, which showed that Bosasa's VIP account was funding the travel benefits of various politicians and officials, including one particular official implicated in the SIU report – Linda Mti.

Bosasa spent anything between R1.7-million and R2.2-million a month with Blakes Travel. Gavin wanted us to get rid of all the evidence as quickly as possible. He told Andries van Tonder and me to meet with Brian Blake at the Blakes Travel offices the following Saturday, collect invoice books and the computers where the booking information relating to Bosasa was stored, and destroy the lot. Gavin promised Brian that Bosasa would compensate him for the computers – which I believe he did.

We were busy revamping the Luipaardsvlei Hostel at the time, so it was the perfect spot to bury the incriminating evidence. Once Brian Blake had handed everything over to us, we headed out to the Luipaardsvlei construction site. We met with the groundsman and asked him to bring us some petrol. We found a large hole, dumped the computers and the invoice books into it, poured petrol over everything, and set it alight. We then asked one of the construction workers to fill the hole using a front-end loader. Problem solved.

Back at the office, we created a fictitious account with Blakes Travel called JJ Venter through which all future VIP travel orders would be placed. After that, things went quiet again, until Gavin received word in 2010 that the SIU report was being promulgated.[61]

At the time, I was entertaining Bosasa's international partners from the USA at Tuningi in the Madikwe Game Reserve on the South Africa/Botswana border. The two ladies were visiting us to better understand our operations. Having spent a considerable amount of time comparing notes on the different standards in place at correctional detention facilities all over the world, they asked me if I could take them out on a safari before they left for the USA the following week.

I had only been to Tuningi once before, and I had travelled in a 4X4. This time, I decided we would be going in my brand-new Audi A6. Now, my guests were not the smallest of ladies – they had plenty of luggage, and it was a low-profile vehicle, but we loaded everything into the car and set off, stopping at all the boring tourist traps along the way.

At around 6 p.m., we arrived at the Abjaterskop gate, just before the Botswana border. It was misty and dark, so we quickly paid our fee, and the guard radioed through to Tuningi to let them know we were on our way. As we drove off the main road, the terrain became somewhat rocky. Worried about the car, I drove a bit, stopped the car, got out, moved the rocks out of the way, got back in, drove a bit further, stopped the car, and moved the rocks. I must have done this for about five kilometres. It was exhausting. When we were about two hundred metres from the lodge, I looked up while moving another boulder to find a large bull elephant staring at

---

61 Papa Leshabane, in the meantime, publicly disputed the SIU's explosive findings, claiming that they were merely "speculative".

me. I quickly got back into the car, trying to be as brave and nonchalant as possible with my American guests.

When we woke up the following morning, we had no cell phone signal, but I was not particularly bothered. At about 11 a.m., when the signal returned, I received numerous missed call alerts and frantic messages from Gavin, asking where I was. I called him immediately and reminded him that I'd taken our guests to Tuningi.

"Angelo!" he shouted down the phone, "I need you to get back here now!"

"What's wrong?" I asked, confused.

"I can't talk now," he said, "the phone is hot.[62] Just get back here." Gavin often suspected that our phones were bugged, so I had no idea whether there was any truth to what he was saying.

I told my guests a long story about there being a crisis at Lindela that I had to attend to. I promised them that I would arrange to have a car or an aeroplane available to bring them back to Johannesburg when the week-end was over. It was extremely embarrassing, but it was all I could do.

Arriving back at the office that afternoon, I found Gavin with Andries. Neither looked well. "What the hell is going on?" I asked.

"Seopela tipped me off that the SIU is coming to raid us on Monday," Gavin said, his face white. He explained that they had already raided Gillingham's house, where they found a Consilium Business Consultants business card with Gillingham's name on it, and quite a bit of cash in his safe. With Consilium being Doc Smith's company, and Doc Smith being a Bosasa employee, it didn't take much for them to connect the dots. Gillingham was still employed by the DCS at the time, so they were planning to get him on a charge of moonlighting for a key supplier.

"I want you to go through the office and clear it out," Gavin said. "Go through everybody's desks and drawers."

"What exactly are we looking for?" I asked.

"The agreement between me, Tony Perry and Mti, and anything to do with Phezulu Fencing. And then I want you to destroy the whole lot."

"Gavin," I said, "you can't just destroy stuff – what if you need it in the future?"

"Okay," he sighed. "Then just get it off-site."

The three of us worked through the night, going through people's drawers and cupboards. We cleared the vault and found quite a lot of stuff in there, including Gavin's antenuptial contract. Once we had everything, we bundled it into the boot of my car and headed out to Mooinooi, an hour and a half away.

---

62 Bugged

That Monday morning, we got hold of Brian Biebuyck and asked him to once again draft a letter to the SIU, tendering our full cooperation. They agreed and (once again) asked to meet with us.

Gavin (unsurprisingly) reneged on attending the scheduled meeting, leaving Leon van Tonder, Max Leeson, Brian Biebuyck, Andries van Tonder, Advocate Laurance Hodes and me to meet with the investigators and remind them that we were willing to cooperate and provide them with any information they might need. They set a date to send a team of people in to mirror our servers, and we, in turn, applied for a postponement to give us enough time to remove any damning evidence.

Gavin was extremely nervous about the documents and contracts that were in the safe at the farm, so he sent us back there to look for the contract he had signed with Mti. Unbeknown to us at the time, this document, if discovered, would have directly implicated him as the mastermind behind the capture of Mti. When we eventually found the contract, we drove back to Johannesburg and handed it to him. He was visibly relieved – almost as if a millstone had been removed from around his neck. He immediately shredded it into tiny pieces, placed everything inside a large Ziploc bag, filled it with water, turned it into paper mache, and flushed it down the toilet.

To this day, I want to kick myself for not having made a copy of it before he pulped it.

CHAPTER 44

Schmoozing the Banks

"I sincerely believe that banking establishments are more dangerous than standing armies, and that the principle of spending money to be paid by posterity, under the name of funding, is but swindling futurity on a large scale."
– Thomas Jefferson

For many years, Bosasa was a force to be reckoned with, and the banks loved us. But with Adriaan Basson's escalating media exposés on the company, eventually the banks started frowning upon us. Gavin thought he had a good relationship with the company's bankers because Paul Harris (the-then CEO of RMB/FNB) used to frequent Bosasa's offices, but after the barrage of newspaper articles, followed by the damning revelations contained within the SIU report, everything changed.

Because Gavin avoided confrontation like the plague, he made it Andries van Tonder and my responsibility to attend the dreaded bank meetings. I would have sleepless nights before walking into the bank's offices. It was a standing joke between Andries and me that when the top echelons of FNB[63] offered us chairs and invited us to sit down with them, we'd say, "We're comfortable on our knees, thank you" – just to break the ice. It was an endless battle to convince them that what the media was portraying was false. But we all knew that it wasn't.

The banks weren't interested in any of our media conspiracy stories. What they *were* interested in was: Was there due diligence? Were the company's financial statements in order? Was there growth in the company? Would its loans be repaid? Was the company clean?

The thing is, we were paying R8-million a year in bank fees and interest,

---

63 First National Bank

and our facilities were running at between R40-million and R60-million a year, so it was probably in the banks' interest to keep us as a client – until such time as we were proven guilty, that is.

It was no different from what happened at SARS. Despite the fact that they audited us year upon year, they never picked anything up. People like George Papadakis, the SARS-contracted forensic auditor who Gavin "persuaded" with a few truck-loads of cement, made most of our problems disappear.[64]

But as time went on, and the more tainted the Bosasa name became, it grew increasingly difficult to secure new lucrative contracts. Gavin would spend millions of rands on trips, conferences and motivational sessions, but the pond of opportunity quickly dried up the minute a person felt compromised. The bribe, when offered upfront, would naturally put the receiver in a difficult position. If they accepted R10 000 in cash, and then openly awarded the contract to Bosasa – what then? Ten years earlier, a bribe could fly under the radar undetected, but as time went on, a procurement officer pushing for a certain service provider – particularly when that service provider was associated with bribery and corruption – could quickly find themselves out of a job.

But, that said, those who were accustomed to receiving bribes did not suddenly start putting their hands behind their backs. When the DCS catering contract came up for renewal in 2011 – and despite pushback from good people like Vernie Petersen, who took over from Linda Mti in 2007 and died in February 2011 – a R5-million bribe ensured that the contract was extended in Bosasa's favour. All that was required was a few external consultants (who had contacts within the DCS) to pull a few strings.

It was only a matter of time before somebody was going to be arrested – it's the natural (and eventual) course of events when a company uses fronting and bribery to secure lucrative business deals, and somebody smells a rat. Arrests would be followed by the seizing of assets and the freezing of bank accounts and, without access to funds to fight any applications against us, we found ourselves in a serious quandary.

---

64 Had I not told SARS where to look, they would have been none the wiser. When SARS began their investigations into Bosasa in 2020 and reported on George Papadakis and Kevin Wakeford's indiscretions, the hounds of Hell were released within the organisation.

CHAPTER 45

Gavin Visits Nkandla

"Rather than justice for all, we are evolving into a system of justice for those who can afford it."
– Joseph E. Stiglitz

It's a well-known fact that Gavin Watson was a close friend of then-President Jacob Zuma, and had visited Nkandla, Zuma's official residence in KwaZulu-Natal.[65] I remember him returning from his first visit in 2009 visibly shocked, not only at the mess the place was in with all the construction going on, but that R250-million had been paid for the work to be done. "The toilets looked like they came from Builders Warehouse," he said condescendingly.

Around the same time, the Hawks' investigation into Bosasa's dealings with government – and Linda Mti in particular – continued to gnaw at Gavin's heels. Patrick Gillingham was also becoming increasingly anxious about the probe – it was only a matter of time before the death knell rang out.

As I would later testify at the Zondo Commission, in a 2010 meeting, Mti recommended that we (Gavin and I) "sort out" three key figures at the NPA: Jackie Lepinka, Nomgcobo Jiba (Deputy National Director of Public Prosecutions), and Lawrence Mrwebi (Special Director of Public Prosecutions). It was agreed that Jiba (code-named "Snake" because she was always on the offensive and poised to strike) would receive R100 000 a month, Lepinka (code-named "Jay") would receive R20 000, and Mrwebi (code-named "Snail") would receive R10 000.

Mti had a code name for everyone. Gavin's code name was *Silver Fox* because of his hair. Andries's code name was *Bald Eagle* because of his lack of hair. My code name was *The Stallion* (because I'm Italian). Patrick

---

65 Jacob Zuma also visited Bosasa's offices.

Gillingham's code name was *Bison* because of his initials (PG = PG Bison). As I indicated in my testimony before the Zondo Commission, Gavin would pack R395 000 in cash into a large haversack with the various monthly payments, and I would make sure that they were delivered to Mti. There was R65 000 for Mti, the three amounts for Jay, Snake and Snail, and two other payments – R100 000 for the Acting Commissioner of Correctional Services, Nontsikelelo Jolingana (codenamed *Middledrift* because she came from that part of the Eastern Cape), and R100 000 for Free State Area Commissioner, Grace Molatedi (codenamed *Groenpunt*, because that was where she worked).

With all parties in agreement, Mti ensured that the monthly amounts were disbursed to the various parties. In return, Snake, Snail and Jay ensured that highly confidential NPA working files on the Bosasa case – including verbal and written documents, minutes of meetings, names of witnesses and people who would be testifying, as well as bank accounts and financial documents that were being investigated – made their way back to Gavin. A document from Glynnis Breytenbach, who at the time was Senior Deputy Director of Public Prosecutions and the head of the Pretoria Regional Office of the Specialised Commercial Crime Unit (SCCU) of the National Prosecuting Authority (NPA), read:

"An issue that needs to be addressed on an urgent basis is the position of Mr Mti who is one of the main suspects and who currently holds the position of Head of Security 2010 World Cup, and the impact that this investigation, once it gains momentum and attracts the attention of the media, might have. Some guidance in this regard would be greatly appreciated."

In a letter dated the 17th of November 2010 from Advocate Marijke De Kock, addressed to the then-National Director of Public Prosecutions, Menzi Simelane, the "limitations" of the SIU report were raised, and read as follows:

"The SIU report makes it clear that their investigation suffered from certain limitations ... It would appear as if the SIU relied on information that was submitted to them without questioning the veracity of the facts that were conveyed to them ... The SIU report would appear to have been drafted in a careless and almost casual fashion. The lack of accuracy and precision with the drafting of the report will give ample opportunity to those seeking to fault it. The SIU has placed themselves and the SAPS investigators in a dilemma by casting doubt upon the reliability of their own report. We will need to establish the veracity of the facts and at least try and ground the conclusions reached by the SIU. We must know what information is reliable and what is not. The "verification process" will take some time ... The admission of the "limitations" experienced by the SIU investigators may not be enough to hide the fact that the report was released at a premature point during the investigation."

This was an example of the extent to which we, at all times, had access to the Bosasa investigation, making it easier to plot every move to make it go away.

Over the course of the next eighteen months, Gavin and I met with Mti regularly to review the various documents supplied to us and plan our next steps. I would later supply the full list of documents to the Zondo Commission.

In November 2012, Mti invited Gavin and me to his home and showed us an email – which appeared to have originated from Jackie Lepinka and which was sent to Silas Ramaite (Deputy National Director of Public Prosecutions) and Lawrence Mrwebi – stating that Nomgcobo Jiba was requesting status reports on various other cases, including that of Bosasa. Mti explained to us that there were four other cases that the NPA was planning on shutting down at the same time as Bosasa's case, so as not to raise any unnecessary suspicion. A section of the email read as follows:

"In terms of the Bosasa case, please be advised that this matter needs to be finalised ASAP as the matter has been investigated for many years and from the submitted reports it is clear, says Ms Lepinka, that there is no evidence and/or prospect of a successful prosecution ... The ANDPP[67] has indicated further that no resource will be allocated to any case for longer duration. You are therefore requested to ensure that Prosecutors focus on cases where there is sufficient evidence as this is fruitless and wasteful expenditure."

A letter dated April 2013 from Advocate Marijke De Kock from the Serious Commercial Crimes Unit, addressed to Advocate M Mokgatle, Acting Regional Head SCCU, stated that Patrick Gillingham was going to be charged with corruption, money laundering and fraud and that a draft charge sheet was being prepared to replace the draft 2010 charge sheet prepared by the SIU. The same letter stated that Danny Mansell and Riaan Hoeksma had been clearly identified as being linked to criminal behaviour and that Angelo Agrizzi (myself), Carlos Bonifacio, Andries van Tonder and Frans Vorster were also being investigated for their corrupt relationship with Patrick Gillingham. Upon considering this letter, Menzi Simelane stated that the SIU had been shoddy in attending to the case and that pursuing the matter in court might be detrimental to the State.

We were handed a copy of the NPA's 2013 draft charge sheet, and I noticed that the one glaring difference between the SIU's 2010 charge sheet and the NPA's 2013 charge sheet was that, this time, Gavin Watson's name appeared loud and clear. Joe Gumede's name also appeared. Miraculously, the 2013 charge sheet omitted the charges against Riaan Hoeksma (Riekele Construction) for the houses they built and furnished – via Mark and Sharon Taverner – for Patrick Gillingham and Linda Mti.

Snake and Jay then approached Mti and told him to pass a message on to us that we should instruct our attorneys to submit a letter to the NPA (addressed to Jiba), challenging the legality of the SIU report, with a particular focus on the manner in which evidence was obtained. We were to sign the letter off, requesting that the case be closed down and not prosecuted. Some of the points, as suggested by Snake and Jay, were that the report should have gone to the President before being made public, which was not the case, because SIU head, Willie Hofmeyr, skipped this step; that the evidence was "fruit of the poisonous tree" – meaning that it was not obtained within the prescript of the law; that the fundamental rights of Bosasa and its employees had been encroached upon in the process of the investigation; that a significant period of time had lapsed since the initial investigation; and, finally, there was reference to the ongoing persecution and harassment of Bosasa personnel.[66]

Brian Biebuyck drafted the letter, which I took back to Mti, and which was then vetted by Snake. Snake then returned the letter to Mti with a list of additional notes that she felt should be added, including the fact that, in terms of the criminal case, there was no complainant's statement from Acting Commissioner Jenny Schreiner; the impact of the investigation on the families of implicated Bosasa personnel; the amount of business that Bosasa was losing as a result of the allegations, and our view that the issue was being politicised.

Then, on the 8th of May 2015, just as we thought we were getting somewhere, Nomgcobo Jiba was accused of fraud and perjury and subsequently suspended.

---

66 Both Nomgcobo Jiba and Lawrence Mrwebi have publicly denied ever receiving bribe money from Bosasa.

Scan here to watch Angelo Agrizzi implicate Nomgcobo Jiba, Lawrence Mrwebi and Jackie Lepinka at the Zondo Commission.

Mti called a meeting at his house to brief us.

"That's it," said Gavin. "We are going to Nkandla next week. We will tell the President what to do and how to sort this out because this is getting a bit too much."

Gavin knew that if there was one person who could make the NPA and their threats to act on the SIU report go away, it was his friend, the President, who consistently did what Gavin told him to do. Gavin planned to set up a meeting at Nkandla, to request that Zuma call for a *nolle prosequi*[67] on the report and close the investigation down entirely.

I had a feeling that one day I might need some evidence and so decided to take a chance and record the conversation from the safety of my shirt's top pocket.

Pacing up and down, Gavin enacted the discussion he planned to have with the President. He started off by saying that Jiba had tried to close the case down twice (by issuing a *nolle prosequi*) but couldn't because Anwa Dramat (who was head of the Hawks between 2009 and 2014) wouldn't release the docket to her. He then suggested that Zuma move Marijke De Kock off the case permanently. Jiba had taken her off the case previously but, as Gavin stated, Glynnis Breytenbach [who wanted Bosasa to be successfully prosecuted] had "smuggled" her back on. In his rehearsal, Gavin went on to remind Zuma that, "You haven't got much time left [the 2012 elections were fast approaching], so you must sort this problem out."

He then spoke about how Willie Hofmeyr and Glynnis Breytenbach were still talking to each other, but that he didn't want to implicate Willie Hofmeyr in any way – "I know he's done things for you, Mr President, but Willie is sitting on the fence.

"We've got such a good relationship, Mr President," Gavin continued. "We can talk to you. I don't just want to give you stories – I want to give you the facts. Now, Mr President," he said, "we need to get this thing [referring to the investigation] closed down."

He went on to suggest that Zuma move people around in the NPA to close the case down. This was not the first time that Gavin had used his

---

67 The formal termination of criminal proceedings on the part of the State.

connections in an attempt to move people around who posed problems for Bosasa – Vernie Petersen, who took over from Mti as National Commissioner, was one of them.

"Now," he continued, rehearsing his Zuma appeal, "we need the right people in the right places. Ntlemeza [referring to Berning Ntlemeza, the new head of the Hawks[68] who was friendly towards Bosasa – and Gavin] is the right guy at doing what he can. Now we need to get the right person at the National Prosecuting Authority. Either we get [Andrew] Chauke or Jiba or the woman down in Natal." [I was unsure of who this woman was that Gavin was referring to.]

Gavin then turned the conversation back to Glynnis Breytenbach. He explained that it was Breytenbach who was discrediting Bosasa in the press and pushing the agenda to move ahead with the prosecution. Gavin knew he couldn't fight Breytenbach, but he felt that if Zuma brought Ntlemeza into the picture, Ntlemeza – being in a more senior position – would neutralise Breytenbach's efforts.

After this protracted rehearsal, Gavin asked that I call Sesinyi Seopela to verify some information. Pulling my phone out of my pocket, I was relieved to see that it was still recording, but, much to my horror, Gavin was looking directly at me holding the incriminating device. My blood ran cold. I immediately tapped on the screen to stop the recording. I put my phone back in my pocket. Gavin, none the wiser, then turned to Mti to explain that he didn't want his discussion with Zuma to compromise Mti, so he wasn't going to mention anything about Jiba and Mti working together.

"I think one them [referring to Jiba] has got to move," Gavin said, going back to his rehearsed conversation with Zuma. "Look at what has happened to Mrwebi – he's been buggered up in the press. He [referring to Zuma] told me that himself," said Gavin, looking at Mti and me.

"Now," said Gavin, "he [referring to Zuma] is going to ask me who he should put in Shaun Abrahams' [National Director of Public Prosecutions at the time] place. I'm going to tell him [referring to Zuma] that "Jiba is your person."

68 Berning Ntlemeza was appointed Acting Head of the Hawks in 2014 and became Hawks Head in 2015.

Gavin turned his attention to me, his dress rehearsal complete. He looked elated. "Angelo, I want you to draw up a spidergram so that I can show this to the President."

Scan here to listen to Gavin Watson's famous dress rehearsal before he went to meet with Jacob Zuma at Nkandla.

Gavin and Joe Gumede headed off to Nkandla the following week to meet with the President – spidergram in hand. Zuma told them that he was on his way to Russia but that he'd arrange for someone from the Hawks to meet with Joe – whom Gavin had decided would be the liaison person – as soon as he returned, and "handle the matter".

A meeting was arranged between Joe and certain senior Hawks and NPA officials. Joe met with me shortly afterwards to debrief me. He told me that they had shown him the 2010 draft charge sheet – which implicated seven people and Bosasa – and the 2013 draft charge sheet, which implicated thirteen people and Bosasa. Pointing out that neither Gavin nor Joe's names appeared on the 2010 charge sheet, they said they planned to proceed with the 2010 charge sheet and conduct their arrests based on that. This meant that everyone on the 2010 charge sheet would be arrested (including me), that everyone would forget about the draft 2013 charge sheet, and that Gavin could ride off into the sunset.

"Angelo, what the Hawks are also saying," Joe explained, "is that you need to come out and admit that you were the kingpin in all of this."

Scan here to listen to Joe Gumede explaining to Jackie Leyds (Bosasa's Youth Development Project Manager), Johan Abrie (Bosasa's HR Manager), Leon van Tonder, Andries van Tonder and Frans Vorster that the Hawks had suggested that Angelo Agrizzi should take the fall for Gavin Watson (together with Patrick Gillingham) but "none of you guys".

My blood ran cold.

I remember about two years earlier, it had been suggested to Gavin that the best way forward would be for "Angelo to take the fall" for orchestrating the bribes and pay a R30-million penalty (with a suspended sentence) as a slap on the wrist. When Gavin approached me with the idea – promising me that I'd be "looked after" if I agreed – I was absolutely furious and refused point-blank. Even though he assured me that I wouldn't end up in jail over the charges, I certainly didn't want to risk walking around with a criminal record against my name for the rest of my life. And besides, while I may have been complicit in the physical transactions, it was Gavin who had initiated all the bribery and corruption in the first place, not me. I remember storming out of the building and feeling utterly betrayed, only for Gavin to pitch up at my house later that afternoon, apologising profusely for having made the suggestion.

Sitting with Joe that day, it was clear that this seed had been planted a long time ago. I was livid.

However, what neither the Hawks, nor Gavin Watson (nor any of us for that matter) failed to envisage (because it seemed implausible at the time), was that Zuma would fall from power in February 2018 and that something called the Zondo Commission would convene six months later.

CHAPTER 46

Closing the Chapter on Bosasa

"When faced with senseless drama, spiteful criticisms and misguided opinions, walking away is the best way to stand up for yourself. To respond with anger is an endorsement of their attitude."
– Dodinsky

I always enjoyed my 4 a.m. drives to the office. The thirty-four-minute journey allowed me time to settle my thoughts and prepare for the day ahead. It was the quietest time of the day and, other than the odd guinea fowl that might decide to cross the road, there was usually little else in my way. Turning the car into Cedar Road, I opened up the Maserati Quattroporte. The V8 GTS, sounding a bit like Pavarotti gargling on rusty nails, uttered its distinctive growl. Driving up the hill past Silverstar Casino, I opened up all the ports, staying close to the bend in the road and allowing the G-force to take the car into the outer lane, keeping its speed, and then topping it at 300km/h down the hill, towards Cedar Lodge. The exhilaration was as priceless as it was stupid, and no two days were ever the same.

But on this particular early August morning in 2016, the drive was laboured, the hill was steeper. The roads no longer held their familiar thrill. The car was lifeless, her handling was twitchy, and she was loose on the bends. Something was wrong, but it wasn't the car, the road, or the hill – it was me.

It is said that the most soul-wrenching battles are the ones that take place between the ears. I was acutely ill at ease. I had had enough of the constant ridicule from people like Papa Leshabane. I was done with the lies and egotistical manipulation of Gavin Watson and the smoke and mirrors that enrobed Bosasa. Deep down, I knew what I had to do. My inner conscience was drumming louder and louder. There was no doubt in my mind that I had sold my soul to Hades himself. I knew the time had come to close the chapter on Bosasa. It was pointless trying to convince Gavin that everything was going to blow up in his face if he didn't change course and face the music. Despite the fact that he freely admitted that the country had gone to the dogs since Zuma rose to power, he was too caught up in his thirst for power and desperate quest to retain political favour.

Arriving at the office that morning, I went straight through to Doc Smith and told him about my exit plans. We must have debated the matter for about two hours. Doc felt that the impact of my departure was going to be far greater than that of Danny Mansell, but he respected my decision and wanted to see me happy. He wasn't entirely comfortable with the idea that he would be the one to break the news of my decision to Gavin, but he wished me well and promised to keep me updated.

I left my letter of resignation on Doc's desk, returned to my car, and drove home. I was resolute – there was no way in hell I was going back. I called Gina to tell her that I'd be away for a while but that we should meet up for a coffee later that week. She had been loyal to my office for over fifteen years, and I didn't have the heart to break the news to her over the phone – she deserved better than that.

It wasn't long before the calls started, but I refused to take them – not even from my closest confidants who would later embark on the same path. Gavin tried every conceivable means to contact me – if it wasn't a family member calling, it was a call from the security guard at our main gate, wanting to know if he could let Gavin in. And then there was the deluge of WhatsApp messages from him, at all hours, playing on my emotions and appealing to my spiritual awareness of the situation, with specific reference to messages he had received from "THE LORD":

1:09 a.m. – "Angelo, I have always said we are in this together. When all the agreements have been signed, and the dust has settled, you and I will plan the way forward. Natasha is busy getting all the signatures in place for Lamozest. So relax you will be rewarded for all the hard work and effort. I have never done anything for you to doubt or question my integrity neither have I ever question[ed] your integrity. So let's not allow the devil to rob us of our destiny we have been called to do. GOD bless."

1:10 a.m. – "GOD has entrusted us to steward Bosasa. Angelo let's sow good seed. Whatever we sow, we are going to reap. Let's sow unity and love. Don't have a hardened heart. GOD shows us mercy, let's have mercy one to another. Don't let the devil disrupt. Discern this misunderstanding correctly. I am waiting for you in the morning. GOD bless."

1:13 a.m. – "You do not have to throw away your inheritance which you have worked hard to accumulate for the last 20 years and do an injustice to yourself. GOD bless you will lead operations and keep your position please. GOD bless."

5:07 a.m. – "Angelo don't reject my calls. I have never rejected yours. As brothers in CHRIST, this is not the way to handle this misunderstanding and confusion. Let's sit down and with respect, honesty and integrity, speak to one another. As I respect you, have never questioned your judgment and integrity, let this be the spirit we resolve this with. We cannot just break down what we as a team have built in 20 years. I have never questioned your operational ability and allowed you to run it as your own. I have given you the space to express yourself and have never undermined you in any way. As leaders, we are responsible for the people of Bosasa."

I spent about eight days at home, contemplating my position, reading Gavin's messages, not responding to them, and generally cutting myself off from the world.

Eventually, it all got too much. I told Debbie to pack her bags, and we headed for OR Tambo. On arrival, I would usually be met by a contingent of security guards, either wanting to greet me or solicit a few rands. I parked my vehicle a long distance away from my regular parking spot, snuck past the Bosasa security personnel, and took the long route to the boarding gates. Sitting down comfortably in seat 2F, with Debbie seated next to me, I breathed a sigh of relief. A bit of time in Ballito, on the Kwa-Zulu-Natal north coast, was all the therapy I needed.

Just as the last of the overhead bins were being clipped shut, who should appear on the passenger boarding bridge but Dudu Myeni. I sank into my seat, wondering whether her presence on the flight was a random coincidence or something Gavin had conjured up. Our eyes met as she approached her seat – which was directly in front of mine – and I greeted her out of courtesy.

"Oh," she remarked. "Where's Gavin?"

I shot a glance at Debbie, looked back at Dudu, and, feeling rather bold, said, "I don't work for him anymore." Dudu, clearly startled by my response, turned around and sat down. I pretended to sleep for the duration of the forty-five-minute flight, just in case she decided to ask any probing questions that I was in no mood to answer.

No sooner had I switched on my phone at King Shaka International Airport than it lit up with messages. It was as if the gates of Hell had opened up with strict instructions to "call me" – news of my impromptu run-in with Dudu Myeni had travelled fast.

Eventually, Debbie and I agreed that I would put the phone away. It was time to find ourselves again and fathom a way forward. I had spent over nineteen years of my life dedicated to Gavin and at his every beck and call. Now, for the first time in almost two decades, I could go to the cinema and watch a movie, uninterrupted. I could sleep without worrying that the phone was going to ring in the early hours of the morning. A twinge of guilt crept in, but I quickly brushed it aside. I had no idea who I was beyond Bosasa and Gavin Watson. I had allowed myself to degenerate. My health was suffering. My children had suffered a pinnacle injustice, growing up with a father who was there in body but nothing more. Now it was time to enjoy seven glorious days of morning walks on the beach, punctuated by long breakfasts at Zaras Cafe, followed by fishing off the rocks or lazing around on oversized beanbags, soaking up the sun and catching up on the latest bestsellers.

As the holiday drew to a close and reality began to set in, I decided to write an email to Brian Biebuyck. I wanted to establish the best possible way to come clean and rid myself of this burden I was carrying. My request, which was largely for advice, was gently weighted with a glimmer of hope that there was some kind of life beyond the Watsons.

I knew that speaking out would have far-reaching consequences. Gavin never signed anything – how would anyone believe that anything I was telling them – as fantastical as it sounded – was even true? I weighed up my options and interrogated each new idea.

With the NPA seemingly captured by the very person I was incriminating, to whom was I to confess? I couldn't help but wonder whether risking it all to expose Gavin Watson might mean that my next meal would either be coming to me from behind bars, or via a feeding tube.

One afternoon after returning to Johannesburg, Brian Biebuyck called me. I waited patiently while he pleaded with me to meet with Gavin and sort things out. He wouldn't back down, no matter how many times I refused, saying that there were issues that needed to be dealt with.

I told Brian there was no way I would entertain meeting with Gavin. I was done with Bosasa. Not long after Brian's call, I received an impromptu call from Cheeky Watson, who told me he was in town and needed to see me urgently. I'd always had a soft spot for Cheeky because he was the black sheep of the family. While I had my trepidations, I agreed to see Cheeky on one condition – that the meeting had nothing to do with Gavin. He assured me that it was a private meeting but said it might take a few hours. After hours of catching up over a fine four-course meal at the Tortellino d'Oro restaurant in Oaklands, Johannesburg, lingering over our second bottle of Lambrusco Amabile, Cheeky steered the conversation towards my relationship with Gavin. I insisted that I wanted no part in the discussion.

"Look," said Cheeky, always the more astute of the brothers, "I know Gavin, and as long as he is there, there are going to be problems. He's an old dog and needs to go home now. You have to rescue the situation, *brother* – you know you're like a brother to us – I want you back in the seat. The wellbeing of thousands of employees is dependent on you right now. Please consider coming back."

I was annoyed. "Cheeky, my friend," I said, looking him directly in the eyes, "it's over –let's take a drive back to the hotel."

We hardly uttered a word to each other as we drove back to the Michelangelo. I dropped him off at the foyer, waved goodbye, and left. After an hour, he called and asked if we could please meet for an early breakfast the following morning – just some unfinished business that he needed to discuss, and then he wouldn't bother me again. I sighed and reluctantly agreed.

I tossed and turned that night. My phone was filling up with a torrent of desperate messages from Bosasa employees who could no longer bear the uncertainty. Whether these messages were initiated by Gavin or not, I will never know, but they certainly served well in unleashing a significant guilt trip on me.

Arriving at the Michelangelo Hotel the following morning, I found Cheeky sitting alongside the Koi pond. I had barely sat down when the subject of returning to Bosasa was raised again. I immediately stood up and made my way to the reception area. This was not what I was there to hear. Cheeky followed me in hot pursuit.

"Just give me thirty minutes to explain, Angelo," he begged. "The least you can do is hear me out. Come on – we are like brothers. I am not doing this for Gavin – I'm doing it because I love you, brother."

I continued walking, but he wouldn't back down. "Please Angelo, just thirty minutes." Eventually, tired of the badgering, I relented. "Thirty minutes and we're done," I said abruptly. I ordered eggs Benedict with extra bacon, sausages, and an extra helping of hollandaise sauce – comfort food in preparation for the long and tempestuous discussion ahead.

"Gavin has agreed to remedy his old ways," Cheeky said.

Supposedly, Gavin had agreed to relinquish power and put an end to the autocratic way in which he managed the company. Cheeky made me a substantial offer – pretty much a set of golden handcuffs – which included a ten-year retention agreement, earnings in the region of R12-million per year, annual bonuses, a 10% shareholding in Bosasa and Lamozes – Lamozest was originally created to look after the "white" management and would invoice Bosasa for "special skills" – as well as a large capital amount to the tune of a quarter of a billion rand, which would be paid out over the ten years. Gavin agreed to dilute his shares to no more than 20% overall.

The proposed ten-year agreement would see a transition from a politically-geared grouping to a purely service-oriented company, ridding Bosasa of the political rubbish that weighed it down. There would be more stakeholder involvement where middle management would actively participate in profit-sharing initiatives that were usually reserved for the top directorate.

I was impressed. This was a mammoth transformation, especially on Gavin's part.

"We are going to give you Professor Martin Nasser [a Wharton University professor and business turnaround strategist], and anyone else you want to work with, to take the business to the next level. And your first project," Cheeky said, realising he was winning me over, "will be to call an imbizo with the staff so that you can introduce the new way forward."

I sat back in my chair and folded my arms. It all sounded phenomenal. If the mighty Gavin Watson had committed to relinquishing power, my shareholding – even as a minority shareholder – would allow me to control any of his future shenanigans and call him to order. Still, I didn't trust Gavin, so there was no way I could trust the offer's authenticity at face value.

"Cheeky, I know Gavin perhaps even a little better than you do," I said. "I will not succumb to promises made. Put a structure in writing – signed by Gavin himself – and I might consider it."

"Brother, I am going to get Brian [Biebuyck] to draw up a watertight agreement," Cheeky assured me. "I'll make sure you have it by the close of business tomorrow."

By 9:30 the following morning, Cheeky sent me a text to tell me the agreement had been drafted, and that he was waiting for his attorney to give it a once-over before handing it over to Brian Biebuyck. I told Cheeky that I was in no particular hurry.

A day later, Cheeky arrived with the agreement. I signed it on condition that the capital amount be paid to my bank account in full before any further dealings. I knew I was pushing the envelope, but I had nothing to lose. It had become a running joke in my family that the more I tried to make my returning unattractive for Gavin, the more he succumbed. Even my brother, super-cynical about the Watsons as he was, was flabbergasted.

Once the money was safely in my account, I (apprehensively) agreed to meet with Gavin at the Michelangelo Hotel. Gavin spent the better part of an hour trying to pour oil over troubled waters, reiterating how he had taken me for granted over the past nineteen years and that he really needed me. He went as far as saying that we were "like David and Jonathan"[69] and that we shouldn't allow misunderstandings to get in the way of the "divine plan" that God had set before us.

"Gavin, wait," I eventually said. "Let's just take this one step at a time. Stop personalising the situation. You and I both know things have to change drastically for this to work."

A deathly silence hung over us for about a minute.

"Angelo, you're right – things have to change," he said. "We will clean the company up. There will be no more politics – you have my word. And besides, I am done with them – they just don't add value."

I was shocked, but on guard.

I spent some time with Professor Martin Nasser developing a turnaround strategy for the group, which we presented to Gavin and the board of directors in mid-September. The plan was to focus primarily on non-government business – we agreed that there was less corruption in the private sector and that there would be a complete cessation of bribe payments moving forward. Gavin appeared to be elated with the new direction and agreed that we would begin the re-engineering process that November.

With that out of the way, all that was outstanding was my share certificate. Even with the SIU and the NPA after us, I was confident that taking on the role of a shareholder posed no risk to me because I had only recently come on board in that capacity to assist with the company's transition.

By November, which is when the signed agreement stipulated I would receive the shareholding agreement, nothing was forthcoming. I emailed Gavin and asked where things were at. "We're facing turbulent times, Angelo," he replied, "but don't worry, I'm working on getting everything finalised."

When I asked again in mid-December, Brian Biebuyck suggested we allow the matter to stand over until January 2017, when we all returned from our annual leave.

---

69 From the Hebrew book of Samuel, where Jonathan made a covenant with David because he loved him as his own soul.

Gavin was the type of person who would throw mountains of money at a problem to make it go away. And so, to keep everyone happy, he paid out massive monthly bonuses to the directors, including himself. On top of his R5.2-million salary, he added on a R5-million bonus. The directors, who were all earning in the region of R200 000 a month at the time, were each given an additional monthly bonus of R2-million. Shortly before the company closed for the year, I asked Andries how much money was in the bank. I was curious because it was the first time we had paid our staff a thirteenth cheque in twenty years. Andries told me that after making provisions for our creditors, we would be left with R240-million in the bank.

Leaving the office that day, Gavin handed me a black bag containing R265 000. He was going away and asked that I drop the payment off on his behalf on the 23rd of December when the recipient, was back in town. Not wanting to get into any form of confrontation at that point, I took the bag, threw it into the boot of my car, drove off, and later locked it in my safe at home.

While I thought we were done with the bribes, it was clear that it was business as usual. I was furious with myself for being naive enough to believe that anything had changed.

PART 8

CHAPTER 47

Doctor's Warning

"Young men, hear an old man to whom old men hearkened when he was young."
– Augustus (63 BC – 14 AD)

Dr Jurgen Smith, or "Doc Smith", as he liked to be called, was a mentor and a father figure within the Bosasa group and one of the few people who had the knack of impacting positively on people he came into contact with. While there may have been the odd dressing-down for failing to comply with SARS regulations, it was usually more of a case of him spending an hour acknowledging everything a person had achieved.

A shrewd businessman and a colleague and personal friend of the late Anton Rupert, multibillionaire co-founder of Rupert & Rothschild, he was well respected in business circles.

As one of the founder members of Meritum, Doc Smith continued, after the sale of the business to Gavin, to oversee the payroll and administer the group's pension funds and medical aid. He would come into the office once a month for four or five days, do the payroll, and then leave. Doc was frugal and conservative, with his philosophy being one of keeping things simple in the business. His passion was ensuring the group's pension and provident funds, while remaining conservative, were maximised for optimum growth at minimal risk. His ethos was: "Pay the taxes and keep the Receiver happy so that he doesn't come and scratch" – something the company stuck to steadfastly until 2016.

If I wanted to purchase a new car, he would try to talk me out of it. "Angelo, do you *really* need a new car?" he'd ask. "What's wrong with the one you have?"

I liked to change cars when they hit one hundred thousand kilometres – I'd always done it like that. Of course, it was my money and not his, so he couldn't stop me, or anybody else, from buying a new vehicle – but he would most certainly discourage the practice. In the end, I learned the hard way that faster is certainly not bigger and better, and most definitely retains none of its original value.

Doc had a deep love and respect for money, especially forex. When I returned from an overseas trip, he was usually the first person to appear in my office. While I liked to believe he had missed me, his first question was usually, "Did you bring any forex back with you?" He'd then promptly buy it all off me at the lowest possible rate.

Doc would often call me after hours to chat. In early 2016, he told me that he had been diagnosed with lung cancer. He had never smoked a day in his life. "Would you mind if I use the company's driver to take me to chemo?" he asked.

I decided to do one better than that and arranged with Peter Rieger – a family member of mine who worked for the company and who was Doc's age and had undergone similar treatment before – to drive him to hospital, keep him company, and drive him home afterwards.

By August 2016, Doc had resigned himself to his fate and the fact that he needed an exit plan. He slowly handed the consultancy side of the business over to Peet Venter, with Gavin's blessing.

Doc lived in a small, upmarket security cluster just off Ontdekkers Road, to the west of Johannesburg. I would often, en route home or on my way to the office, pop in to see how he was doing, usually with a good bottle of whiskey or a nice Italian wine. While driving back to the office one afternoon early in December 2016, I suggested to Gavin that we pay Doc a visit. Doc was visibly shocked to find me in his house with Gavin, who was not one for hospital-type visits to people at death's door. He invited us into the sunroom – as he liked to call it – and told us about a dream he'd had the night before. It contained a myriad of work-related revelations, which left Gavin feeling somewhat perturbed. Eventually, after about two hours, we left.

Doc, when on a roll – and especially if he had you backed up against the wall – was not one to mince his words. "Gavin," he said, "when we started this some twenty-three years ago," referring to the company's pension and provident fund, "we said the people must benefit because it is the people who built this company. One of our stars is Nicholas Kgotse. He has managed the Group's payroll for years and years, yet every time I want him promoted, the directors block it."

Gavin shuffled uncomfortably in his seat, but Doc refused to back down. "And those directors do bugger-all all day. They always have a lot to say for themselves, but I never see results. Nicholas deserves better and the staff all look up to him. *He's* director material if ever I saw it."

An eerie silence descended over Gavin and I as we drove back to the office. Pulling into the parking area, Gavin turned and looked me in the eyes. "Go on, Angelo, say it – I know you want to say it." I looked at him and smiled. There was no need to utter the words "I told you so" because he knew exactly what I was thinking.

"Don't switch off," Gavin said, "I'm going to a meeting in Sandton." And with that, he abruptly left. Andries was still at the office, so I immediately went to debrief him as to what had transpired.

Suddenly, my cell phone rang. It was Doc. "Angelo," he said, "we need to meet – not now, but next week. I want to have an open discussion with you. I need to bring you up to speed."

"Sure, Doc," I responded. "Just let me know when, and I'll be there – and I'll make sure Gavin is there too."

The phone went silent. "Doc? Are you there?"

Silence.

I was about to put the phone down when Doc spoke. "It's late, Angelo. I'm sorry I bothered you. I'll call you on Tuesday." I put the strange tone of the call down to the medication he was on. It concerned me how quickly his health had declined.

The days that ensued were filled with last-minute arrangements for family who were visiting from across the globe, and I hardly gave Doc a second thought. He called me again on the 15th of December and asked that I stop by his house. "I haven't got much longer to go, Angelo," he said. "I really need to see you."

I told him I had a prior engagement with Sam Sekgota, a consultant who had connections in Correctional Services, about an extension on the existing DCS catering contract and that I couldn't cancel the meeting because it was important.

I told Doc I would see him at 9 o'clock the following morning. Although the 16th was a public holiday, I knew that Doc wouldn't have been as persistent if the matter up for discussion wasn't important.

I arrived at his home with a box of pastries I had bought en route from Fournos Bakery, as well as the annual gift of Panettone I always bought for him and his wife, Annetjie. And then, of course, the bottle of whiskey I had received from Hanlie Carstens at CGM Insurance Brokers. It was a tradition that I would give him my bottles of whiskey when I received them as gifts because I didn't drink the stuff.

He didn't look well – the cancer was clearly in charge, and the sudden change in his condition saddened me deeply. What I thought would be a quick meet-and-greet evolved into an in-depth discussion that ran on for hours. Never before had I seen Doc speak about other people with such conviction and passion. In fact, I had never heard Doc speak badly of anyone.

"Angelo, I want to show you this because it's going to come out eventually and Gavin is going to deny it," said Doc, trying to maintain a sense of composure. "He's going to accuse me of stealing money from the company through the payroll. Here are all the warning signs of his intentions and what he plans to do – and I refuse to be a part of it.

"Look at this," he said, pointing to the paperwork in front of him, "I'm paying this one and that one, and the only one that knows is Gavin. And Danny Mansell is signing all the invoices off."

He took me through everything, including the hidden companies that Gavin had set up to siphon money out of Bosasa through fictitious payrolls, payments, and schemes. I was impressed with how meticulously Doc had worked everything out, how he had minuted every meeting, and how he had a record of every decision made.

"He's also planning on moving millions of rands into a non-related party's account," Doc continued, his hands trembling. "Please, Angelo, make sure this doesn't happen. I refuse to die without a clear conscience. I need you to protect my name."

I took his hand and promised him that he wouldn't take the knock for Gavin's unscrupulous behaviour. "Please Angelo," he said, "guard against those "gifappeltjies"[70] from getting their hands on what rightfully belongs to the people." You're the only person standing between Gavin and the company's pension funds. Under no circumstances can you allow Roth Watson and Kevin Wakeford to suggest an alternate pension fund."

I nodded.

"Do you recall what happened in 2008 when Kevin Wakeford told us to cancel our short-term insurance policies and hand them over to a friend of his to manage? Remember what a complete and utter balls-up it was?" he said, his voice dry and rasping. "We ended up with no insurance at all."

I remembered it well. According to Kevin, Bosasa would "save millions". Gavin, thrilled with the idea, immediately referred Kevin to me with one instruction: "Implement the changeover as soon as possible". Against the better advice of Tony Perry, Doc Smith and Andries van Tonder – and despite Natasha Olivier, Bosasa's Company Secretary, warning us that this new company had no credentials – Gavin went ahead and cancelled the

---

70 Poison apples

company's existing policies.

At the eleventh hour, we received notice that the proposed insurance underwriters could neither meet our criteria nor deal with the volumes, leaving me with no choice but to sheepishly return to our old insurers and beg them to take back our account. Not only did the switch put Bosasa at risk of non-compliance, but it also cost the company almost R2-million in over-insurance fees and double commission structures.

Fully aware of my reasons for resigning three months earlier, and my subsequent return to the company, Doc was concerned. "Angelo, I'm warning you, he's not going to honour his agreement with you in terms of the share structure he promised you in Lamozest."

Doc told me that it bothered Gavin that he could no longer strong-arm me and that he was going to do whatever it took to neutralise me. "Angelo, I'm counting on you not to let up on Gavin – be hard on him. Please, promise me that? If you don't, he's going to pin all the corruption on you."

"I've had enough," I said, deflated. "I don't blame you," Doc sighed. "You should get out while you can." Then he sat back and looked at me, "Angelo, you're not looking good at all."

He was right. I didn't feel well. I was drained. I was listless. I hadn't told a soul, not even Debbie. I didn't want anyone to worry. This had been going on for months. I had blacked out behind the wheel of my car on more than one occasion. Thank goodness for the car's lane-keeping assist feature – I'd usually come to while the car was still driving. I kept putting off going to see the doctor, hoping it was nothing serious. I stopped taking all my medication, thinking that it was the blood pressure and blood sugar pills that were making me feel like shit. I wasn't concerned about my blood sugar, and I was eating too much – meat, carbs, sugar – all of the bad stuff. I remembered reading that aspirin thins the blood, so I began popping four to five pills a day, and pushed on, despite feeling deadly. I was under a great deal of pressure, working nineteen-hour days, not wanting to drop the ball. Giancarlo and Nikita's wedding was around the corner, and we had a house full of international visitors. The last thing I wanted to do was cause an upset.

"Please don't leave this," Doc Smith said as I left his home that day. "You need to see a doctor."

The information disseminated to me in those long hours proved invaluable, setting out the modus operandi for the plan that Gavin had masterminded with his new "team". He truly believed he was immortal and didn't have to answer to anyone. Although I was shocked, I was glad I had been let in on Doc's painful secret. Now I could plan ahead, think smarter, and finally stop believing that Gavin might change.

"Doc," I said, "I'd like to come and see you after Christmas with Andries van Tonder so that we can make detailed notes and copies of everything you've shared with me today. That way we can carefully unpack it for the other guys to see."

He smiled weakly. "Sure, Angelo, let's do that." I hugged Doc on my way out. "I'll see you on the 26th, Doc," I said warmly, "and I'll bring us something nice to eat if that's okay?"

As I made my way back to the highway, I was overcome with a feeling of complete horror that one human being could plan another's demise in the manner that Gavin Watson had. Doc was the last person to deserve this. I had sacrificed my freedom and my family for the Watson name, yet everything Gavin had orchestrated was for him and his family's benefit alone.

As I drove home, I wept, overwhelmed with anger, grief and utter contempt for what I felt was the ultimate betrayal. But deep down inside, I wept for the man I had become, the puppet who'd been supremely played by Gavin Watson. The bitter pill of accountability had come to rest with me.

CHAPTER 48

Seeing the Light

"We are not here to curse the darkness, but to light a candle that can guide us through the darkness to a safe and sure future."
– John F. Kennedy

Although I gave Doc Smith my word, I never made an appointment for that check-up with my GP. Debbie and I took our visitors to the Kruger National Park, and suddenly Christmas was upon us. By Christmas morning, I was feeling dreadful. I still hadn't told anyone. Chef Allister Esau had gone to a great deal of trouble to set up an extravagant Christmas lunch for us at the Michelangelo Hotel in Sandton. Allister had grown to be a close friend of mine, a true brother in arms, and I wasn't about to let him down just because I wasn't feeling great. I decided that after lunch, Debbie and I were going to go directly through to the hospital and find a doctor on duty to give me a once-over. I packed an overnight bag, tossed it into the boot of my car, and headed off to celebrate Christmas with the family.

"We're admitting you," the staff at the hospital told me, handing Debbie various forms to complete. "We think you're having a heart attack, at this very moment." The doctor suspected I had an enlarged heart. Dr George Dragne, a specialist cardiothoracic surgeon, was called in, but he wasn't convinced. My oxygen saturation levels were sitting at 75%, and according to Dragne's diagnosis, I was the walking dead. After numerous scans, including an MRI, the problem child was discovered. Not only was there water on my lungs, but there was a large pancake-shaped tumour that had made itself at home in my heart.

After that, everything was a blur. I was whisked through to theatre for emergency surgery, equivalent to that of a triple bypass. Dragne initially tried to access my heart through my left lung, but, with the lung filled with water, he was unable to collapse it. Every time he tried, I flatlined. He eventually performed a thoracotomy, cutting me open from my chest, working his way up and around to my back, peeling me open like a banana. I was given so much adrenaline that the doctors could see my heart pumping from under my gown. The tumour was the size of a fist, but it was finally out. The anaesthetist told Dragne that he had five minutes to close me up. One hundred and seventy-eight staples later, and the worst was over, or so I thought. I slipped into a coma in ICU, where I remained for five days. I was attached to five different machines, each with four lines, and each pumping intravenous fluid into my body. There was a five-litre drain on either side of my bed. With my kidneys having gone into renal failure, I was also attached to a dialysis machine.

I don't recall much about my time in the coma, but, as I began surfacing, I remember being overcome with a feeling that somebody was trying to steal my kidneys. In my confused state, I ripped out the nasogastric tube that was being used to feed me, followed by every other pipe that was attached to my body. It took six nurses to pin me down and convince me that nobody was trying to steal my organs. By day three, all I wanted was a decent shower, and so I sneaked out of ICU in search of one. I came upon an unused ward, and there it was, the shower of my dreams. I remember looking out of the window at the grass and trees outside. And then I turned on the taps.

I was soaking wet and buck naked when the nurses eventually found me, having raised a code blue alarm when they realised I wasn't in my bed. I was loaded onto a trolley and returned to ICU, feeling much better after the long-awaited shower.

Unbeknown to me, while I was in the coma, Dragne had approached Debbie and asked her a question that had left her dumbfounded: "Don't you think it's a little soon for Gavin to be making a claim on your husband's life insurance?"

CHAPTER 49

Leaving Bosasa

"It's usually hard to let go and move on, but once you do, you'll feel free and realise it was the best decision you've ever made. I've often tried to explain it and now realise some things can never be explained, nor should you waste your time trying. Just walk away."
– Ellie Borak

It was early January 2017. I had been discharged from hospital. I was sitting in my dining room, drip in hand, oxygen mask on, going through paperwork that Brian Biebuyck had left with me. Bosasa had launched an application against the Department of Correctional Services for negligence on their part that saw the company losing over forty percent of our catering contract. As I later testified, Sam Sekgota had insisted that Gavin pay R5-million into his account in 2016 to secure a six-month extension on the existing contract. The extension was duly awarded, but Sekgota then requested an additional R10-million to handle the actual renewal of the contract. Gavin initially agreed but then subsequently retracted his offer. Sekgota, who we thought was on top of things, neglected to apply for the renewal, and we lost a huge chunk of our existing contract. The papers were due to be served on the DCS the following day.

Brian Biebuyck arrived at my house, followed by Gavin Watson and his quasi-board of directors – Joe Gumede, Ishmael Dikane, Sesinyi Seopela, and Papa Leshabane. I was so angry, I could barely look Gavin in the eyes. The first thing Gavin asked for was Mti's R265 000 that I had been unable to deliver in December, so I sent Debbie upstairs to retrieve the money from the safe. At that point, Brian and Gavin informed me that Bosasa was withdrawing their application against Correctional Services after being told that taking the DCS to court would be tantamount to political suicide.

I was furious – the new contract was completely above board, and I couldn't understand why Gavin was taking this lying down. This was a legitimate application that we had every right to make.

Perhaps it was the medication I was on, but I was convinced that Gavin was lying to me.

"You're all a bunch of idiots!" I shouted, my blood pressure reaching a crescendo. At that point, Debbie came through and chased everyone out of the house, reminding them that I was supposed to be in bed recovering, not working.

It wasn't fifteen minutes later when a text message beeped on my phone. It was Gavin, apologising profusely for upsetting me. "Gavin, it's not about upsetting me," I wrote back. "It's about doing what is right."

Something fishy had happened between December 2016 and March 2017. The company was suddenly R50-million into its overdraft. Gavin was maintaining a low profile and refusing to meet with me – he knew I had it in for him. When somebody you've known and worked with closely for almost twenty years attempts to claim against the company's key man insurance on your life while you're still hooked up to ventilators in ICU, you know exactly where you stand. The insurance was forty-two million rands. I was pissed off, and I wasn't prepared to let the matter go until he had the decency to acknowledge what he'd done and explain himself. When I finally confronted him about it face-to-face, his answer was simple – "We had to do what we had to do."

With the stark reality of Gavin's true motives sinking in, I was in a quandary. I had signed the agreement, and I had already used some of the money to pay off the bond on my house. Even if he still wanted me on board, I couldn't go through with it. I wanted nothing more to do with him. I also knew that I couldn't simply sit back and let it all go, like I had done so many times in the past.

My near-death experience gave me renewed courage. I realised it was now or never. I had had enough – Gavin had proved over and over again that he did not have my interests at heart. But it was definitely the life insurance claim that tipped the scales. With no proper management in place at Bosasa, it was clear that the company would eventually fold. The country was going to the dogs, and Bosasa had a large role to play in it. What kind of a legacy was I leaving my children and grandchildren if I sat back and watched South Africa being plundered even further, knowing that I'd reaped the benefits without making reparations? I could not stand by and do nothing.

The more I thought about it, the more resolute I became. If the Master himself wasn't prepared to come clean, I was going to do it for him. For me. There was a chance that I would go to jail for my involvement, but there were forces outside the law that were threatening to take me down anyway. If spilling the beans and whistleblowing against Bosasa meant serving myself a death sentence on a silver platter, it was a chance I was prepared to take.

And so the hard conversations began. Andries van Tonder was nervous when we met. "What does the future hold for me with you gone?" he asked.

"I don't know," I replied, "but I'm going all out with this."

"Then I'm doing the same," he insisted.

"No," I said. "Let's be strategic about this. We need someone on the inside. Wait for things to settle down, and then start gathering evidence for us."

Andries agreed. "We should think about bringing Peet Venter on board." Peet had taken over from Doc Smith and was looking after the tax affairs of Consilium and Lamozest.

"Perfect," I replied. "Bring him along, and bring Carlos Bonifacio too."

It started with five of us – me, Andries van Tonder, Leon van Tonder, Frans Vorster, and Richard Le Roux – and by the end of it, forty-eight other senior people in the company were on board. Peet Venter and Carlos Bonifacio were still sitting on the fence. Of course, we couldn't guarantee anything – not a job, and certainly no money – anyone who was willing to blow the whistle on Bosasa needed to understand that this was a con-science-clearing exercise only. I was prepared to lead the way. My soul was thirsting for redemption.

That February, I left on a trip abroad with the family. While 35 000 feet above the ground on an Emirates flight, I received a heads-up that there was a board meeting that morning. Gavin had my itinerary but booked the meeting anyway. As a (supposed) shareholder, I was legitimately allowed to be present. I knew the call was going to cost at least R3 000, but I swiped my company card and asked Natasha Olivier to patch me into the meeting.

Part of the meeting revolved around the group's strategy moving forward, but something else that was discussed was retrenchments. I already had some inkling as to what Gavin's motives were – this had everything to do with laying-off of the "problem people" in the company and nothing to do with the company's so-called "poor performance".

I had always been a stickler for the staff's wellbeing, and it was certainly not the first time that Bosasa had embarked upon retrenchments, so I made it clear that any retrenchments should be conducted with due process – which included allowing those affected ninety days to find a new job, or looking for ways to accommodate them elsewhere. It didn't go down well. I was constantly told that they were struggling to hear me (although I later discovered that they could hear me perfectly), but I could hear everything that was being discussed.

Arriving back in South Africa, Brian Biebuyck asked that I meet with him.

"I think it's best that you and Gavin go your separate ways," he said. "Gavin wants to make you an offer to buy you out of the contract."

Well, well, well, I thought, the Master is going to pay to get rid of me. "Let's take a look at it," I said.

Brian put the offer down in front of me. It was for R29.6-million, with a R1.2-million incentive if I signed before midday the following day. I motioned for a pen. "It's fine," I said. "I'll accept his offer."

PART 9

CHAPTER 50

The Evidence is Clear

"If you dare nothing, then when the day is over, nothing is all you will have gained."
– Neil Gaiman, *The Graveyard Book*

We had no idea where to start, extricating ourselves out of the web of Bosasa, but we had to start somewhere – and I had to be careful. There was a dustbin for people who knew too much or raised their voices or had served their purpose. People – especially white males – who became a problem would have their names thrown into that dustbin. Gavin was the master of veiled threats. First, their salaries would be cut. Then they would be demoted. Their offices would be moved. They would be ignored. If they threatened him for trying to dispose of them, he would remind them that he had never signed anything – because he hardly ever signed a thing – and that nobody could pin anything on him. And then they would be fired. By that stage, the person lacked the financial resources to take matters further, and so the problem would neatly disappear. Once they were gone, the naming and shaming would start. It was a classic Gavin Watson modus operandi.

Whatever evidence I managed to gather, it had to be selective. I had already begun the process in 2016 before I resigned, and things were easier then because nobody suspected anything was untoward when I requested information. Asking for a loan agreement was pushing it, and I didn't want to raise any red flags, so I kept my requests low-key. I'd usually send Gina off to find what I was looking for, but she had no idea of – and never questioned – my motives. As I gathered information, I stored it safely in the office of the Company Secretary – Natasha Olivier – among the different files. I planned to start the process of collating and copying everything as soon as I had a chance. But then the coma threw me a curveball.[71]

Although Andries van Tonder was still working at Bosasa, he didn't know where I had hidden the information, and I didn't want to compromise him in any way by asking him to obtain it.

The only way to catch Gavin out would be to obtain video footage of him in action, and the vaults were a perfect place to start. He was regularly in the vault in the Company Secretary's office, counting and packing money, so it was simply a matter of finding an opportune moment and hitting the record button at the right time.

"Andries," I said, "there's one specific recording I need you to get. You need to get Gavin on camera acknowledging the cash."

"And how exactly am I going to get him to do that?" Andries asked.

"He's going to be counting the bundles of cash out loud before he packs it into the safe," I explained, "so make sure you do the counting with him – and make sure he says exactly how much is there."

It was a plan fraught with danger, but Andries agreed to do it. Not long afterwards, he was instructed to carry a box of cash from Natasha Olivier's office to Gavin's vault. It was now or never. He hit the record button on his cell phone, made sure the camera was facing outwards, placed the phone in the top left pocket of his shirt, walked down the passage, and entered through the two false doors leading to the vault.

Gavin was seated at the desk inside – which was used primarily for counting and packing cash – with Joe Gumede. Papa Leshabane was standing inside the vault, on a call, while simultaneously trying to hide two large bags of cash in his hand from Andries.

"Morning," said Gavin, followed by Joe.

"Morning," said Andries, audibly out of breath. He placed the box of cash down on the table. After a brief discussion with Joe, Gavin waited a minute or two as Andries counted the bundles of cash.

"Must be a million," Gavin said after it was counted a second time.

While Andries sounded as if he might hyperventilate at any moment, Gavin was blissfully unaware, and even laughed about the cash being "Monopoly money", with which Andries agreed.

While Andries could not always face the camera in Gavin's direction, he managed to get footage of Joe and Papa, partial footage of Gavin, the grey security bags that were laid out on the desk, along with several bundles of R100 notes, all going out for delivery.

---

71 At the time of writing this book, this information was still on the Bosasa African Global Operations' premises and included detailed expenditure sheets explaining certain transactions, plus numerous video recordings.

Scan here to watch Andries van Tonder at the Zondo Commission explaining how he filmed the footage in the Company Secretary's vault.

Gavin then counted the heavy bundles of cash, and at this point, Andries had the camera aimed directly at him. "One, two, three, four, five, six ..." Gavin counted, " ... seven, eight, nine, ten ... brother ... one million exactly. How much is Patrick?" Gavin asked (referring to Patrick Gillingham).

"One ten, isn't it?" Andries muttered. Gavin then told him that, "Brian Biebuyck and Angelo [are] to handle Patrick independently" and that Andries was responsible for getting the money to Brian every month.

It was priceless and crucial footage. Unfortunately, it was the only video footage he was able to obtain.[72] Soon Gavin began to realise that there were weak links in his chain of command and started side-lining various people. Andries was among those identified. Suddenly, there was an information lockdown and, right before my eyes, I could see my emails being read and then marked as unread again.

 Scan here to watch Andries van Tonder's video recording from inside the vault, implicating Gavin Watson as the Kingpin of Bribes.

Brian Biebuyck called on me again in November 2017, this time sounding a little desperate, demanding that I intervene at Bosasa. Apparently, the other whistleblowers had broken rank – they had left the company and sent notice to Brian that they would be whistleblowing.

The bribery and corruption were going to be disclosed – there was no escaping that – but Gavin wanted it to be done his way. The idea was to initiate a process that would govern how the disclosures were made. For instance, Bosasa would admit guilt directly to SARS, saving the company the

---

72 Jared Watson, upon seeing the footage, claimed that the video was staged and that the amount of cash being handled in the clip was unrealistic. This is despite Gavin's clear instructions to Andries at the end of the video. He has also laid criminal charges against me and Andries, accusing us of channelling Bosasa funds into shell companies.

embarrassment of having the whistleblowers divulge the details in an open forum.

I reminded Brian that I no longer worked for the company, nor was I reporting to anyone there. But he was hearing none of it and insisted that we meet for lunch the following day so that he could explain everything in more detail.

Seated at the restaurant, Brian told me that it was Gavin who had asked that I intervene – or else. "Angelo," he said, "I know you don't want to get involved, but you have no option. Gavin has turned this whole thing around. He's going to implicate you as the kingpin and mastermind behind Bosasa's shady dealings. He's saying that you're all going to go down. You need to get these guys under control."

Joe Gumede, Jackie Leyds and the Human Resources Manager, Johan Abrie, had apparently called Andries van Tonder, Leon van Tonder and Frans Vorster into a meeting and threatened them, stating unequivocally that if they were planning on whistleblowing, that they were all heading down a dark and dangerous road. He also told them that arrangements had been made to "sort me out".

"You guys are safe [as long as you don't whistleblow]," said Jackie Leyds. "Don't be like Angelo."

Leon van Tonder recorded the whole thing and gave it to Brian. I was disgusted. I remember struggling to eat the penne arrabbiata I had ordered. I told Brian that there was no way in hell I would intervene. "If you don't intervene, Angelo," Brian said, "you will be in direct breach of your exit contract."

"How interesting," I remarked. "It's the first time I've heard of an exit contract stipulating that I do something illegal like speaking to whistleblowers."

Suddenly, every Bosasa employee was being tracked. Everything felt super-suspicious. Nobody was allowed to take work home. All laptops were to stay in the office. Full-body searches were performed on exiting the premises. It was a bit like the old South African apartheid regime. Every time I posted something remotely offensive or controversial on Facebook, Brian Biebuyck would call me to say that I was upsetting the Watson family and that I must take the post down.

Where do you draw the line and say enough is enough? I had stood against bullies my entire life, and I refused to allow myself – or anybody else for that matter – to be subjected to that level of treatment.

People were also being retrenched left, right and centre. Gavin went on a targeted, focussed approach to purge the company of anyone who had anything to do with me. People were constantly calling me for help – they had no income, and they were afraid that they were going to lose their houses. Some people lost all hope. I received a call one night from a guy's wife. She was hysterical. Her husband was holding a gun in his hand, and he was seconds away from pulling the trigger. He was the breadwinner, and now he could no longer afford to feed his family. I got into my car and drove out to Krugersdorp to sit with him, to take the gun out of his hand, and to reassure him that he would get his life back. I sent some of the staff for counselling, just to help them through.

I wasn't prepared to allow people to lose their homes because they were brave enough to come forward and whistleblow on the company, so I used a large part of my retention bonus and savings to assist them. We gave them money every month, we fed them, and we made sure the bonds on their houses were paid. Some people received R10 000 a month; others R35 000. We tried to help every family that was affected. I sat at my laptop night after night, making sure that everybody had money and that everybody received food. At one stage, between five whistleblowers, we were looking after forty-eight ex-Bosasa families.

Over time, we created opportunities for all the staff. We started businesses for them. We found them work at other companies. We helped every one of them get back on their feet, even if it meant paying their salaries for two years.

CHAPTER 51

A Humble Pawn –
Richard Le Roux

"Some people may fool you for the moment, but be patient and see what happens. In time, a person's true colours will always reveal themselves."
– Anon

Richard Le Roux, his wife Christine, and my family go back many years to when we started a church together in Auckland Park, Johannesburg. Richard and Christine later emigrated, and when they decided to return to South Africa, I offered Richard a position as the Technical Manager for Sondolo IT in charge of special projects. A large part of Richard's job involved installing Bosasa-sponsored CCTV systems in various government ministers' homes – Nomvula Mokonyane, Gwede Mantashe, and the Deputy Minister of Corrections, Thabang Makwetla, to name but a few. He knew exactly when and where the systems were installed.[73]

Richard and Christine lived in the residential complex adjacent to the Bosasa premises (which was also owned by Bosasa), so Richard also served as quasi-groundsman, looking after the birds, pheasants, ducks and other wildlife on the sprawling property. Christine's brother, Chris Herbst, also lived with them. He suffered from depression, had no income and, by default, was privy to the many conversations and discussions that took place under their roof.

When Gavin discovered that Richard was thinking about joining the whistleblowers – and knowing that Chris Herbst was a soft target – he devised a plan to extract information from him. Gavin apparently hired

---

73 To date, Nomvula Mokonyane, Gwede Mantashe and Thabang Makwetla have denied these allegations.

someone by the name of Andries de Jager to meet with Chris and offered him R6 500 a week (plus other fringe benefits) to provide information on what Richard and Christine were up to, and how much information the couple was feeding over to me. So Chris met with Andries de Jager weekly to share everything he had uncovered the previous week.

Then Christine Le Roux was hijacked outside of their house. She was not injured – only her handbag was stolen. On a regular basis, the Le Roux's electricity would be switched off in the middle of the night and then turned back on again. To me, these were all scare tactics employed to mess with their heads.

Richard was accused of stealing leftover conduit pipe. He kept the piping in a storeroom at his house, just in case he was called to do an installation. While this was a standing arrangement with the company, it was the perfect opportunity to take things to the next level and have Richard arrested. Once the charges were brought to my attention, I called in Solidarity[74] to fight the case, and the charges were subsequently dropped.

Richard had cottoned on to what his brother-in-law, now turned informant, was up to, and he was furious.

Before Richard had a chance to confront Chris, Chris was "relocated" to The Country Cottage, a guest lodge in Krugersdorp. According to Richard, Bosasa paid the bill upfront for a fixed period of time and threw in R10 000 for booze.

One Saturday morning, three weeks after Chris had moved out, Richard and Christine received a call from Andries de Jager to tell them that Chris was dead.

When Richard and Christine went to see Andries de Jager, they insisted on seeing the autopsy report. De Jager told them that no autopsy had been performed and that the body had already been moved from the State mortuary to the funeral parlour. He told them that he had a hunch that a girlfriend who had visited Chris might have poisoned Chris with the pesticide, "Two-Step" – because when you ingest that stuff, you take two steps and you die. He also presented them with the receipt from the funeral parlour. "It's all covered," he said. "Bosasa has paid AVBOB for the cremation, and it's taking place on Monday."

Richard and Christine called the Krugersdorp Police Station to arrange for the body to be returned to the State mortuary. I told them to make sure that the cremation was stalled and that they open a case of murder. The station commander refused to open the docket, saying that there was nothing suspicious surrounding Chris's death. Eventually, a case was opened and

74 Solidarity is a South African trade union

the cremation was halted. The autopsy was approved, but the body was kept on ice for almost a month, while nothing happened. We then received a recommendation to call Mike Bolhuis – a top-class investigator whom everyone calls Johnny Bravo because he looks, walks and talks just like the cartoon character – to speed things up. He charged me R220 000 to obtain statements from the owner of the lodge to gain access to the body and to arrange a toxicology report and an autopsy before it was cremated, but he was blocked from all corners. He did, however, ask me to appear on his KykNET television show.

In the meantime, Andries de Jager was growing steadily more impatient, insisting that the cremation go ahead because it was costing the company money to keep the body on ice. After kicking up a storm, the autopsy was performed a few days later. Nothing untoward was discovered, and the case was declared cold. Blocked on all sides, the family finally ordered the cremation to go ahead.

Shortly after Chris's body went up in smoke, Gavin called Richard in and asked him to sign an affidavit stating that it was me who instructed Richard to install the CCTV systems in all the various ministers' houses.

"Angelo," Richard said when he called me later that day, "I can't do that – it's all lies."

Gavin used various tactics to put pressure on Richard to sign the affidavit, including threatening to evict him and Christine from their house. The whistleblowers also received strange phone calls and messages at all hours of the day and night from anonymous people. While we did not know who was threatening us, we made sure that every single one of them was recorded. I was also warned that Mikey Schultz had been hired to protect the Watsons and that my life was in danger. (I have subsequently seen reports in the media where Schultz strongly denies being hired by Gavin or Bosasa.)

But I had a plan. "Richard," I said, "right now you need to protect your job. As much as this goes against everything you believe, I want you to write the affidavit, and I want it to read as follows:

'Angelo Agrizzi instructed me to do all the ministers' CCTV installations. Signed, Richard Le Roux'

"When you're done, I want you to go and hand it to Gavin's daughter [Lindsay Watson]. And then, I want you to get into your car and drive to my house," I continued. "You're going to sit with me and write a new affidavit stating that you wrote the first affidavit under duress to stop Gavin from intimidating the whistleblowers."

Richard delivered the first affidavit to Lindsay, and then we wrote the new one. Richard signed it, I signed it, and we got two witnesses to sign. "Now," I said, "take this piece of paper down to the police station and have it stamped by a Commissioner of Oaths."

We kept the affidavit aside so that if – or when – Gavin ever tried to use the first affidavit against us, this one would be available to counter it.

CHAPTER 52
Confronting the Dregs

"Don't sacrifice your peace trying to point out someone's true colours. Lack of character always reveals itself in the end."
– Mandy Hale

During this time, the incessant threats and bullying continued. It was obvious that there was a witch-hunt on the go against me and anybody linked to me. There is nothing more soul-destroying than receiving a message in the middle of the night, reminding you that your wife and children are being watched. Most of the time, I had no idea who was on the other end of the line or who had sent the text message. Sometimes it was Joe Gumede who called me. On one occasion – and I spoke about this during my testimony at the Zondo Commission – Joe told Brian Biebuyck, "Tell Agrizzi that we don't want a funeral anytime soon – and he knows what I am talking about."

On another occasion, Andries van Tonder and Frans Vorster sent me a voice recording of Joe casually saying something along the lines of, "We'll just open the doors of Westville prison and get somebody to take [Angelo] out," – adding that they'd return the prisoner to his cell when the deed was done. The other whistleblowers were warned to watch out for the window-washers at traffic lights – there might be petrol in their water bottles. One spray and a match and ka-boom, you're incinerated. I had worked with Gavin for nineteen years – our families even went on holiday together – and here he was, reduced to *this*.

Scan here to listen to Joe Gumede speaking about releasing a prisoner from Westville prison for the night.

It would have been easy to keep quiet and watch the country haemorrhage hundreds more millions of rands to Bosasa, but enough was enough. Either I was going to be Gavin's fall guy, or I was going to try and beat him at his own game. I had already written my statement – it was just a matter of finding the right people to help bring the matter into the public arena. At that stage, there was no direct channel through which matters of this nature could be brought into the light. While the term "State Capture" was bandied about in local media from 2016, a formal Commission of Inquiry was yet to be established. The question of who to report the matter to was a subject of much consternation.

To begin with, I knew that we were going to need political support, so I contacted Dennis Bloem from COPE and Glynnis Breytenbach (who was now a Member of Parliament for the DA) to bring them into the picture. Glynnis and I met at the Sheraton Hotel in Pretoria, and I explained my plans. She was unable to point me in the right direction – or any direction for that matter. Then I went to see Willie Hofmeyr at the National Prosecuting Authority for advice, but he told me he was preoccupied with "the Nkandla issue" and that he couldn't help me. He also added that the NPA was in such disarray that it would be safer for us to wait until things had "settled down". It was clear that every NPA employee who was on the right side of the law was too afraid to step out of line. We couldn't go to the President for obvious reasons – Gavin was already having regular one-on-one meetings with the man. The Hawks had been captured. The NPA had been captured. Without a change in leadership, who was going to listen to us besides God himself? It was utterly infuriating.

In the meantime, Gavin had devised a new tactic to completely sideline the suspected whistleblowers. Anyone whose name appeared on the SIU's 2010 charge sheet was systematically moved out of the way or replaced. Only those who pledged their allegiance to him were looked after. He told Andries van Tonder to relocate his office to one of the off-site companies. To Frans Vorster, he'd say, "I want you to focus on other things, so I'm going to move you around."

Eventually, they were all like frogs in a pot of cold water. The heat was slowly being turned up, and, by the time they realised it, they were being cooked alive. Andries didn't resign – he just stopped going to work. He asked that I get involved and help the guys. They needed to get out; they wanted to whistleblow, they needed to earn an income outside Bosasa – but they needed my support.

I called a meeting at my house one evening in mid-November 2017. Andries van Tonder, Leon van Tonder, Richard Le Roux, Frans Vorster, Carlos Bonifacio and Peet Venter all showed up. I checked that they were all still on board. They assured me they were. Before I spoke, I made everyone leave their mobile phones outside.

"Guys," I said, "if you want to whistleblow, then you are going to need to do it properly. If you want to be taken seriously, you each need to write a formal statement in the form of an affidavit."

I explained the process and handed everyone a copy of my affidavit to use as a template. They each grabbed a spot somewhere in the house or out on the patio, plugged their laptops in and began typing out their version of events. The following evening, we continued, and the next, and the next. Every night, Debbie and I cooked up a storm, making sure the guys were well fed.

Next began the process of compiling all the physical proof. There were files and documents everywhere. We typed out transcripts of the threats that had been recorded. Every piece of evidence had a written testimony supporting it. There was annexure, upon annexure. It was a mammoth task, but, three weeks later, everyone's affidavit was complete. Carlos submitted his but neglected to sign it. That should have been a warning bell.

The following morning, Leon van Tonder called me to tell me that he had seen Carlos Bonifacio sitting with Gavin in deep discussion, and it later emerged that Carlos had spilt the beans on us. Carlos told Gavin that "the grouping" was having regular meetings, and that Peet Venter was in on it too.

Gavin got into his car and drove to Peet's office.

"I believe you're going to whistleblow," Gavin said, "but I'm asking you not to do it."

Peet denied all knowledge of being involved. Gavin then arranged for Peet to come to the Bosasa offices to "meet some people". When Peet arrived, he was confronted by a bunch of heavies who showed him photographs of Andries van Tonder's nephew and nieces. Peet had young children too. He called up Andries as soon as he was back in his car. "Andries, I'm not going to whistleblow," he said, nervously. "And I don't think you should either. You and Angelo need to go and have a chat with Gavin."

Peet Venter arrived at my house one evening while the other whistleblowers were there. He approached me and told me – despite literally swearing on the Bible that we wouldn't say a word about what we were doing – that

Gavin had threatened him and that he had 'fessed up.

Peet was the eternal draadsitter[75]. He couldn't make up his mind about whether he was going to blow the whistle or not. He then approached Andries. "Andries, you need to be careful," he said. "They showed me photos of your brother's kids – these are dangerous people."

Andries was highly annoyed and so decided to gather intel to see who these heavies were. It transpired that a surveillance company was being paid R424 000 a month for surveillance services. We Googled them and discovered their offices were in Krugersdorp. Frans drove past the house, but there was no sign of a business operating from the premises.

In the meantime, Gavin managed to convince Peet not to sign any affidavits. Carlos pulled the plug on us, too. When I saw him a few years later, he was dishevelled, depressed and more cynical than he'd ever been. He was convinced that he was going to jail. Even though I'd reached out to him, offering full assistance and access to our legal team, he had refused. He was a man running scared, and no amount of support from the whistleblowers was going to get him out of the hole he was in.

It wasn't long before all the whistleblowers stopped going into the office. Daily, they gathered at my house. Gavin, realising the guys weren't at their stations, completely lost it. In the end, there were forty-eight employees inside the company who wanted to speak out. I was paying the whistleblowers' salaries out of my own pocket. I arranged to have a house owned by the Le Roux family renovated so that they could move in there if the shit hit the fan. I must have paid about R1-million from my quasi-shares to cover the costs. It was all getting a bit too much for me.

"What do you guys want?" I asked them one morning. "Do you want a separation agreement? Do you want a pay-out?"

The guys weren't looking for a pay-out – all they wanted was for Gavin to agree to allow them to start a new business to take over the catering operations at DCS. This would form part of their retrenchment package and, that way, they'd be helping Gavin clean up all his dirty laundry. I suggested that the takeover be structured in such a way that when Bosasa Operations sold their catering division to this new company, all existing liabilities would be taken care of, and Gavin would receive R10-million a month for the rest of his life. The business model was completely different from the existing one. First of all, it was set up as a genuine BB-BEE company.

---

75 Fence-sitter

Secondly, food would continue to be prepared and cooked on-site, but that part of the business would be run by women from the local areas who would grow fresh produce specifically for the prisons' kitchens. And finally, the women would hold a genuine 51% share in the business.

The guys wanted me involved in the new business, but I wasn't interested. I agreed to help them draw up a cash-flow analysis and a business plan detailing the proposed takeover, and to visit Brian Biebuyck to handle the legal side of things, but that was where my involvement would end.

Brian saw the new business as a win-win for everybody. He suggested that we send the agreement to Professor Martin Nasser to check before he presented it to Gavin. Martin Nasser subsequently sent it on to Ian MacMillan in the USA. MacMillan replied to say that Gavin would be a fool not to accept the proposal, so Brian sent it through to Gavin.

Pending Gavin's approval, the next step would be to get DCS to approve the transfer of the contract. I decided to write to the National Treasury for their approval first, and, two days later, approval was granted. All we had to do was set up a meeting with the DCS, and the guys were good to go.

"Angelo, are you okay?" It was one of the ladies in the Accounts department.

"I'm fine," I said. "What are you worrying about?"

I had always nurtured an open-door policy with the people in Accounts, and they continued to check in with me long after I left. They all had a soft spot for me. Even when I was sick in hospital and Gavin told them that nobody was allowed to speak to me, they went over his head anyway.

"We're making payments to a company called Blue Delta Security," she explained, "and the amounts aren't small."

"How much?" I asked.

"One million rand a week," she responded.

"Send me the paperwork." I was curious.

A few minutes later, photos of Blue Delta Security's invoices were on my phone. I scanned through them. "Towing Services" read the line item, not "Security". I remembered having cut a deal with the Automobile Association for breakdowns – R36 000 a month covered all the company's towing services. My lady in Accounts was right – it made no sense to pay R1-million a week for the same service.

Next thing, Arthur Hand pitched up at my house. Jason Stoltz (who had once headed up Bosasa's Marketing department) was with him. They looked concerned. "Angelo," Arthur said frantically, "we've been trying to get hold of you. Do you know that the motorbike gangs are after you? Some guys from a motorbike club visited me and warned me not to have any dealings with you. They're going to take you out."

Arthur was part of the motorbike club. Apparently, they had rocked up at his house and told him that his life was in danger and that he would be wise not to have any dealings with me.

At that stage, I was ready for anything. I wrote to Brian Biebuyck and my personal attorney, but they told me not to worry – that nothing was going to happen to me. Gavin pleaded ignorance when Brian confronted him, and Joe Gumede said that he had nothing to do with it.

I got hold of my brother, Claudio. I knew he knew people who operated in those circles, so he would probably know something. He made some calls and phoned me. "Angelo, I wouldn't worry – these motorbike gangs are Mickey Mouse."

Next thing, I received a call from Tim Blackman – an old school friend of Claudio. "Mikey Schultz [the self-professed murderer of mining tycoon Brett Kebble] wants to take you out," he told me. Tim just so happened to live next door to the notorious Mr Schultz.

Great, I thought – of all people, Gavin would pick Mikey Schultz. But I wasn't scared – I'm a big boy – so I called up Claudio and asked where I would be able to find Mikey. I thought it was high time that I met the man in person. Quite coincidentally, Mikey's sons went to the same school as Tim Blackman's sons. As did Claudio's.

"Tell Tim to tell Mikey that I'll meet him outside the school at 3 p.m. this Friday. I'll be there to pick up my nephews."

At 3 p.m. sharp, Mikey was standing outside the school with his friends, Faizel "Kappie" Smith and Nigel McGurk. They were tattooed from head to toe and wearing shorts and T-shirts. I was dressed in a suit, sans the jacket.

I walked up to Mikey. "I believe you want to take me out," I said.

"No, no, no," said Mikey. "We don't."

"Well, I have it on good authority that what you're saying is not the case," I said. "So, shoot me now if you want to. I'll stand still so that you don't miss me – I won't be like Brett Kebble and move around."

"What's the story, Mikey?" I asked. "What do you guys want from me?"

"Get the whistleblowers to sign their separation agreements, and we'll leave you alone," he said.

I returned home and lodged a complaint with the Hawks. I told them that I was on the receiving end of numerous death threats. I wrote an affidavit to back up my claims, including details of Blue Delta Security and the recordings of Joe Gumede and the rest of the team (the same recordings I testified about at the Zondo Commission), warning Brian Biebuyck that they were arranging to have me taken out by a Westville prisoner who would allegedly be released for the day to kill me. I explained how I'd gone as far as replacing Debbie's car so that she wasn't tracked. The threats levelled against the other whistleblowers were added in: the pieces of paper with death threats written on them, stuck under our windscreen wipers; the anonymous calls in the middle of the night; and how we were told that people who refused to remain silent on sensitive matters often disappeared, only to be found dead later with a bullet in their head.

I was visited by two members of the Hawks – Joey Tijane and his assistant – who were genuinely concerned for my safety and promised to get to the bottom of the matter. And then it all went quiet. I later discovered that a *nolle prosequi* was raised against the case.

Brian Biebuyck called me to tell me that Gavin had just let slip that he was liquidating the company. He had even obtained a tax amnesty declaration. All the key people were gone. The company's bank balance was sitting at about R50-million in the red. FNB and Absa had pulled all of Bosasa's facilities. Apparently, a voluntary liquidation was planned – where Gavin could choose his own liquidator who would happily look the other way if you asked him to – this would tidy everything up quite nicely.

We called the DCS to set up a meeting, but they weren't interested. Gavin had already told them not to meet with us – that "Angelo and his team want to take over Bosasa". Firstly, I wasn't even part of the transaction, and secondly, the guys only wanted to take over one business unit within Bosasa. Gavin was always one step ahead of us – his plan to close the company's doors meant making sure that nobody benefitted except him. He would get off scot-free, and the whistleblowers – who were all on the 2010 charge sheet – would take the fall for his crimes.

Eventually, the guys approached me. "Angelo, it's enough – please stop fighting for us," they said. "We'll take what we can get." At that point, they just wanted to leave on peaceful terms. There was nothing left to do except to negotiate their retrenchment packages (sans the new business) and sign their separation agreements.

Gavin put an offer on the table to pay each of the guys part of a R40-million lump sum. R20-million would be paid out that August and the other half would be paid that November. I knew that no separation agreements could be legally enforceable if they were covering up an illegal deal.

Me (16) as a trainee chef.

A staff pic taken soon after I joined Bosasa.

Gavin Watson

The Bosasa reception area.

One of Gavin's favourite board-rooms. The puzzle pieces were there to remind staff of the Bosasa ethos.

With Gavin at the Lamborghini factory in Italy. Gavin indicating that two Lambo Venenos should be ordered.

After a business meeting with Gavin and the Bosasa crew.

Gavin in the newly launched Ferrari 488 GTB in Maranello, Italy. He would later order one for me.

In my garage with my Ferraris and Ferrari memorabilia.

The Bosasa Group's bank balance in 2016, updated daily by an app on my phone.

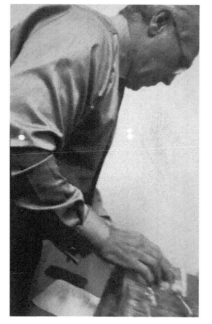

Screenshots of Gavin counting bribe money in the Company Secretary's vault.

Having dinner at my home in 2016 with whistleblower brothers Andries and Leon van Tonder.

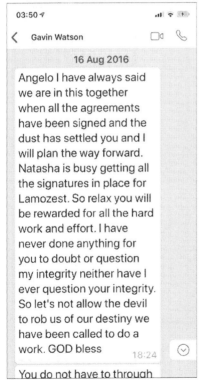

03:50

< Gavin Watson

16 Aug 2016

Angelo I have always said we are in this together when all the agreements have been signed and the dust has settled you and I will plan the way forward. Natasha is busy getting all the signatures in place for Lamozest. So relax you will be rewarded for all the hard work and effort. I have never done anything for you to doubt or question my integrity neither have I ever question your integrity. So let's not allow the devil to rob us of our destiny we have been called to do a work. GOD bless   18:24

You do not have to through

03:50

< Gavin Watson

have been called to do a work. GOD bless   18:24

You do not have to through away your inheritance which you have worked hard to accumulate for the last 20 years and do an injustice to yourself. GOD bless you will lead operations and keep your position pls.
GOD bless   18:24

Angelo don't reject my calls. I have never rejected yours. As brothers in CHRIST this is not the way to handle this misunderstanding and confusion. Let's sit down and with respect, honesty and integrity speak to one

WhatsApp messages from Gavin, pleading with me not to leave Bosasa. (August 2016)

A chess game of corruption.

Playing chess in 2019.

PART 10

CHAPTER 53
The Press Release

"The way to right wrongs is to turn the light of truth upon them."
– Ida B. Wells-Barnett

In July of 2018, I found myself sitting at the Irene Village Market at a quaint Greek restaurant, waiting patiently for Prof Martin Nasser to arrive. He had asked that I meet with him and Gavin – presumably to facilitate some sort of negotiation between the two of us, to bridge the impasse. He hoped that, in some way, he could act as a stabilising force.

Martin and I chatted about an online property platform I was developing while we waited for Gavin to arrive. Within fifteen minutes of Gavin sitting down with us, he was waxing lyrical about Bosasa's new name – African Global Operations (AGO).

He went on and on, to the point that I started fiddling with my phone, knowing how it annoyed him when people did that in his presence. He looked at me in disbelief. I had made it abundantly clear that any hold he had over me had dissipated, that I was not interested in discussing his issues, and that I was merely there as a courtesy to Martin Nasser. I promptly finished my meal, paid the bill, and left.

Gavin appeared behind me just as I was getting into my car. He was sweating profusely. His face was blood red. "What are you going to do, Angelo?" he asked, breathing heavily from the exertion. "Are you really going to blow the whistle on us all? Do you realise who you are dealing with?"

I ignored him. He was in my personal space, so I gently moved him aside with my forearm. "Never, Gavin, will you ever, ever threaten me again," I said, looking him dead in the eyes. "I will do what I feel is right, and you must do the same. I am not beholden to you, and you are not my master. I will no longer tolerate your idle threats – so if you wish to threaten me, make sure you finish the job."

Gavin stood back as I got into my car. He motioned for me to stop as I drove away, but I pushed my foot down on the accelerator, turned up the volume on Pavarotti's rendition of "Ave Maria", and let out a deep sigh of relief. It was the last time I saw Gavin Watson.

As he grew smaller and smaller in my rear-view mirror, I knew that I no longer had to put up with this over-controlling narcissist, who was prepared to do anything to protect his image, his empire and his ego.

On the 17th of December 2017, Former Public Protector, Advocate Thuli Madonsela, made a finding – based on her October 2016 "State of Capture" Report – that required then-President Jacob Zuma to establish a Commission of Inquiry to investigate allegations of State Capture (and various matters relating to corruption in the public sector). The Commission was given 180 days in which to comply with her "remedial action" and complete its work, starting the 1st of March 2018.

On the 23rd of January 2018, Jacob Zuma signed a proclamation appointing Justice Raymond Mnyamezeli Mlungisi Zondo, Deputy Chief Justice of the Republic of South Africa, to establish and chair a judicial Commission of Inquiry into allegations of State Capture, corruption and fraud in the public sector – including organs of State. At that stage, the Inquiry appeared to be wholly focussed on the Gupta family and their involvement in the alleged capture of the State.

In a media statement issued by the Commission of Inquiry into State Capture on the 24th of July 2018, it was advised that the Gauteng Division of the High Court had granted an order extending the time allocated to the Commission to complete its work by the 1st of March 2020.[76]

On the 8th of August 2018, I learned that the Commission had opened its doors to non-Gupta-related matters. If ever there was an opportunity to purge my conscience, this was it. Not only would the Commission provide me with an opportunity to come clean in a public forum, but anything raised within the Commission could not be used against me in a court of law.

I did some digging around on the Internet to find out how to apply to the Commission. Reverend Mbuyiselo Stemela's name – with the title "Media Enquiries" – appeared in the footer of the Commission's 24th of July media statement, together with his mobile number and email address, so I wrote him a brief text message.

---

76 This was subsequently extended.

Dear Sir,

I was given this number when asked if I could furnish information on the Bosasa Group of Companies, known also as African Global Operations (Pty) Ltd.

I would like to confirm who the correct people are that I must converse with regarding the matter.

I have retired after having been the Chief Operations Officer for 18 years.

Kind Regards,
Angelo Agrizzi

Within a matter of minutes, my phone pinged.
Hi Angelo, who gave you this number?

I replied, explaining that somebody in the press had sent it to me.
Radio silence.

I sent several more messages in the days that followed. No response. I did some more digging. Dr Khotso De Wee's name came up as the Commission's Secretary. De Wee's name had been mentioned to me on several occasions while I was still at Bosasa.

That Sunday, the 19th of August 2018, I sat in church listening to Eric Tocknell's[77] sermon. I was restless and looking for answers, but none were forthcoming. It felt like one brick wall after another. As the service ended, Debbie and I got up to leave, but Pastor Tony Sivewright hurried over to me.

"Angelo," he said, "there's somebody here who wants to meet you," upon which he introduced me to Eric Tocknell. Eric and I stepped away from the other churchgoers. I don't know how he knew or how much he knew, but his words to me that morning went as follows: "You're sitting on a minefield of information. You need to get it out there – and the sooner, the better. Please get off your butt and do something about it."

I was more apprehensive than I was afraid. I knew I no longer wanted to be party to the corruption that plagued the country. I had a grandchild coming into the world. How was I going to answer to her one day and say that I was directly involved in bringing the country of her birth to its knees, that I directly benefitted from its poisoned fruit, but I did nothing about

---

77 Eric Tocknell started Wimpy in South Africa.

it? I knew the information needed to come out. But how? Nobody seemed to want to listen.

I called up my old nemesis, Adriaan Basson. He suggested I go public with it – draft a press release, unpack the whole bloody thing, and send it out to the media. It was the only way I was going to get anybody to sit up and take notice.

At 5 p.m. on the 21st of August 2018, I called my family together – my brother Claudio, Debbie, and our two children. We sat down for an early dinner, but I was too nauseous to eat. While they knew about the threats, they didn't know the full extent of them. Besides Debbie, nobody knew about Gavin's claim against my life insurance while I was in hospital. They had no idea that Gavin was trying to frame me.

I told them that enough was enough – that I was coming clean. I explained my plans to put out a press release – which I had already drafted earlier that day – to the national media. At 6.30 p.m., with my family's approval, I hit the "send" button.

Date:	Tuesday 21 August 2018 at 6:30:57 PM South Africa Standard Time
From:	Angelo Agrizzi
To:	Nellis Wolmarans C.A.(S.A.), Adriaan Basson, nicky@carteblanche.co.za, news@huffpostsa.com, Claudio Agrizzi, Daily Maverick, Denise, Debbie Agrizzi, Brian Biebuyck, Gerhard Wagenaar, derek@carteblanche.co.za, Mannie Witz, Daniel Witz, Anandh, Deon, Brian Biebuyck, Gavin Watson, Kyle Cowan
CC:	

Dear All,

PUBLIC ANNOUNCEMENT AND PRE-PRESS RELEASE NO-TIFICATION ON AFRICAN GLOBAL OPERATIONS, GAVIN WATSON, BOSASA GROUP OF COMPANIES

I have decided pursuant to great thought, prayer and consideration, to provide comprehensive details on all the activities at the Bosasa group of companies and myself whilst I was employed there. I have tried to not report on the activities in an attempt to potentially save the jobs of the people concerned. It is however in my best interest to disclose the matters to all involved, and I think the most appropriate platform would be the judiciary and the free press which I will be using.

I am also fully aware that I have been aware of all the wrongdoings but will tender my full cooperation in resolving the matter, and bringing both clarity and truth to the matter regarding the racketeering, corruption and money laundering that I have been aware of over the last 18 years.

---

78 African Global Operations

At 9 p.m. that Wednesday evening, while all hell was breaking loose in the media over my press release, I received a call from Security at the main gate to tell me I had visitors – Ronnie Watson, Valence Watson, his son Jared Watson, and Brian Biebuyck. I told the guard to let them in.

The meeting continued into the early hours of the following morning. Of primary concern was the potential reputational damage to Valence and Jared's recent (and substantial) investment in a new lifestyle property development in Port Elizabeth, called Royalston Coastal Wildlife Estate. The Watsons pleaded with me to retract my intention to blow the whistle in return for a substantial settlement. I was not interested. I stood firm, and they left without success.

Earlier that evening, I received a text message from Gavin – "Don't throw away your inheritance, Angelo. Keep quiet, and you will be well looked after."

The following evening, they were back – this time with an offer. In return for my silence, they presented me with R50-million as a full and final settlement, and, to sweeten the deal, they wanted to give my son's real estate agency, Hamptons Realty Group, the sole mandate on all property sales at Royalston. I was not even remotely interested in the R50-million – because not even God Himself was going to silence me at that point – but I wanted to play them for a while by using the property part of the equation as evidence of how the Watsons operated when they wanted people to shut up. I told them that I doubted Giancarlo would want anything to do with them or the deal, but they could send me their formal offer in the meantime. I decided to string them along until that Saturday afternoon.

The Friday morning, Valence and Jared were back – apparently, they were "in the area" attending another meeting. While Valence was insistent that I give him the signed agreement before he flew back to Port Elizabeth later that afternoon, I told him it would not be possible, but I would make sure he had it no later than that Saturday afternoon. In the meantime, and to buy myself some time, I decided to thoroughly nit-pick the document. One email after another, requesting changes, went back and forth. I suspected that by Saturday afternoon, they would be so frustrated, that not only would I have their signature on the dotted line, but I'd also have a strong piece of evidence to add to my arsenal. Brian assured me that he would have the document finalised by Saturday morning.

Jared Watson mentioned earlier on the Friday that Gavin's kids, Lindsay and Roth, wanted to come around and make amends. At about 5.30 p.m., I received a call that they were at the main gate. "You can let them in," I said. The house was empty, save for the domestic worker and me.

As they drove up into my driveway, I noticed that Jared was with them. I welcomed them into the house and invited them to sit down in the lounge. They were all in their late twenties and early thirties – I had watched them growing up. Roth and Lindsay were overly apologetic, telling me that the situation was "so confusing" and that they didn't know what had got into their father. "We must sort this out as a family and work together," Lindsay said.

Of course, they were mollycoddling me, and, after three gin and tonics and a slice of carrot cake, my blood sugar levels were going through the roof. We spoke about Bosasa, and I asked them what went wrong. They admitted their father was guilty of making numerous mistakes, and told me that the business was struggling. Out of the corner of my eye, I could see Jared fiddling. He eventually excused himself to go to the bathroom. I called up my daughter, Natasha, and asked her to order us something to eat from a local lady who specialised in Indian cuisine. Arriving home and sensing that something was awry, Natasha went upstairs and listened to our conversation from there.

At around 11 p.m, Jared pulled out his phone to show me a ten-minute video[79] of a black pastor and professor, Dr James David Manning, belittling black people for waiting for others to help them, instead of doing something for themselves or paying it forward after being shown benevolence. I had already seen the video because Gavin had already passed it on to various people, including me. Jared then showed me another video about a Stanford University study on the IQ levels of different ethnic groups. Indian women led the way, followed by Indian men, then Europeans, then Canadians, and finally, Americans. The study – which was absolute hogwash – measured borderline "retard" IQ at 76 ("normal" sits between 85 and 115), and the study said most black Africans came in at 76.

It was only much later that I realised that I'd been set up that night.

The three of them started to ask me questions about Papa Leshabane and Joe Gumede and what I thought of them and their relationship with Gavin. They had heard that the black directors were trying to control Gavin by insisting that he didn't take outside advice. They [the directors] had gone as far as approaching an attorney as a collective to prevent Gavin from seeking alternative legal counsel. The alcohol was flowing. It was at that point that I should have kept my mouth shut, but instead of practising some self-restraint, I said, "You know, I will personally go into that company, with or without permission, and fuck each of those [insert derogatory K-word – plural] out of there." That outburst was recorded. And

---

79 Dr Manning: God is sick of Black People! https://youtu.be/aasMbwKFtes

little did I know how it would come back to haunt me.

I have listened to it many times, and I am deeply, deeply ashamed. I have never considered myself to be a racist, but on that recording, I sounded like the worst kind. I can try and defend myself until I am blue in the face, but there is no defence for the things I said that night.

Eventually, they got up to leave, along with the recording that they would later release to the public. As we said our goodbyes, I told them I'd sign the agreement the following morning. I handed Jared three kilograms of coffee beans that I'd had roasted (knowing how much he enjoyed that particular brand) and sent them on their way.

When Saturday afternoon came around, I sent the family an email and copied Brian Biebuyck in.

By 3 p.m., pressure to sign the agreement was mounting. I tried my luck again and asked who was going to stand surety. Ronnie quickly offered to sign on behalf of the family. When I had run out of ideas to play them any longer, I asked them to return the agreement to me once they had signed it, after which I would return the countersigned copy to them. Brian told me it wouldn't be necessary since the agreement would be signed in counter-part (I would sign my side, and they would sign theirs, and the two signed documents would make up one legal agreement). Brian advised that I should go ahead and sign the document first, and the Watsons would sign their side of the agreement afterwards. He also added that he needed the agreement signed "now", and that I should send him the banking details into which he could deposit the initial R10-million down payment in a show of good faith.

"You must think I'm an idiot," I replied. My arsenal of evidence would be blown to smithereens if I signed it first. I wrote my final email on the subject to the Watsons and copied Brian in.

"Thank you for your offer" – it read – "but I will not be signing it. You have insulted my intelligence, and I am not prepared to sell my soul to the devil – even if you paid me." I hit the send button, reclined in my chair, and waited for all hell to break loose.

At 7 p.m., there was a call from the security gate to tell me there were "two upset gentlemen" who wanted to come in. It was Roth and Jared Watson. "Please," said Roth, "we just need to see you for two minutes."

I told the security guard to send them away. Not long afterwards, I received a WhatsApp message from Lindsay Watson.

Angelo. What changed? We had such a nice evening. We thought we had made progress?

This was followed by a message from Brian Biebuyck, saying that Gavin was flying up from Port Elizabeth to sign the agreement, and could we please set up another meeting with the brothers to sort the matter out.

By then, it must have been about 9 p.m. I switched off my phone and went to bed.

CHAPTER 54

Somebody's Finally Listening

"As leaders, we have to discern issues facing your organisation. The easiest way to discern is by listening. Sometimes, leadership skills translate to listening skills."
– Janna Cachola, *Lead by Choice, not by Checks*

The day after my press release was published, I received a call from Frank Dutton, an investigator working for the State Capture Commission. He asked if he could please come and see me. We set up a meeting, and I asked Andries van Tonder to be there.

I did some background checks on Frank Dutton and found that he spent the greater part of his career prosecuting people found guilty of committing crimes against humanity during South Africa's apartheid years. He also spent some years abroad working for the International Criminal Tribunal in the former Yugoslavia. He was involved with the local Truth and Reconciliation Commission and went on to join South Africa's elite police force, the Scorpions. He had even been personally recognised by Nelson Mandela for his work. I felt sure that I could trust this man.

Frank Dutton arrived at my home with a Hawks investigator by the name of Colonel Herby Heap. I explained everything to them – how Bosasa had been involved in deep State Capture, and why I had taken so long to come forward. I told him how long I had been trying to get somebody to listen, and how everybody had looked the other way – including the Commission itself.

Frank raised his eyebrows over my last point. My press release was the first time my story had been brought to his attention. I showed him my correspondence with Reverend Stemela. He could not understand why Stemela had failed to respond to me. While Khotso De Wee was later placed on special leave, Stemela had no ties to the company. "You need to get this out in the open," Frank said. "This [the Commission] is the perfect forum in which to disclose everything."

He told me that he would be putting me in touch with the Commission's evidence leader, Advocate Paul Pretorius. He went on to explain that I would need to write an affidavit and provide a full statement to the Commission on exactly what happened and how it had happened. Once my statements were complete, they would analyse everything and corroborate the evidence, after which I would be called in to provide a witness statement. Finally, I would be given the dates on which I would be testifying.

On the 31st of August, I received a call from a journalist by the name of Pinky Khoabane, and then another journalist called, claiming to work for *City Press*. Pinky's name sounded familiar – I suspected that she was one of the journos Gavin had paid to write positive articles about Bosasa, during the height of Adriaan Basson's media exposés. After I mentioned this at the Zondo Commission, Pinky went public with strong denials. Nevertheless, she told me that she had just met with Joe Gumede and Papa Leshabane and wanted to ask me some questions. She said that Joe and Papa had lodged a complaint against me at the Douglasdale Police Station for some racist comments I'd made about them.

I had no idea what she was talking about until she mentioned that I had used the K-word in reference to them. The Watson children had clearly recorded me ranting about Papa and Joe the night they visited. No wonder Jared had been so fidgety. And now they'd leaked the tape to the media in a last-ditch attempt to discredit me. While any normal person might have found it strange that the media knew that Joe and Papa had pressed charges before I got to hear about it, I didn't. What I found most frustrating was that the part of the recording leading up to my using the racist word was never transcribed, let alone published. While I cannot deny that my outburst was deeply racist, it was obvious that the Watson children's visit was a set-up designed to entrap me.

I called the Douglasdale Police Station to confirm whether there was a charge against me, and they confirmed that indeed there was. They also said that they had been trying to reach me – which was a lie because both my telephone number and my address is known. I immediately went to see the investigating officer and told her that I was tendering my full cooperation. She seemed happy enough, agreed to keep me posted as the case progressed, and I left it at that.

In order to prepare my statements for the Commission, I needed to work with an attorney who understood this particular game. I called Glynnis Breytenbach, explained where things were at, and asked that she meet with me at my house. She recommended that I work with Gerhard Wagenaar (who represented her during the NPA's case against her in 2017) and Barry Roux. I was familiar with Barry Roux from the Oscar Pistorius case, but I had never heard of Gerhard Wagenaar. I met with both men. Andries van Tonder joined me at the meetings. Gerhard Wagenaar seemed nice enough, and he was available to take on my case. All he needed was for me to agree to his starting fee of R1.3-million, which I honoured by paying in full upfront.

He told me that I would have to relinquish working with Frank Dutton and Herby Heap and that he would meet with them on my behalf. I found him to be quite overbearing and strangely intimidating. I said I wanted to be at the meetings. "You can't," he said matter-of-factly. "It's just the way things work."

I handed him my original affidavit. It was four-hundred-and-eight pages long. All he had to do was clean it up and make it sound more legal. While asking me about my story, I found it disturbing that he questioned the facts as I put them to him.

Eventually, I lost my cool. "Gerhard," I said, "you are my attorney. I'm telling you the truth. If I say there are forty-two grapes in a pile, don't decide that you're going to count them for yourself. Either you accept what I'm saying as the truth, or we don't work together."

Soon, bills against the budgeted R1.3-million started flying in. For example, the first one was for R50 000, followed by another for R220 000 – for counsel fees and the like – and then another one in mid-November, 2018 for R 220 000. Along with forbidding me to meet with Frank Dutton or Herby Heap, he also didn't want me involved in any meetings with the NPA. He billed me R35 000 for consulting with Glynnis Breytenbach for eight hours when, as far as I was concerned, all he needed to do was hand her documentation from my dossier that I'd given.

Months passed without any sign of an affidavit. It started to bug me that nothing appeared to be happening, even though Gerhard Wagenaar assured me that he was "working on it". I decided to continue communicating with Frank Dutton and Colonel Herby Heap behind the scenes, without telling Gerhard.

"Frank," I said, "I know Gerhard said we shouldn't talk, but I'd like to keep the lines of communication open."

Frank had no problem with this arrangement. I continued to filter information through to him and Herby Heap so that, no matter what Gerhard was – or wasn't – up to, the Commission was confident that we were tendering our full cooperation and assistance. Frank Dutton and Paul Pretorius met to go through all my material and ascertain whether it was suitable for the Commission or whether it should be handled by somebody else. There was a debate about whether it was a State Capture issue since they would need to have substantial evidence to bring the case forward. As the Commission was going to be streamed on live television across the world, they couldn't have somebody testifying with insufficient evidence to corroborate their claims.

Eventually, it was confirmed – I would appear before the Commission in the middle of January 2019.

By the time Gerhard Wagenaar's R200 000 November bill landed in my inbox, I'd had enough. I told Andries that I was going to give Gerhard notice and find somebody else to work with. But Gerhard was having none of it and told me that he didn't have far to go before the affidavit was complete, adding that there would be one final bill.

"And how much will that be?" I asked him.

"R60 000," he said.

When I went through the invoice, I noticed he'd charged me for an additional five hours in consultation with Glynnis Breytenbach. I found this strange – what more did they need to discuss?

Andries and I debated how to move forward. Do we start from scratch with another attorney, or do I wait for him to complete it? The thing is, I'd already paid the R1.3-million upfront, so I basically had no choice. We agreed that it would be easier just to go with Gerhard, seeing as he was so close to the finish line anyway. Or so we thought. The agreement was that he would be given until December. He was going away on holiday, but he assured us that his daughter – who worked with him – would complete the affidavit and have it ready for submission to the Commission in January. He said he would be back in town by the 9th of January. The Commission was in contact with him right through December, and his response was always the same – "You will have your affidavit in January."

In the background, Gavin was still fighting tooth and nail to get the whistleblowers and me not to speak out. I refused to speak to him, which clearly infuriated him. He decided to try another approach and get to me through my friends and acquaintances. Gavin was under the impression that Andries van Tonder and I had fallen out of favour with each other. He appeared desperate to get the three of us in one room together.

Early in December, Andy Grudko, a close friend of mine who is involved in private security – and with whom I had worked on various projects for Bosasa – called me up. He had just received a phone call from someone called Dave, asking him if he had managed to speak to Gavin, Andries and me. Andy responded by saying that the only person he knew personally was me and that he had no desire to speak to Gavin. Dave said he wanted to make it clear that there was no extortion and that "it's jail time for these guys" and "we can rather just call it consultancy fees" and "consult in the best way possible for them not to be doing jail time". Dave told Andy that "we need to get the three of them [referring to Gavin, Andries and me] together because "it's in their best interests to get talking with each other". Dave went on to recommend that Andy pass on a message to me that the three of us should "fall in rather than fall out".

Andy had recorded the call, so he played it back to me. I could hear that "Dave" was blocking his nose to disguise his voice – and yet, his voice was vaguely familiar. Andy and I put a tracker out on the phone. It turned out to be a throw-away phone, and while we knew where he'd bought it and where he'd filled it up with airtime, we still couldn't work out who this "Dave" was.

Sadly, I had to purposely dissociate myself from good people like Andy because I didn't want to compromise them in any way.

 Scan here to listen to the Andy Grudko recording.

Peet Venter, in the meantime, got cold feet about staying on Gavin's side of the fence and decided he was going to join the whistleblower family again. He signed his affidavit on the 18th of December while on holiday with his family in Mossel Bay, drove over fifty kilometres to George to have the affidavit stamped by a Commissioner of Oaths, and then emailed it through to me the following day. I was quite surprised that he had changed his mind, but glad nonetheless that he was prepared to offer his testimony.

Around the same time, Gavin's relationship with Brian Biebuyck appeared to have broken down. Brian reached out to me in a text message. "Angelo," the message read, "please forgive me." I took his message with a pinch of salt. "I can't say I didn't warn you," I wrote back.

January came around, and Frank called me in to meet with him and Paul and the rest of the team at Hill House – the Commission's offices in Parktown, Johannesburg. Gerhard Wagenaar was also there.

The first thing I noticed when I arrived at Hill House that day was that Bosasa security equipment was everywhere, from the CCTV, to the metal detectors, to the refurbished Nuctech x-ray scanners that had originally been purchased for the 2014 FIFA World Cup in Brazil. It was a classic case of the thief watching the guardian.

I immediately disclosed this information to Judge Zondo and Paul Pretorius.[80] "It seems as if even the Commission has been captured," I laughed.

The Commission of Inquiry into Allegations of State Capture appeared to have paid one of the top capturers of the State to install their CCTV and access control systems. The two men were clearly embarrassed. Within a few hours, everything had been removed and replaced with equipment from Fidelity.

"Where is my affidavit?" I asked Gerhard Wagenaar the minute I saw him. He assured me that his daughter was busy putting the finishing touches to it, but that he would hand it to the Commission later that day. I nagged him about it throughout the morning. When his daughter finally submitted it, it was filled with incorrect references and amounts. I'd paid him almost R1.3-million in total for one affidavit that he never prepared. When I got the final bill, it came to R1 296 000.

"Gerhard," I said, looking at it, "this is rubbish – we can't use this."

Now, the whole team was upset. It was Thursday afternoon. I was due to testify at the Commission the following Monday, and we didn't have an affidavit. "That's it," I said, "we're done. I'm no longer using you."

"What do you mean?" he asked. "I'm not being paid to work with the Commission – I'm being paid to do an affidavit for you."

"I've paid you almost R1.3-million to prepare an affidavit, and you couldn't even deliver that," I reminded him.

---

80 Khotso De Wee, who had been the one to sign off the Bosasa order, subsequently took special leave.

He was furious.

"Gerhard," I said, "you're out of here. I don't want to see you ever again."
I now had only a few days to compile the document. I suspected that
Gerhard hadn't even started on Andries van Tonder's testimony – and I'd
paid him for that too. Things didn't look promising.

I called up Advocate Mannie Witz from Witz Incorporated, who I knew
through my brother, and with whom I had been working on a separate
matter since 2018. Gavin had defaulted on several payments (in terms of
our agreements), both to the other whistleblowers and me, and Mannie
(and his son, Danny) were working on recovering the monies for us.

Mannie Witz is a well-respected senior counsel – and probably one of
South Africa's top criminal law experts – who knows something about
everything. He has worked on numerous high-profile cases, including un-
packing the Oscar Pistorius trial. He's also quite a character – as down-
to-earth as you can get – short, Jewish, untidy hair, and he always wears
a suit. His son, Danny, is the polar opposite. Mannie doesn't believe in
technology, so he has a little black book that he writes everything down in.
He doesn't bother to save numbers on his phone – they're all in his little
black book. He calls it his iCloud and, every year, he starts a new one.

Despite his eccentricities, he genuinely has the interests of his clients at
heart, and regularly checks up on them. He was away at the time when I
called him, as was Danny, but he assured me that he would meet me at Hill
House first thing on the 14th of January – the day on which I was scheduled to testify – to go through my statement before I took the stand, and
hold my hand in general.

In the days that ensued, Paul Pretorius and I sat together until well after
midnight in the Hill House boardroom, writing up my statement from
the beginning. It was a tedious process. We gave each other a hard time
agreeing on what would be included and what was going to be omitted.

In the end, there must have been about eight people on the team. Gerhard fobbed us off, refusing to release any of my documents – the original affidavits in particular – to the Commission or me. Fortunately, I had
some of the evidence with me that I'd taken from him in November when
I fired him the first time. Other documents were saved on my computer,
so we used those. We added in annexures, addendums and anything else
we could find. While my testimony was initially scheduled to take place
over two days, Paul Pretorius found more and more information that he

wanted to be included. I knew I was in it for the long haul. There was so much to verify and check up on, that we eventually ran out of time, leaving the rest of the team to work on the case in the background.

The Saturday before I was due to appear at the Commission, and while Paul and I were finalising the compilation and writing of my affidavit, someone from the Commission approached me and told me that they had received intel that there were threats out on my life.

"I'll live with it," I said.

They refused to debate the subject and said they would arrange for me to be driven to and from the Commission every day. That evening, a detail of eight security personnel escorted me home in a protected vehicle. I told Debbie, Giancarlo and Natasha that they were going to have to be extremely careful over the next few weeks until I was done testifying.

That Sunday, Debbie and I attended church for what would be the last time in several weeks. While I was enjoying the pastor's sermon, my eight bodyguards were seated in between the members of the congregation, watching over me. It was then that the enormity of it all hit me. I realised that this was going to be my life for the next while. The mere thought of it made me deeply uncomfortable.

I had arranged to have breakfast with ten of my friends from my church after the service so that I could explain why they wouldn't be seeing Debbie and I for a while. The eight bodyguards drove us to Tashas in Bryanston and sat down at various tables around us.

That Sunday afternoon, back at Hill House, Judge Zondo popped his head into the boardroom and told us that, in terms of Rule 33 of the Commission's rules, all implicated parties were to receive notice two weeks before their names were mentioned in public – but he was concerned for my safety and the safety of my family. The only way this rule could be bypassed would be if the judge was presented with substantive reasoning not to notify the implicated parties – in other words, that witnesses' lives were at risk. He said that he would be forfeiting the notification of all implicated parties in my matter and that the Inquiry was being postponed from the Monday to the Wednesday.

On Monday the 14th of January, my statement was leaked to the media. We were still working on it – I hadn't even signed it off yet. While the Commission put mechanisms in place to watermark my statement so that they could identify it if it was ever leaked again, news of my Wednesday appearance seemed to be spreading like wildfire.

Chapter 55

In the Gladiator's Arena

"A Maximus, the Gladiator, lies in every human being. When the time comes, your Maximus within you will come out. It is not called destiny – it is an extended automatic self-reflex."
– Anoop Raghav

My testimony in the days and weeks ahead was the culmination of many arduous days and nights, working alongside the country's top investigators and acclaimed legal minds at the Commission. The team had worked tirelessly, corroborating statements, sources and evidence, committed to getting at the truth, all while Gavin Watson hosted a burn and destroy festival at the Bosasa premises across town.[81] I wondered how much of the evidence, pointing to the facts, was going to end up in that inferno.

I spent a total of nine days on the stand in January 2019, and a further two at the end of March. Every day, we started at around 9 a.m. and finished up at about 4 p.m. Wherever I walked, there were police watching me. Bottles of water would be pre-opened and checked before I could drink from them. Food was served separately. Even visiting the bathroom was impossible without an officer going in ahead of me to inspect each of the cubicles. I found it all extremely overbearing and uncomfortable.

Walking into that room for the first time on the 16th of January was like walking into a gladiator's arena. Many people from different walks of life were present, each one uniquely interested in the country's affairs. The eyes and ears of the local and international media were trained on me. While I was battle-scarred and had no idea which gate would open next or who my opponent would be, I carried with me one powerful weapon – the truth.

---

81 When Gavin received word of the impending Hawks' raid (which never happened) he arranged for incriminating evidence to be burnt to a cinder in skip bins on the Bosasa premises. Other paperwork was moved offsite to various people's houses.

Advocate Paul Pretorius, the Commission's evidence leader, was unashamedly frank in his questioning. Only the facts were stated – there was no room for embellishments of any kind. Piece by piece, the detailed history of my nineteen years in the employ of the Bosasa Group of Companies was dissected and ripped apart.

Day one and day two were pivotal moments in the Inquiry. Day one encompassed my employment history before Dyambu, followed by my time at Dyambu and then Bosasa, and how, in the years that followed, the company began to take on the form of a cult with prophets and pastors – and what a mockery it all was. My salary was discussed at length, especially the fact that, for five years (between 1999 and 2004), a significant chunk of it was paid to Debbie, who was employed by Bosasa on paper only. While it was a discretionary mechanism suggested by Doc Smith that made sense at the time, I eventually asked for the arrangement to be terminated. "Besides," I explained to Judge Zondo, "[Debbie] was getting all my money anyway."

While checking the news that evening, it suddenly dawned on me how big this whole thing was. Social media was going crazy. My face was on the front pages of major newspapers with headlines like "Agrizzi Checkmates Watson" and "Bosasa Bribery Scandal". Zapiro had a field day with his cartoons. While the Gupta saga had had its time in the sun at the Commission, the Bosasa case put the topic of State Capture squarely on the map again.

By the end of day one, we had barely scratched the surface of the beast. By day two, the dirt was being brought out by the shovel-load, as I exposed the murky dealings behind which over R12-billion in government contracts were awarded to Bosasa, during my incumbency. Andries van Tonder's video footage of the cash being counted and packed in Gavin's vault was dissected frame-by-frame. I uncovered how the R4-million to R6-million left the company's safe in grey security bags every month, and how bruised my hands got from depositing cash into Gavin's drop safe when he wasn't around to do it himself.

Later that morning, I happened to spot an ex-Crime Intelligence Colonel speaking to the police officers who were guarding the entrance to the main room in which I was giving testimony. I knew this Colonel was employed by Bosasa and worked with Gavin Watson and Joe Gumede. No sooner had I brought the matter to Paul Pretorius's attention than I was whisked away and taken home. A security threat was declared, and the afternoon session abandoned.

Scan here to watch as Thursday afternoon's hearing is canned due to the security threat.

"My God," said Paul Pretorius as I arrived at Hill House the following morning, "we've got the whole nation on the edge of their seats."

He was right. It was as if the world as I knew it had stopped spinning. Everyone appeared to be focussed on State Capture. Nobody could have prepared themselves for the rot that I was about to expose. The BBC wanted to interview me. Then Sky News. Then Fox. I was under oath, so I couldn't speak to anyone.

Dr Denise Bjorkman said something to me that made me think that something positive was eventually going to come out of Bosasa's sordid history. "Angelo," she said, "I don't think you quite realise what you've done. People don't tell the truth anymore – and they certainly don't put their lives on the line to do it either."

Word from Bosasa was that Gavin wasn't coping well. I was told that he was so stressed about what I might say next that somebody would have to get on the road at about 5 a.m. and bend the cardboard news headline posters stuck up on street poles on the routes that Gavin was likely to take, so that he couldn't read them.

While the questioning increased in intensity as the days wore on, the routine had become monotonous. I was feeling run-down and exhausted. Each morning started the same way. I would wake up, put on a suit and a tie (to look the part), go downstairs, meet my security detail at 8 a.m., get into their van, and head off to Hill House. As we moved through the early morning traffic, the blue lights would swing into action, sirens would scream, and the road ahead of us would open up. Nobody could stop us from pushing through the commuters – not even the police. A trip that would have usually taken an hour took twenty-five minutes. I couldn't help but feel guilty. Once at the venue, we would sit and wait for Judge Zondo to enter the room, after which I would be escorted past the same old journalists and the same flashing cameras, to the same uncomfortable chair, in the same dock. The ill-functioning air-conditioning did little to improve my mood amid the sweltering summer heat.

The more flustered I became, the more my blood sugar levels roller-coastered. There were times when people must have thought I was

302

drunk. Sometimes, I'd sit back and close my eyes in rebellion against the absurdity of some of the questions. Having quit smoking twenty years earlier, I was still chewing Nicorette gum to manage the withdrawal symptoms. Since chewing it in the dock wouldn't have been a pretty sight, I had to settle for gritting my teeth instead. While I was able to answer every question put to me – because everything in my affidavit was the truth – I was astounded at how Paul Pretorius expected me to remember the minutiae of what happened on a particular date, off the top of my head, without giving me any context within which to answer the question. Or exactly how much money I may have handed over to a certain individual on a particular day. Sometimes he would ask me the same question in five different ways.

"But, Mr Pretorius," I'd say, visibly annoyed, "I just told you that. Why are you asking me the same question again? Are you trying to get something else out of me – because if that's your intention, you won't."

Once I got my blood sugar under control, I became more level-headed. I was determined to see the nine days through and leave no stone unturned. I couldn't allow myself to crack, no matter how draining it was.

But by day eight, the 28th of January, I'd reached near-breaking point. Part of the day's questions revolved around whether a damaging *Sunday Times* article published the previous day held any water in so far as its suggestion that I was selling up my house and other memorabilia so that I could skip the country. While I was in the process of downscaling, my only plan to leave the country was for the sole purpose of attending my annual fly-fishing trip in Italy, which I'd already had to postpone so that I could appear at the Inquiry. I certainly did not go through all the effort to testify at the Commission to leave the country, never to return. I was not a criminal on the run.

To add insult to injury, my son and daughter-in-law were welcoming our second granddaughter, Avery Ruth, into the world that morning – and I couldn't be there. My intentions were honourable and the truth had to be told. My disconnect that day was palpable. Try as I might, I couldn't contain my emotions.

As the day drew to a close, my only solace was that I would soon be making my way to the Sunninghill Hospital to meet the latest addition to the Agrizzi family. It was quite surreal, entering the building and having people silently or overtly acknowledge me. While it was clear that some people must have known who I was, my security detail did little to shield me from the attention. The newsstand at the hospital gift shop that I popped into, to buy balloons and flowers, boasted four different tabloids, all emblazoned with images of myself staring back at me.

The thought crossed my mind as I walked along the corridors about how different life might have been had I failed to speak out and had I – together with the other whistleblowers – succumbed to Gavin Watson's offers to buy our silence. The truth is, the country would have been none the wiser. Bosasa would have continued to pillage state resources with reckless abandon, with the country's revenue services giving the company a silent thumbs-up from the sidelines.

Entering the maternity ward on the first floor, my heart leapt as I laid my eyes on Nikita holding Avery Ruth in her arms, tiny and precious, innocent and untainted by the world into which she had been born. Giancarlo and Sophie Ella, my older granddaughter, were there too, taking in the miracle of this new life, only a few hours old. My heart melted as Avery Ruth was placed in my arms. Overcome with pride, relief and joy, tears flowed from my eyes, unabated. If baring it all at the State Capture Inquiry meant there would be a turnaround for every other child born into this beautiful country of hope, that they might find opportunities for success, growth and security, then it was all worth it.

I spent that evening sitting on the patio, feeling more content with my life than I had in a long time. I realised I had spent so much time and energy chasing what I thought were the important things with the long-term financial benefits, that I had lost sight of what was *really* important. Everything else paled in comparison to the moment when my newborn granddaughter looked up into my eyes.

How many cars can one actually drive, I asked myself. Does it really matter whether it's a Ferrari, a Maserati or a Volkswagen Polo? What difference does it make if we have a collection of 888 Edition Montblanc pens or a simple Bic pen – are the words any different when we write them down? All those flashy material objects I had been collecting were nothing more than a show of ego and vanity. It no longer sat comfortably with me, and I wanted to rid myself of the excesses – it was time to declutter. Over the next few weeks, I began giving my once prized possessions away – saying goodbye to them felt like a long-overdue sense of liberation. More importantly, my soul was beginning to feel free for the first time in decades.

CHAPTER 56

"Chair, I am a Racist."

"In order to change the external situation, we must first change within ourselves."
– The Dalai Lama

I woke up the following morning with a new spring in my step. It was my final day of testimony. I was looking forward to packing my fly-fishing gear and heading off to Italy to forget about everything for a while. But I should have known that life sometimes throws a curveball or two at you, just when you think that you're out of the woods and the worst is behind you.

Paul Pretorius began the day by examining the events of the 23rd of August 2018, when Lindsay, Roth, and Jared Watson pitched up at my house to "make amends". What bothered me about the proceedings was that Paul Pretorius wanted to discuss my racist rant that took place on that evening. I was furious. As far as I was concerned, while I knew it was abhorrent, calling someone the K-word after one too many gin and tonics in the privacy of my own home had absolutely nothing to do with State Capture.

Except, according to Paul Pretorius, it did. I was annoyed as much as I was embarrassed. Here I was, laying bare the truth about rotten politicians, and all the Commission wanted to focus on that morning was a protracted discussion over whether or not I was a racist.

I sat back in the dock, my blood boiling, and listened to the recording – which Paul Pretorius described as "nakedly racist and grossly offensive, both to the individuals you refer to and to the country at large". It was clear that Judge Zondo was upset about the rant. I apologised to him and everyone in the room. I admitted I was a racist. I believe, if the truth be told, most white South Africans are racist to a varying degree. But, as a white South African, the worst word you can call a black person is the

K-word, and I did – and on numerous occasions during my drunken out-burst. I know that none of my explanations could ever justify my rant. While I felt like a serial murderer in the dock that day, it also seemed as if the racist accusation was getting in the way of State Capture evidence.

It was easier for ANC spokespersons like Dakota Legoete to refer to me as a "racist" and a "bigot" who was dead set on damaging the electoral fortunes of the party than it was to admit that some of the party's own members had been captured by Bosasa and been part of a network of cor-ruption and plunder. What would have been different about the capture of the State had I not been recorded making that racial slur? The answer is simple – absolutely nothing.

"I am happy, Chair," I said. "You can rule I am a racist; you can rule I am a liar; you can rule that I am fat and ugly. What I am asking the Commis-sion to do is to rule on the facts that I have presented."

All I wanted was for my testimony and my racist remarks to be judged separately – not for one to supersede the other or cloud the facts surround-ing my reasons for being at the Commission in the first place.

"I will still examine your evidence and consider it properly," Judge Zon-do replied. "[I will] consider the evidence of those who will come and give evidence about what you have said, and deal with it in the way a judge should deal with it."

I was subsequently instructed to meet with Buang Jones from the South African Human Rights Commission, who explained that I could either fight the charges or sort the matter out. I told him I wasn't going to fight it. I was slapped with a R200 000 fine and told to pay it over to the Bar-ney Mokgatle Foundation. After meeting with Barney, we became firm friends, and I decided to invest my time in developing and empowering him – something I continue to do to this day. My financial support, in fact, exceeded the initial agreement of R200 000.

Numerous people, having known me for many years, approached me af-ter I gave testimony, annoyed that I had admitted to being a racist, despite the fact that they had never witnessed me behaving like one before. But, as white South Africans, we are all in some way guilty of being racist, and the sooner we admit it and deal with it, the better.

Scan here to watch Angelo Agrizzi at the Zondo Commission admitting to being a racist.

Arriving home from the Commission on the 29th of January, I thanked my security detail for their service and waved them goodbye. I was looking forward to my long-awaited fly-fishing trip to Italy. All I had to do was make sure that I was back in time to return to the Commission for a further two days at the end of March, to provide supplementary evidence on the government officials I had implicated in my affidavit.

No sooner had I sat down than I received a call from Mannie Witz, asking that I urgently attend a meeting with him and Frank Dutton at Daniel Witz's office. Debbie decided that she was coming with me – she didn't want me driving there on my own.

Much to my dismay, I was asked to postpone my fly-fishing trip by five days. It was the fourth time I had been forced to postpone my flights.

"Are you planning on arresting Angelo ?" Debbie asked, out of the blue.

"No, of course not," Frank insisted.

He explained that Shamila Batohi was taking up office as the new National Director of Public Prosecutions and wanted to meet with me, due to the high-profile nature of the case.

"Fine," I said, "I'll postpone again, but I'm heading off to Gariep Dam next week to fish there instead. If you're looking for me, that's where you'll find me."

 Scan here to watch Angelo Agrizzi apologising to the public for his racist remarks.

CHAPTER 57
Getting Arrested

"If you do things, whether it's acting or music or painting, do it without fear – that's my philosophy. Because nobody can arrest you and put you in jail if you paint badly, so there's nothing to lose."
– Anthony Hopkins

Andries van Tonder, who was present for every day that I testified, picked up from where I left off and took the stand on the 30th of January. Part of his testimony involved going into detail about the failed SeaArk aquaculture project that was relocated from Port Elizabeth to Krugersdorp, for the sole purpose of writing off profits made in other business units belonging to the Bosasa Group of companies. Frans Vorster testified the following day, followed by Richard Le Roux and Leon van Tonder. Mannie and Daniel Witz were there throughout, supporting the whistleblowers.

On the 5th of February, halfway to Gariep Dam in the Free State, my phone rang. It was Colonel Lazarus from the Hawks. He asked that I visit his office the following day. I explained that I wasn't in town, but that I would turn around and meet with him.

"Please bring your passport along with you," he added.

I immediately phoned Mannie Witz. He had no idea what the meeting was about. I phoned Frank Dutton. He knew nothing about it either. But still, I had to be at Visage Street at 7 a.m. the following morning.

"Draw some cash," Mannie Witz suggested. "If they're going to arrest you, you're going to need money for bail."

I called my brother and asked him to draw R100 000 in cash and meet me at the Hawks' headquarters the following morning.

When I arrived, I found Patrick Gillingham, Linda Mti, Carlos Bonifacio, Frans Vorster, and Andries van Tonder standing there with Mannie

Witz. I walked up to Colonel Lazarus.

"What the hell's going on?" I asked.

"It's just a formality," the Colonel said.

We were taken through to the Commercial Crimes Unit, where we were fingerprinted and arrested. The small courtroom was filled with people from the media, which I found strange. Who had given the media the heads-up? And then the penny dropped – this was a publicity stunt. It was the eve of the State of the Nation address, so whoever had arranged for the media to be there, had only one person's agenda in mind.

Our arrests were all over the news. The Hawks had used the SIU's 2010 charge sheet. Everyone had been arrested – except, of course, Gavin Watson, whose name appeared nowhere. My family was freaking out, thinking I was going to spend the night in jail, but I was already on my way home, having been released on R20 000 bail. Driving back, I couldn't help but wonder how many other potential whistleblowers changed their minds after hearing our stories at the State Capture Inquiry and then seeing us being arrested afterwards.

Scan here to watch as the whistleblowers are arrested.

The media started questioning why Gavin hadn't been arrested – and what about Joe Gumede and Papa Leshabane? The facts were out there. The video evidence was damning enough on its own. But nothing was happening. Even at the time of writing this book – eighteen months later – there has still been no progress.

We later found out that certain members of the Hawks had gone over Shamila Batohi's head to have us arrested. I was due to appear at the Mokgoro Commission later that month to give testimony on Lawrence Mrwebi and Nomgcobo Jiba's fitness to hold office. It seemed obvious to me that the sole purpose of our conveniently timed arrest was to make sure we kept our mouths shut. While I never physically appeared at the Mokgoro Commission that February, my testimony from the State Capture Inquiry was used as evidence, and Mrwebi and Jiba were subsequently disbarred. The Supreme Court of Appeal later overturned the 2016 ruling, and they were reinstated.

On Monday the 18th of February, Gavin Watson applied for voluntary liquidation, claiming that FNB and Absa had moved to close Bosasa's bank accounts after the previous month's damning testimony, making it impossible to continue operating. I suspected that Gavin didn't want anybody to see the dirt in Bosasa's financial records, and a friendly liquidator – whom Gavin had already appointed – could quickly sweep everything under the rug.

When I got wind of this, I was furious. There was no way I was going to allow Gavin to get away with murder, ruining the lives of the remaining Bosasa employees in the process. After sending an urgent letter to the Master of the Supreme Court, contesting the voluntary liquidation and requesting that an independent liquidator be put in place alongside the friendly one, I emailed Cloete Murray, Werner Human and Gideon du Plessis from Solidarity, asking them to tender their assistance. While only some of Bosasa's staff belonged to Solidarity, the union agreed to act on behalf of all the employees.

It wasn't long before an independent liquidator arrived on Bosasa's doorstep and Gavin was in checkmate. He tried to overturn the voluntary liquidation, but it was too late – the liquidation was going ahead, and it wasn't going to be an amicable one.

CHAPTER 58

Back in the Dock

"If you tell the truth, you don't have to remember anything."
– Mark Twain

Peet Venter testified at the Inquiry over two days – the 26th and the 27th of March 2019. On day two, he completely changed his story. Paul Pretorius asked Peet whether he was sure he hadn't spoken to Gavin Watson, or me, or anyone at Bosasa since his appearance the previous day because his persona had completely changed. Gavin probably got hold of him and worked him over that night, demanding that he retract some of his statements, which is exactly what Peet did. I don't think he did his credibility any favours, especially considering his testimony was being broadcast on live television all across the world.

On Thursday and Friday, the 28th and 29th of March 2019, I was back in the gladiator's arena. Part of Thursday's agenda centred around the computers on which Danny Mansell had stored Grande Four Trust's[82] records. Gavin had instructed that they be wrapped in plastic and buried. They were buried in a great, big hole in the sand somewhere at SeaArk in Coega, Port Elizabeth, between all the prawns. After the SIU threatened to come sniffing in 2010, the computers were dug up and stored elsewhere. Amusingly, I had received a call from a journalist from *The Herald* newspaper on the 7th of February, a week after my first round of testimony was complete, enquiring whether I was aware that the Hawks were digging up the Port Elizabeth coastline looking for the computers. Apparently, they had received "intelligence" about the buried treasure – probably after my affidavit was leaked to the media mid-January – but had clearly missed the latter part of the story.

---

82 Grande Four was the vehicle used to pay for the construction of Patrick Gillingham and Linda Mti's houses, along with a string of other benefits.

"The holes are so big and so deep that you could bury a whale inside them," the journalist said. Why the Hawks didn't just phone me and ask me where the computers were, is beyond me.

I spent the Friday providing detailed evidence on the bribes (in the form of cash and home upgrades) given to Cedric Frolick, Vincent Smith, Linda Mti, Nomvula Mokonyane, Dudu Myeni and Gwede Mantashe, as well as the numerous bribe-related contracts awarded to Bosasa by, among others, the Department of Education (a R10.5-million contract for access control with an additional R1.25-million paid out as an "administration fee"), the Department of Justice and Constitutional Development (where a monthly maintenance contract was being paid, but no service was being provided), Randfontein Municipality (where the same video surveillance system was installed at the home of the person who signed off the order without it going through the regular tender process), and the Mpumalanga Department of Health (where a "success fee" was paid to the individual who awarded the contract to Bosasa).

With my final day of testimony having drawn to a close, my only hope was that the justice cluster would finally pick up the pace and not only take appropriate action against those who were implicated but follow up on the leads I had given them. It boggled my mind that, despite the fact that the relevant authorities were given ample warning that Gavin and Co. were destroying information, vital to proving our innocence – including manipulating and removing live data – nobody was rushing to the scene of the crime.

The Hawks, for instance, were in possession of search and seizure warrants to investigate the installation of CCTV equipment (on Bosasa's account) at the homes of Vincent Smith, Thabang Makwetla (who was Deputy Minister of Justice and Correctional Services at the time), Dudu Myeni, Nomvula Mokonyane, Gwede Mantashe and various other politicians. The first house they decided to inspect was that of Vincent Smith; only, when they arrived, they found the equipment had already been removed. The ironic part of the saga was that the Bosasa staff who rushed over to take everything off-site neglected to remove the DVR (the recording equipment). Not only that, but the DVR was running when the equipment was being removed. Vincent Smith could be seen walking around while the Bosasa people were removing the cameras.

Next up was Dudu Myeni's house in Empangeni, KwaZulu-Natal. Bosasa had done four separate installations there to the tune of R700 000.

Richard Le Roux accompanied the Hawks to her home. His job was to identify the serial numbers on the security equipment so that it could be tied up to the invoices on which they were originally purchased. While the Hawks were in possession of a court order from the Randburg Magistrate's Court, they decided to obtain a second one from the local authorities in Empangeni – just to cover themselves in case anything went wrong. Two court orders in hand, they arrived outside Dudu Myeni's home the following morning. And then, after receiving a warning from her that they dare not enter her property, search warrants or not, they got cold feet. Three days later, they were back in Johannesburg, empty-handed.

As whistleblowers, are we simply wasting our time by coming forward? We have gone out of our way to tender our assistance to the Hawks, the SIU, SARS and The People's Tribunal on Economic Crime. These services are tendered at no cost to the State, but at considerable and undue stress to ourselves. As whistleblowers, we speak the truth. We have pointed things out and indicated where the information is being hidden. We have written up synopses of the day's events and sent them out the following morning. The information is there, yet nobody has come back to ask more questions. One cannot help but ask one simple question – why?

Eventually, we resolved to accept that the investigators and the audit teams simply did not understand the extent of the beast they were dealing with – or perhaps they did; we'll never know. Those who are guilty have chosen not to come forward and defend themselves, and those who do want to come forward to corroborate my claims, are being threatened. It's a classic catch-22.

While the Judicial Commission of Inquiry into Allegations of State Capture is a brilliant concept in principle, it begs the question – what next? A door has been opened for our President, but what remains to be seen is whether his government will act without fear or favour and bring the guilty parties to book.

Either way, and whatever does or does not happen, I know that, as whistleblowers, we did what was right for our souls – and for the country.

Gavin was later subpoenaed to testify at a SARS inquiry into his tax affairs. The case was set down for the 27th of August 2019, with various meetings to take place before the planned court date. I got wind of the fact that Gavin refused to appear at the first inquiry, and sent his daughter Lindsay to appear on his behalf. Lindsay was turned away, and the subpoena was reissued with a warning that if he did not present himself in person, he would face arrest.

On the morning of Monday the 26th of August, I received a text from an unknown number asking me if I was aware that Gavin had died. Putting it down to fake news, I ignored the message. My phone rang incessantly after that – the same unknown number – but I was in a meeting, so I ignored the calls. When I eventually answered, it was Kyle Cowan, a journalist from News 24. He confirmed that Gavin Watson was dead.

"I'm so sorry," I said, confused. "What happened?"

"He was in an accident on his way to OR Tambo International Airport at 5 a.m. this morning."

Contrary to how I might normally respond when informed of a person's death, I found myself instantly overcome with feelings of anger. "Coward," I thought to myself. "Just as the net is closing in on you, you decide to go to the grave with the truth in your heart. How evil can one person be?"

Gavin had, without a doubt, taken the easy way out. As far as I was concerned, this was no accident. For Gavin Watson, even death was more appealing than facing the consequences of his actions.

Chapter 59

Master No More

"What we call the beginning, is often the end.
The end is where we start from."
– T.S. Eliot

I knew Gavin Watson for well over nineteen years, and we must have spent up to sixteen hours in contact with each other, every day. While many people thought our relationship was close because we spent so much time in each other's presence, it wasn't. In fact, I spent a significant amount of time checking in with myself, making sure that I did not allow him to get to me, or that familiarity would breed contempt. The thing is, I realised, from early on, that Gavin was a user. He reminded me of a vampire. I watched how he treated those he called his friends – people who were, in truth, nothing more than business associates, and moveable pawns.

His memorial service in Johannesburg took on the form of a business presentation, with Papa Leshabane playing the role of Master of Ceremonies. Jacob Zuma, who also made an appearance, referred to Gavin as "a comrade and a friend", adding, "The reports that the family gave me have a number of gaps in the manner in which Comrade Gavin was found and how he died. Since the investigation is still ongoing, I hope there will be a report that will satisfy all of us."

While some suspected Gavin's death to have been an assassination, many thought it was a suicide. When Kyle Cowan explained that Gavin had lost control of his vehicle before crashing into the pylon outside OR Tambo International Airport, I was shocked – not because Gavin had crashed (Gavin wasn't the best driver) but because he was behind the wheel of one of the company's pool vehicles, a low-spec, manual-drive Toyota Corolla. Why didn't he just take one of the many German luxury sedans parked at the Bosasa offices, all with sophisticated safety and tracking systems? There were no less than twelve other vehicles, ranging from double-cab premiums to a Mercedes E-class, available for him to choose from.

Why did he not take one of his favourites, the BMW, which was, according to remote diagnostics performed after the accident, in perfect running condition? After all, he was driving around in it the day before the accident. Gavin couldn't stand driving manuals – in fact, he could hardly drive a car with a manual transmission. Why, when there were other vehicles available, did he opt for this one? The Corolla didn't even have a tracking device. In all the time I knew and worked with him, Gavin would have a fit if I hired anything less than an E-Class or a 5-Series BMW for us to drive around in when we were travelling for business. I'll never forget how he once made me return an Avis rental because it was a lower-group vehicle.

Why was Gavin driving at that unearthly hour of the morning? In a Toyota Corolla? And why was he even driving to the airport? He certainly wasn't flying anywhere because there were no tickets booked under his name on any airline. The earliest flight he could have taken would have been at 7 a.m. If he was travelling to Port Elizabeth, his flight would be booked for 10 a.m. or later. Was he dropping somebody off instead? That might explain why his briefcase and cell phone were missing, and why his last activity on WhatsApp was at 4:30 a.m.

Gavin was a real pest when it came to money – he always wanted a substantial amount of cash on him. When he died, reports stated that he had R70 in his wallet. I don't believe that for one second. He would have had at least R30 000 in his briefcase. Strangely, one of the first responders on the scene was an employee of a security company. Was his car ransacked before the paramedics arrived?

There were allegations that his cell phone was in my possession, that I killed him, and that his death was staged. In other reports, his cell phone was tracked to just outside Germiston, close to where my brother works. Was someone trying to frame him too? Whatever the rumours, perhaps it is those making the loudest rumblings that should be questioned.

Looking at the vehicle itself, the passenger side – barring the deployed airbags – was remarkably intact, so if there was a passenger, who was it? And if there was, why did they flee the scene?

I found it odd, after viewing photographs of the accident scene (and of Gavin's body in particular) that there was so little blood, despite the obvious gash to his carotid artery. Other than the wound to his neck, his face and body were largely unscathed. He was slumped over the steering wheel, both hands holding onto it, his seatbelt plugged in behind him. Was he killed before the time and then placed in that position before driving into the concrete pylon? Did he have an argument with somebody the previous evening that ended badly? Could someone else have driven the car at high speed and jumped out just before it crashed? Was Gavin's body perhaps placed inside the smashed Corolla after the fact, having been transported to the scene in another vehicle?

There have even been rumoured reports that Gavin Watson is still alive. In March 2020, a private detective doing unrelated work in the Maldives claims to have seen a man on three occasions — who he is convinced is Gavin Watson — now going under the name of Michael Johnson and travelling on an American passport.

While the conspiracy theories of a cover-up abound, one irrevocable fact remains – Gavin Joseph Watson is no more.

Was his death pre-meditated? Possibly. Was it suicide? Personally, I think Gavin was too much of a narcissist to take his own life – he was far too proud to be another Brett Kebble. But I could be wrong.

The truth of the matter is that something was going to give eventually. The situation was a pressure cooker waiting to explode. While Gavin was invited to oppose my testimony at the Zondo Commission, he chose not to. Not once did he dispute the submissions made. There is no doubt that Bosasa was a fully-fronted BEE company. If he did indeed end his life, perhaps his conscience eventually got the better of him. As he said in one of his messages to me before his untimely demise – "I was wrong, I was wrong. Please forgive me."

Unfortunately, we cannot turn back time, but, as it is with the many other tragedies that have unfolded throughout history, Gavin's life – and his death – is a lesson to me (and hopefully many others), on how not to do things.

With the final curtain drawn, I have come to believe that Gavin Watson was – nothing more and nothing less – a mirror to the beast that resides in all of us.

Acknowledgements

To Debbie, for continuously pushing me to write this book, and to Natasha, for the painstaking debates that ran late into the night about what should or should not be included – I owe you both my eternal gratitude.

To Phillipa Mitchell, who spent many months with me, putting together the pieces and writing my tell-all.

To Jennifer Mathews, who tirelessly summarised hours and hours of Zondo Commission transcriptions so that we might verify the facts.

To Julius Botha for building the book's website and your patience in dealing with my daily requests to add yet another QR code.

To Claudio, Vivien, and the boys Roberto, Allessandro and Daniello – thank you for making us laugh when things got a bit too much.

To Andries van Tonder, Leon van Tonder, Frans Vorster, Richard Le Roux and everyone who played a role in bringing years of darkness into the light, I thank you. It is you who are the true heroes. You have done South Africa proud.

To my publisher and force behind TBTP, for your inspiration and enthusiasm. Grazie mille.

And finally, to Daniel and Mannie Witz of Witz Incorporated, a legal team second to none. Not only are you true gentlemen, but you are also icons on the South African legal landscape. You have risked so much and given so much of your time to me. It is people like you who bring the hope of a solid judicial oversight in South Africa.

Printed in Great Britain
by Amazon